# French Children
# Don't Throw Food

## Pamela Druckerman

## Doubleday

LONDON • TORONTO • SYDNEY • AUCKLAND • JOHANNESBURG

TRANSWORLD PUBLISHERS
61–63 Uxbridge Road, London W5 5SA
A Random House Group Company
www.transworldbooks.co.uk

First published in Great Britain
in 2012 by Doubleday
an imprint of Transworld Publishers

This book is a work of non-fiction based on the experiences and recollections of
the author. In some cases names of people and identifying details have been changed
to protect the privacy of others. The author has stated to the publishers that, except
in such minor respects, the contents of this book are true.

A CIP catalogue record for this book
is available from the British Library.

ISBN 9780385617611

Addresses for Random House Group Ltd companies outside the UK
can be found at: www.randomhouse.co.uk
The Random House Group Ltd Reg. No. 954009

The Random House Group Limited supports the Forest Stewardship Council
(FSC®), the leading international forest-certification organization. Our books
carrying the FSC label are printed on FSC®-certified paper. FSC is the only forest-
certification scheme endorsed by the leading environmental organizations, including
Greenpeace. Our paper procurement policy can be found at
www.randomhouse.co.uk/environment.

Typeset in 11/15pt Goudy by Falcon Oast Graphic Art Ltd.
Printed and bound in Great Britain by Clays Ltd, Bungay, Suffolk

8 10 9 7

For Simon, who makes everything matter

*Les petits poissons dans l'eau,*
*Nagent aussi bien que les gros.*

The little fish in the water,
Swim as well as the big ones do.

French children's song

# Contents

# Prologue

# French Children Don't Throw Food

WHEN MY DAUGHTER IS EIGHTEEN MONTHS OLD, MY husband and I decide to take her on a little summer holiday. We pick a coastal town that's a few hours by train from Paris, where we've been living (I'm American, he's British). We book a hotel room with a cot. She's our only child at this point, so forgive us for thinking: how hard could it be?

We have breakfast at the hotel. But we have to eat lunch and dinner at the little seafood restaurants around the old port. We quickly discover that two restaurant meals a day, with a toddler, deserve to be their own circle of hell. Bean is briefly interested in food. a piece of bread, or anything fried. But within a few minutes she starts spilling salt shakers and tearing apart sugar packets, then demanding to be sprung from her high chair so she can dash around the restaurant and bolt dangerously towards the docks.

Our strategy is to finish the meal quickly. We order while we're being seated, then we beg the server to rush out some bread and bring us all of our food, appetizers and main courses, simultaneously. While my husband has a few bites of fish, I make sure that Bean doesn't get kicked by a waiter or lost at sea. Then we switch. We leave enormous, apologetic tips to compensate for the arc of torn napkins and langoustines around our table.

On the walk back to our hotel we swear off travel, joy and ever having more kids. This 'holiday' seals the fact that life as we knew it eighteen months earlier has officially vanished. I'm not sure why we're even surprised.

After a few more restaurant meals, I notice that the French families all around us don't look like they're in hell. Weirdly, they look like they're on holiday. French children the same age as Bean are sitting contentedly in their high chairs, waiting for their food or eating fish and even vegetables. There's no shrieking or whining. Everyone is having one course at a time. And there's no debris around their tables.

Though I've lived in France for a few years, I can't explain this. In Paris, kids don't eat in restaurants much. Anyway, I haven't been watching them. Before I had a child, I never paid attention to anyone else's. And now I rarely pay attention to any child but my own. In our current misery, however, I can't help but notice that there seems to be another way. But what exactly is it? Are French kids just genetically calmer than ours? Have they been bribed (or threatened) into submission? Are they on the receiving end of an old-fashioned seen-but-not-heard parenting philosophy?

It doesn't seem like it. The French children all around us don't look cowed. They're cheerful, chatty and curious. Their parents are affectionate and attentive. There just seems to be an invisible, civilizing force at their tables – and, I'm starting to suspect, in their lives – that's absent from ours.

Once I start thinking about French parenting, I realize it's not just mealtimes that are different. I suddenly have lots of questions. Why is it, for example, that in the hundreds of hours I've clocked at French playgrounds, I've never seen a child (except my own) throw a temper tantrum? Why don't my French friends need to end a phone call hurriedly because their kids are demanding something? Why haven't their living rooms been taken over by teepees and toy kitchens, the way ours has?

And there's more. Why is it that so many of the Anglophone kids I meet are on mono-diets of pasta or white rice, or eat only a narrow menu of 'children's' foods? Meanwhile, my daughter's French friends eat fish, vegetables, and practically everything else. And how is it that, except for a specific time in the afternoon, French kids don't snack?

I hadn't thought I was supposed to admire French parenting. It isn't a *thing*, like French fashion, or French cheese. No one visits Paris to soak up the local views on parental authority and guilt management. Quite the contrary: the British and American mothers I know in Paris are horrified that French mothers barely breastfeed, and let their four-year-olds walk around with dummies.

So how come they never point out that so many French babies start sleeping through the night at two or three months old? And why don't they mention that French kids don't require constant attention from adults, and that they seem capable of hearing the word 'no' without collapsing?

No one is making a fuss about all this. But quietly and en masse, French parents are achieving outcomes that create a whole different atmosphere for family life. When British or American families visit our home, the parents usually spend much of the visit refereeing their kids' spats, helping their toddlers do laps around the kitchen island, or getting down on the floor to build Lego villages. There are always a few rounds of crying and consoling. When French friends visit, however, we grown-ups have coffee, and the children play happily by themselves.

French parents are very concerned about their kids. They know about paedophiles, allergies and choking hazards. They take reasonable precautions. But somehow they aren't panicked about their children's well-being. This calmer outlook seems to make them better at both establishing boundaries and giving their kids some autonomy.

I'm hardly the first to point out that middle-class Britain and America have a parenting problem. In hundreds of books and articles, this problem has been painstakingly diagnosed, critiqued and named: pushy-parent syndrome, hyper-parenting, helicopter parenting and, my personal favourite, the kindergarchy. One writer defines the problem as 'simply paying more attention to the upbringing of children than can possibly be good for them'. Another, Judith Warner, calls it the 'culture of total motherhood'. (In fact, she realized this was a problem after returning from France.) Nobody seems to like the relentless, unhappy pace of Anglophone parenting, least of all parents themselves.

So why do we do it? Why does this way of parenting seem to be hard-wired into our generation, even if – like me – you've left the country? First, starting in the 1980s, there was a mass of data and public rhetoric saying that poor kids fall behind in school because they don't get enough stimulation, especially in the early years. Middle-class parents took this to mean that their own kids would benefit from more stimulation too.

Around the same period, the gap between rich and poor Britons began to widen. Suddenly, it seemed that parents needed to groom their children to join the new elite. Exposing kids to the right stuff early on – and ahead of other children the same age – started to seem more urgent.

Alongside this competitive parenting was the growing belief that kids are psychologically fragile. Today's young parents are part of the most psychoanalysed generation ever, and have absorbed the idea that every choice we make could damage our kids. We also came of age during the divorce boom in the 1980s. We're determined to act more selflessly than we believe our own parents did.

What's more, we feel that we're parenting in a very dangerous world. News reports create the impression that children are at greater risk than ever, and that we must be perpetually vigilant about their safety.

The result of all this is a parenting style that's labour-intensive and exhausting. But now, in France, I've glimpsed another way. A blend of journalistic curiosity and maternal desperation kicks in. By the end of our ruined beach holiday,

I've decided to figure out what French parents are doing differently. It will be a work of investigative parenting. What is the invisible, civilizing force that the French have harnessed? Can I change my wiring, and apply it to my own offspring? Why don't French children throw food? And why aren't their parents shouting?

I realize I'm on to something when I discover a research study led by an economist at Princeton, in which mothers in Columbus, Ohio, said childcare was more than twice as unpleasant as comparable mothers in the city of Rennes, France, did. Or to put it more positively, while the French mums were doing childcare, they spent more of that time in a pleasant state. This bears out my own observations in Paris, and on trips to Britain and America: there's something about the way the French do parenting that makes it less of a grind and more of a pleasure.

I'm convinced that the secrets of French parenting are hiding in plain sight. It's just that nobody has looked for them before. I start stashing a notebook in my nappy bag. Every doctor's visit, dinner party, play date and puppet show becomes a chance to observe French parents in action, and to figure out what unspoken rules they're following.

At first, it's hard to tell. French parents seem to vacillate between being extremely strict and shockingly permissive. Interrogating them isn't much help either. Most parents I speak to insist that they're not doing anything special. On the contrary, they're convinced that France is beset by a 'child-king' syndrome in which parents have lost their authority. (To which I respond: 'You don't know child kings. Please visit New York.')

For several years, and through the birth of two more children in Paris, I keep uncovering clues. I discover, for instance, that there's a 'Dr Spock' of France, who's a household name throughout the country but who doesn't have a single English-language book in print. I read this woman's books, along with many others. I interview dozens of parents and experts. And I eavesdrop shamelessly during school drop-offs and trips to the supermarket. Finally, I think I've discovered what French parents do differently.

When I say 'French parents', I'm generalizing of course. Everyone's different. The parents I meet mostly live in Paris and its suburbs. Most have university degrees and professional jobs. But I'm struck that, despite individual differences, French parents all seem to follow the same basic principles. Well-off lawyers, caregivers in French nurseries, state-school teachers and old ladies who approach me in the park all say more or less the same things. So does practically every French baby book and parenting magazine I read. It quickly becomes clear that having a child in France doesn't require choosing a parenting philosophy. Everyone more or less takes the fundamental rules for granted. That fact alone makes the mood less anxious.

Why France? I certainly don't suffer from a pro-France bias. *Au contraire*, I'm not even sure that I like living here. I certainly don't want my kids growing up into sniffy Parisians.

But for all its problems, France is the perfect foil for the current anxieties in British and American parenting. On the one hand, French parents have values that look very familiar to me. Parisian parents are zealous about talking to their kids, showing them nature, and reading them lots of books. They take them to tennis lessons, painting classes and interactive science museums.

Yet somehow, the French have managed to be involved without becoming obsessive. They assume that even good parents aren't at the constant service of their children, and that there's no need to feel guilty about this. 'For me, the evenings are for the parents,' one Parisian mother tells me. 'My daughter can be with us if she wants, but it's adult time.' French parents want their kids to be stimulated, but not continually. While some Anglophone toddlers are getting Mandarin tutors and pre-literacy training, French kids are – by design – just toddling around.

The French are getting lots of practice at being parents. While its neighbours are suffering from population declines, France is having a baby boom. In the European Union, only the Irish have a higher birth rate. The French have all kinds of public services that surely make parenting more appealing and less stressful. French parents don't have to pay for nursery school, worry about health insurance or save for university. Many get monthly allowances from the state – sent straight to their bank accounts – just for having kids.

But these public services don't explain the differences I see. The French seem to have a whole different framework for raising kids. When I ask French parents how they discipline their children, it takes them a few beats just to understand what I mean. 'Ah, you mean how do we *educate* them,' they ask. *Discipline*, I soon realize, is a narrow, seldom-used term that refers to punishment, whereas *éducation* (which has nothing to do with school) is something they imagine themselves to be doing all the time.

For years now, headlines have been declaring the demise of the current style of Anglophone child-rearing. There are dozens of books in English offering helpful theories on how to parent differently.

I haven't got a theory. What I do have, spread out in front of me, is a fully functioning society of good little sleepers, gourmet eaters and reasonably relaxed parents. I'm starting with that outcome and working backwards to figure out how the French got there. It turns out that to be a different kind of parent, you don't just need a different parenting philosophy. You need a very different view of what a child actually is.

# 1

# Are You Waiting for a Child?

IT'S TEN IN THE MORNING WHEN THE MANAGING EDITOR summons me to his office and tells me to get my teeth checked. He says my dental plan will end on my last day at the newspaper. That will be in five weeks, he says.

More than two hundred of us are laid off that day. The news briefly boosts our parent company's stock price. I own some shares, and consider selling them – for irony rather than profit – to cash in on my own dismissal.

Instead I walk around lower Manhattan in a stupor. Fittingly, it's raining. I stand under a ledge and call the man I'm supposed to see that night.

'I've just been laid off,' I say.

'Aren't you devastated?' he asks. 'Do you still want to have dinner?'

In fact, I'm relieved. I'm finally free of a job that – after nearly six years – I hadn't had the guts to quit. I was a reporter for the foreign desk in New York, covering elections and financial crises in Latin America. I'd often be dispatched at a few hours' notice, then spend weeks living out of hotels. For a while, my bosses were expecting great things from me. They talked about future editorships. They paid for me to learn Portuguese.

Only suddenly they aren't expecting anything. And strangely, I'm OK with that. I really liked films about foreign correspondents. But actually being one was different. Usually I was all alone, shackled to an unending story, fielding calls from editors who just wanted more. I sometimes pictured the news as a mechanical rodeo bull. The men working the same beat as me managed to pick up Costa Rican and Colombian wives, who travelled around with them. At least they had dinner on the table when they finally slogged home. The men I went out with were less portable. And anyway, I rarely stayed anywhere long enough to reach the third date.

I'm relieved to be leaving the paper. But I'm unprepared for becoming socially toxic. In the week or so after the lay-offs, when I still come into the office, colleagues treat me like I'm contagious. People I've worked with for years say nothing, or avoid my desk. One workmate takes me out for a farewell lunch, then won't walk back into the building with me. Long after I clear out my desk, my editor – who was out of town when the axe fell – insists that I return to the office for a humiliating debriefing, in which he suggests that I apply for a lower-ranking job, then rushes off to lunch.

I'm suddenly clear about two things: I don't want to write about politics or money any more. And I want a boyfriend. I'm standing in my three-foot-wide kitchen, wondering what to do with the rest of my life, when Simon calls. We met six months earlier at a bar in Buenos Aires, when a mutual friend brought him to a foreign correspondents' night out. He's a British journalist who was in Argentina for a few days, to write a story about football. I'd been sent to cover the country's economic collapse. Apparently we were on the same flight from New York. He remembered me as the lady who'd held up boarding when, already on the gangway, I realized that I'd left my duty-free purchase in the departure lounge and insisted on going back to fetch it. (I did most of my shopping in airports.)

Simon was exactly my type: swarthy, stocky and smart. (Though he's of average height, he later adds 'short' to this list, since he grew up in Holland among blond giants.) Within a few hours of meeting him, I realized that 'love at first sight' just means feeling immediately and extremely calm with someone. Though all I said at the time was, 'We definitely must not sleep together.'

I was smitten, but wary. Simon had just fled the London property market to buy a cheap apartment in Paris. I was commuting between South America and New York. A long-distance relationship with someone on a third continent seemed a stretch. After that meeting in Argentina, we exchanged occasional emails. But I didn't let myself take him too seriously. I hoped that there were swarthy, smart men in my time zone.

Fast-forward seven months. When Simon calls out of the blue and I tell him that I've been sacked, he doesn't emote or treat me like damaged goods. On the contrary, he seems pleased that I suddenly have some free time. He says he feels that we have 'unfinished business', and that he'd like to come to New York.

'That's a terrible idea,' I say. What's the point? He can't move to America because he writes about European football. I don't speak French, and I've never considered living in Paris. Though I'm suddenly quite portable myself, I'm wary of being pulled into someone else's orbit before I have one of my own again.

Simon arrives in New York wearing the same beaten-up leather jacket he wore in Argentina, and carrying the bagel and smoked salmon that he's picked up at the deli near my apartment. A month later I meet his parents in London. Six months later I sell most of my possessions and ship the rest to France. My friends all tell me that I'm being rash. I ignore them, and walk out of my fixed-rent studio apartment in New York with three giant suitcases and a box of South American coins, which I give to the Pakistani driver who takes me to the airport.

And poof, I'm a Parisian. I move into Simon's two-room bachelor pad, in a former carpentry district in eastern Paris. With my unemployment cheques still arriving, I ditch financial journalism and begin researching a book. Simon and I each work in one of the rooms during the day.

The shine comes off our new romance almost immediately, mostly because of interior-design issues. I once read in a book about *feng shui* that having piles of stuff on the floor is a sign of depression. For Simon, it just seems to signal an aversion to shelves. He has cleverly invested in an enormous unfinished wooden table that fills most of the living room, and a primitive gas-heating system, which ensures that there's no reliable hot water. I'm especially irked by his habit of letting spare change from his pockets spill on to the floor, where it somehow gathers in the corners of each room. 'Get rid of the money,' I plead.

I don't find much comfort outside our apartment either. Despite being in the gastronomic capital of the world, I can't figure out what to eat. Like most Anglophone women I know, I arrive in Paris with extreme food preferences (I'm an Atkins-leaning vegetarian). Walking around, I feel besieged by all the bakeries and meat-heavy restaurant menus. For a while I subsist almost entirely on omelettes and goat's-cheese salads. When I ask waiters for 'dressing on the side', they look at me like I'm nuts. I don't understand why French supermarkets stock every American cereal except my personal favourite, Grape-Nuts, and why cafés don't serve fat-free milk.

I know it sounds ungrateful not to swoon over Paris. Maybe I find it shallow to fall for a city just because it's so good-looking. The cities I've had love affairs with in the past were all a bit, well, swarthier: São Paulo, Mexico City, New York. They didn't sit back and wait to be admired.

Our part of Paris isn't even that beautiful. And daily life is filled with small disappointments. No one mentions that 'springtime in Paris' is so celebrated because the preceding seven months are overcast and freezing (I arrive, conveniently, at the beginning of this seven-month stretch). And while I'm convinced that I remember my year of schoolgirl French,

Parisians have another name for what I'm speaking: Spanish.

There are many appealing things about Paris. I like it that the doors of the Métro open a few seconds before the train actually stops, suggesting that the city treats its citizens like adults. I also like it that, within six months of my arrival, practically everyone that Simon and I know in Britain and America comes to visit, including people I'd later learn to categorize as 'Facebook friends'. We eventually develop a strict admissions policy and rating system for houseguests. (Hint: If you stay a week, leave a gift.)

I'm not bothered by the famous Parisian rudeness. At least that's interactive. What gets me is the indifference. No one but Simon seems to care that I'm there. And he's often off nursing his own Parisian fantasy, which is so uncomplicated it has managed to endure. As far as I can tell, Simon has never visited a museum. But he describes reading the newspaper in a café as an almost transcendent experience. One night at a neighbourhood restaurant, he swoons when the waiter sets down a cheese plate in front of him.

'This is why I live in Paris!' he declares. I realize that, by the transitive property of love and cheese, I must live in Paris for that smelly plate of cheese too.

To be fair, I'm starting to think that it's not Paris: it's me. New York likes its women a bit neurotic. They're encouraged to create a brainy, adorable, conflicted bustle around themselves – à la Meg Ryan in *When Harry Met Sally*, or Diane Keaton in *Annie Hall*. Despite having nothing more serious than man troubles, many of my friends in

New York were spending more on therapy than on rent.

That persona doesn't fly in Paris. The French do like Woody Allen's movies. But in real life, the ideal *Parisienne* is calm, discreet, a bit remote and extremely decisive. She orders from the menu. She doesn't blather on about her childhood or her diet. If New York is about the woman who's ruminating about her past screw-ups and fumbling to find herself, Paris is about the one who – at least outwardly – regrets nothing. In France 'neurotic' isn't a self-deprecating half-boast; it's a clinical condition.

Even Simon, who's merely British, is perplexed by my self-doubt, and my frequent need to discuss our relationship.

'What are you thinking about?' I ask him periodically, usually when he's reading a newspaper.

'Dutch football,' he invariably says.

I can't tell if he's serious. I've realized that Simon is in a state of perpetual irony. He says everything, including 'I love you', with a little smirk. And yet he almost never actually laughs, even when I'm attempting a joke. (Some close friends don't know that he has dimples.) Simon insists that not smiling is a British habit. But I'm sure I've seen Englishmen laugh. And anyway, it's demoralizing that when I finally get to speak English with someone, he doesn't seem to be listening.

This not-laughing also points to a wider cultural gulf between us. As an American, I need things to be spelled out. On the train back to Paris after a weekend with Simon's parents, I ask him whether they liked me.

'Of course they liked you, couldn't you tell?' he asks.

'But did they *say* they liked me?' I demand to know.

In search of other company, I trek across town on a series of 'friend blind dates', with friends of friends from back home. Most are expatriates too. None seems thrilled to hear from a clueless new arrival. Quite a few seem to have made 'living in Paris' a kind of job in itself, and an all-purpose answer to the question, 'What do you do?' Many show up late, as if to prove that they've gone native. (I later learn that French people are typically on time for one-to-one meetings. They're only fashionably late for group events, including children's birthday parties.)

My initial attempts to make French friends are even less successful. At a party, I hit it off reasonably well with an art historian who's about my age, and who speaks excellent English. But when we meet again for tea at her house, it's clear that we observe vastly different female bonding rituals. I'm prepared to follow the Anglo-American model of confession and mirroring, with lots of comforting 'me too's. She pokes daintily at her pastry and discusses theories of art. I leave hungry, and not even knowing whether she has a boyfriend.

The only mirroring I get is in a book by Edmund White, an American writer who lived in France in the 1980s. He's the first person who affirms that feeling depressed and adrift is a rational response to living in Paris. 'Imagine dying and being grateful you'd gone to heaven, until one day (or one century) it dawned on you that your main mood was melancholy, although you were constantly convinced that happiness lay just around the next corner. That's something like living in

Paris for years, even decades. It's a mild hell so comfortable that it resembles heaven.'

Despite my doubts about Paris, I'm still pretty sure about Simon. I've become resigned to the fact that 'swarthy' inevitably comes with 'messy'. And I've got better at reading his micro-expressions. A flicker of a smile means that he's got the joke. The rare full smile suggests high praise. He even occasionally says 'that was funny' in a monotone.

I'm also encouraged by the fact that, for a curmudgeon, Simon has dozens of devoted, long-time friends. Perhaps it's that, behind the layers of irony, he is charmingly helpless. He can't drive a car, blow up a balloon or fold clothes without using his teeth. He fills our refrigerator with unopened tins of food. For expediency's sake, he cooks everything at the highest temperature. (University friends later tell me he was known for serving drumsticks that were charred on the outside and still frozen on the inside.) When I show him how to make salad dressing using oil and vinegar, he writes down the recipe, and still pulls it out years later whenever he makes dinner.

Also to Simon's credit, nothing about France ever bothers him. He's in his element being a foreigner. His parents are anthropologists who brought him up all over the world and trained him from birth to delight in local customs. He'd lived in six countries (including a year in America) by the time he was ten. He acquires languages the way I acquire shoes.

I decide that, for Simon's sake, I'll give France a real go. We get married outside Paris at a thirteenth-century chateau, which is surrounded by a moat (I ignore the symbolism). In the name of marital harmony, we rent a larger apartment. I place a massive order with Ikea for bookshelves, and position spare-change bowls in every room. I try to channel my inner pragmatist instead of my inner neurotic. In restaurants, I start ordering straight from the menu, and nibbling at the occasional hunk of *foie gras*. My French starts to sound less like excellent Spanish and more like very bad French. Before long I'm almost settled: I have a home office, a book deadline, and even a few new friends.

Simon and I have talked about babies. We both want one. I'd like three, in fact. And I like the idea of having them in Paris, where they'll be effortlessly bilingual and authentically international. Even if they grow up to be geeks, they can mention 'growing up in Paris' and be instantly cool.

I'm worried about getting pregnant. I've spent much of my adult life trying, very successfully, not to, so I have no idea whether I'm any good at the reverse. This turns out to be as whirlwind as our courtship. One day I'm Googling 'How to get pregnant'. The next, it seems, I'm looking at two pink lines on a French pregnancy test.

I'm ecstatic. But alongside my joy comes a surge of anxiety. My resolve to become less Carrie Bradshaw and more Catherine Deneuve immediately collapses. This doesn't seem like the moment to go native. I'm possessed by the idea that I've got to oversee my pregnancy, and do it exactly right. Hours after telling Simon the good news, I go online to scour English-language pregnancy websites. Then I rush to buy some pregnancy guides, at an English bookstore near the Louvre. I want to know, in plain English, exactly what to worry about.

Within days I'm on prenatal vitamins and addicted to BabyCentre's 'Is it safe?' column. Is it safe to eat non-organic produce while pregnant? Is it safe to be around computers all day? Is it safe to wear high heels, binge on sweets at Halloween, or holiday at high altitudes?

What makes 'Is it safe?' so compulsive is that it creates new anxieties (Is it safe to make photocopies? Is it safe to swallow semen?) but then refuses to allay them with a simple yes or no. Instead, expert respondents disagree with each other and equivocate. 'Is it safe to get a manicure while I'm pregnant?' Well yes, but chronic exposure to the solvents used in salons isn't good for you. Is it safe to go bowling? Well, yes and no.

The Anglophones I know also believe that pregnancy – and then motherhood – come with homework. The first assignment is choosing from among myriad parenting styles. Everyone I speak to swears by a different book. I buy many of them. But instead of making me feel more prepared, having so much conflicting advice makes babies themselves seem enigmatic and unknowable. Who they are, and what they need, seems to depend on which book you read.

Another consequence of this independent study is that we Anglophone mothers-to-be become experts in everything that can go wrong. A pregnant Englishwoman who's visiting Paris declares, over lunch, that there's a five in one thousand chance her baby will be stillborn. She says she knows that saying this is gruesome and pointless, but she can't help herself. A Londoner I know, who unfortunately has a doctorate in public health, spends much of her first trimester cataloguing the baby's risks of contracting every possible malady.

I'm surrounded by this anxiety when we visit Simon's family in London (I've decided to believe that his parents adore me). I'm sitting in a café when a well-dressed woman interrupts me to describe a new study showing that having a lot of caffeine increases the risk of miscarriage. To stress her credibility, she says she's *married to a doctor*. I don't care who her husband is. I'm just irritated by her assumption that I haven't read that study. Of course I have; I'm trying to live on one cup a week.

With so much studying and worrying to do, being pregnant increasingly feels like a full-time job. I spend less and less time working on my book, which I'm supposed to hand in before the baby comes. Instead, I commune with other pregnant Anglophones in due-date-cohort chat rooms. Like me, these women are used to customizing their environments, even if it's just to get soy milk in their coffees. And like me, they find the primitive, mammalian event happening inside their bodies to be uncomfortably out of their control. Worrying – like clutching the armrest during aircraft turbulence – at least makes us feel like it's not.

The English-language pregnancy press, which I can easily access from Paris, seems to be lying in wait to channel this anxiety. It focuses on the one thing that pregnant women can definitely control: food. 'As you raise fork to mouth, consider: "Is this a bite that will benefit my baby?" If it is, chew away . . .'

explain the authors of *What to Expect When You're Expecting*, the famously worrying – and bestselling – pregnancy manual.

I'm aware that the prohibitions in my books aren't equally important. Cigarettes and alcohol are definitely bad, whereas shellfish, cold meat, raw eggs and unpasteurized cheese are only dangerous if they've been contaminated with something rare like listeria or salmonella. But to be safe, I take every prohibition literally. It's easy enough to avoid oysters and *foie gras*. But – since I'm in France – I'm panicked about cheese. 'Is the Parmesan on my pasta pasteurized?' I ask flabbergasted waiters. Simon bears the brunt of my angst. Did he scrub the chopping board after cutting up that raw chicken? Does he really love our unborn child?

*What to Expect* contains something called the Pregnancy Diet, which its creators claim can 'improve fetal brain development', 'reduce the risk of certain birth defects' and 'may even make it more likely that your child will grow to be a healthier adult'. Every morsel seems to represent potential SAT points. Never mind hunger: if I find myself short of a protein portion at the end of the day, the Pregnancy Diet says I should cram in a final serving of egg salad before bedtime.

They had me at 'diet'. After years of dieting to slim down, it's thrilling to be 'dieting' to gain weight. It feels like a reward for having spent years thin enough to nab a husband. My online forums are filled with women who've put on forty or fifty pounds over the recommended limits. Of course we'd all rather resemble those compactly pregnant celebrities in designer gowns, or the models on the cover of *Fit Pregnancy*.

Some women I know actually do. But a competing message says that we should give ourselves a free pass. 'Go ahead and EAT', says the chummy author of the *Best Friends' Guide to Pregnancy*, which I've been cuddling up with in bed. 'What other joys are there for pregnant women?'

Tellingly, the Pregnancy Diet says that I can 'cheat' with the occasional fast-food cheeseburger or glazed doughnut. In fact, pregnancy seems like one big cheat. Lists of pregnancy cravings read like a catalogue of foods that women have been denying themselves since adolescence: cheesecake, milk-shakes, macaroni and cheese and ice cream cake. I crave lemon on everything, and entire loaves of bread.

Someone tells me that Jane Birkin says she can never remember whether it was '*un* baguette' or '*une* baguette', so she just orders '*deux baguettes*'. I can't find the quote. But whenever I go to the bakery, I follow this strategy. Then – surely unlike the twiggy Birkin – I eat them both.

I'm not just losing my figure. I'm also losing a sense of myself as someone who once went on dinner dates and worried about the Palestinians. I now spend my free time studying new-model buggies and memorizing the possible causes of colic. This evolution from 'woman' to 'mum' feels inevitable. A fashion spread in a pregnancy magazine that I pick up on a trip to New York shows big-bellied women in floppy shirts and men's pyjama bottoms, and says that these outfits are worthy of wearing all day. Perhaps to get out of ever finishing my book, I fantasize about ditching journalism and training as a midwife.

Actual sex is the final, symbolic domino to fall. Although it's technically permitted, books like *What to Expect* presume that sex during pregnancy is inherently fraught. 'What got you into this situation in the first place may now have become one of your biggest problems,' the authors warn. They go on to describe eighteen factors that may inhibit your sex life, including 'fear that the introduction of the penis into the vagina will cause infection'. If a woman does find herself having sex, they recommend a new low in multitasking: using the moment to do pelvic-floor exercises, which tone your birth canal in preparation for childbirth.

I'm not sure that anyone follows all this advice. Like me, they probably just absorb a certain worried tone and state of mind. Even from abroad, it's contagious. Given how susceptible I am, it's probably better that I'm far from the source. Maybe the distance will give me some perspective on parenting.

I'm already starting to suspect that raising a child will be quite different in France. When I sit in cafés in Paris, with my belly pushing up against the table, no one jumps in to warn me about the hazards of caffeine. On the contrary, they light cigarettes right next to me. The only question strangers ask, when they notice my belly, is *Vous attendez un enfant?* – are you waiting for a child? It takes me a while to realize that they don't think I have a lunch date with a truant six-year-old. It's French for 'Are you pregnant?'

I am waiting for a baby. It's probably the most important thing I've ever done. Despite my qualms about Paris, there's something nice about doing this waiting in a place where I'm practically immune to other people's judgements. Though Paris is one of the most cosmopolitan cities on earth, I feel like I'm off the grid. In French I don't understand name-dropping, school histories and other little hints that, to a French person, signal someone's social rank and importance. And since I'm a foreigner, they don't know my status either.

When I packed up and moved to Paris, I never imagined that the move would be permanent. Now I'm starting to worry that Simon likes being a foreigner a bit too much. After living in all those countries while he was growing up, it's his natural state. He confesses that he feels connected to lots of people and cities, and doesn't need any one place to be his official home. He calls this style 'semi-detached', like a house in a London suburb.

Already, several of our Anglophone friends have left France, usually when their jobs changed. But our jobs don't require us to be here. The cheese plate aside, we're really here for no reason. And 'no reason' – plus a baby – is starting to look like the strongest reason of all.

# 2

# Paris Is Burping

OUR NEW APARTMENT ISN'T IN THE PARIS OF POSTCARDS. It's off a narrow street in a Chinese garment district, where we're constantly jostled by men hauling rubbish bags full of clothes. There's no sign that we're in the same city as the Eiffel Tower, Notre-Dame or the elegantly winding river Seine.

Yet somehow this new neighbourhood works for us. Simon and I stake out our respective cafés nearby, and retreat each morning for some convivial solitude. Here, too, socializing follows unfamiliar rules. It's OK to banter with the staff, but generally not with the other patrons (unless they're at the bar, and talking to the barman too). Though I'm off the grid, I do need human contact. One morning I try to strike up a conversation with another regular – a man I've seen every day for months. I tell him, honestly, that he looks like an American I know.

'Who, George Clooney?' he asks snidely. We never speak again.

I make more headway with our new neighbours. The

crowded street outside our house opens on to a quiet cobble-stone courtyard, where low-slung houses and apartments face each other. The residents are a mix of artists, young professionals, mysteriously underemployed people and elderly women who hobble precariously on the uneven stones. We all live so close together that they have to acknowledge our presence, though a few still manage not to.

It helps that my next-door neighbour, an architect named Anne, is due a few months before me. Though I'm caught up in my Anglophone whirlwind of eating and worrying, I can't help but notice that Anne and the other pregnant French women I come to know handle their pregnancies very differently.

For starters, they don't treat pregnancy like an independent research project. There are plenty of French parenting books, magazines and websites. But these aren't required reading, and nobody seems to consume them in bulk. Certainly no Frenchwoman I meet is comparison-shopping for a parenting philosophy, or can refer to different techniques by name. There's no new, must-read book, nor do the experts have quite the same sway.

'These books can be useful to people who lack confidence, but I don't think you can raise a child while reading a book. You have to go with your *feeling*,' one Parisian mother says.

The French women I meet aren't at all blasé about mother-hood, or about their babies' well-being. They're awed, concerned, and aware of the immense life transformation that they're about to undergo. But they signal this differently from

Anglophone women. We typically demonstrate our commitment by worrying, and by showing how much we're willing to sacrifice, even while pregnant. French women signal their commitment by projecting calm, and flaunting the fact that they haven't renounced pleasure.

A photospread in *Neuf Mois* shows a heavily pregnant brunette in lacy ensembles, biting into pastries and licking jam from her finger. 'During pregnancy, it's important to pamper your inner woman,' another article says. 'Above all, resist the urge to borrow your partner's shirts.' A list of aphrodisiacs for mums-to-be includes chocolate, ginger, cinnamon and – this being France – mustard.

I realize that ordinary French women take these calls to arms seriously when Samia, a mother who lives in my neighbourhood, offers me a tour of her apartment. She's the daughter of Algerian immigrants, and grew up in Chartres. I'm admiring her soaring ceilings and chandeliers, when she picks up a stack of photographs.

'In this one I was pregnant, and here I was pregnant. *Et voilà*, the big belly!' she says, handing me several pictures. It's true, she's extremely pregnant in the photographs. She's also extremely topless.

I'm shocked, first of all, because we've been using the formal '*vous*' with each other, and now she's casually handed me naked pictures of herself. But I'm also surprised that the pictures are so glamorous. Samia looks like one of those lingerie models from the magazines, *sans* most of the lingerie.

Granted, Samia is always a bit dramatic. Most days she drops off her two-year-old at daycare looking like she just stepped out of a film noir: a beige trench coat clinched tightly at the waist, black eyeliner and a fresh coat of shiny red lipstick. She's the only French person I know who actually wears a beret.

Nevertheless, Samia has merely embraced the conventional French wisdom that the forty-week metamorphosis into mother shouldn't make you any less of a woman. French pregnancy magazines don't just say that pregnant women can have sex; they explain exactly how to do it. *Neuf Mois* maps out ten different sexual positions including 'horseback rider', 'reverse horseback rider', 'the greyhound' (which it calls '*un grand classique*') and 'the chair'. 'The oarsmen' has six steps, concluding with 'In rocking her torso back and forth, Madame provokes delicious frictions . . .'

*Neuf Mois* also weighs in on the merits of various sex toys for pregnant women (yes to 'geisha balls', no to vibrators and anything electric). 'Don't hesitate! Everyone wins, even the baby. During an orgasm, he feels the "Jacuzzi effect" as if he was massaged in the water,' the text explains. A father in Paris warns my husband not to stand at the 'business end' during the birth, to preserve my feminine mystique.

French parents-to-be aren't just calmer about sex. They're also calmer about food. Samia makes a conversation with her obstetrician sound like a vaudeville routine:

'I said, "Doctor, I'm pregnant, but I adore oysters. What do I do?" He said, "Eat oysters!"' she recalls. 'He explained to me, "You seem like a fairly reasonable person. Wash things well. If you eat sushi, eat it in a good place."'

The stereotype that French women smoke and drink through their pregnancies is very outdated. Most women I meet say that they had either the occasional glass of champagne, or no alcohol at all. I see a pregnant woman smoking exactly once, on the street. It could have been her once-a-month cigarette. I leave her alone.

The point isn't that anything goes. It's that women should be calm and sensible. The French mothers I meet distinguish between the foods and substances that are almost definitely damaging and those that are only dangerous if they're contaminated. Another woman I meet in the neighbourhood is Caroline, a physiotherapist who's seven months pregnant. She says her doctor never mentioned any food restrictions, and she never asked. 'It's better not to know!' she says. She tells me that she eats steak *tartare*, and of course joined the family for *foie gras* over Christmas. She just makes sure to eat it in good restaurants, or at home. Her one concession is that when she eats unpasteurized cheese, she cuts off the rind.

I don't actually witness any pregnant women eating oysters. If I did, I might have to throw my enormous body over the table to stop them. They'd certainly be surprised. It's clear why French waiters are baffled when I interrogate them about the ingredients in each dish. French women generally don't make a fuss about this.

The French pregnancy press doesn't dwell on unlikely worst-case scenarios. *Au contraire*, it suggests that what mothers-to-be need most is serenity. 'Nine months of spa' is the headline in one French magazine. *The Guide for New*

31

*Mothers*, a free booklet prepared with support from the French health ministry, says its eating guidelines favour the baby's 'harmonious growth', and that women should find 'inspiration' from different flavours. 'Pregnancy should be a time of great happiness!' it declares.

Is all this safe? It sure seems like it. France trumps the US and Britain on nearly every measure of maternal and infant health. The infant mortality rate is 29 per cent lower in France than it is in the UK, and the under-five mortality rate is 50 per cent lower in France. According to Unicef, about 6.6 per cent of French babies have a low birth weight, compared to about 7.5 per cent of American babies.

What really drives home the French message that pregnancy should be savoured isn't the statistics or the pregnant women I meet. It's the pregnant cat. She's a slender, grey-eyed cat who lives in our courtyard and is about to deliver. Her owner, a pretty painter in her forties, tells me that she plans to have the cat spayed after the kittens are born. But she couldn't bear to neuter the cat before she had gone through a pregnancy. 'I wanted her to have that experience,' she says.

Of course French mothers-to-be aren't just calmer than we are. Like the cat, they're also skinnier. Some pregnant French women do get fat. In general, body-fat ratios seem to increase the further you get from central Paris. But the Parisians I see all around me look alarmingly like those celebrities on the red carpet. They have basketball-sized baby bumps, pasted on to skinny legs, arms and hips. Viewed from the back, you usually can't tell they're expecting.

Enough pregnant women have these proportions that I stop gawking when I pass one on the street or in the supermarket. This French norm is strictly codified. English-language pregnancy calculators tell me that – with my height and build – I should gain up to 35 pounds during my pregnancy. But French calculators tell me to gain no more than 26.5 pounds (by the time I see this, it's too late).

How do French women stay within these limits? Social pressure helps. Friends, sisters and mothers-in-law openly transmit the message that pregnancy isn't a free pass to gorge. (I'm spared the worst of this because I don't have French in-laws.) Audrey, a French journalist with three kids, tells me that she confronted her German sister-in-law, who had started out tall and svelte.

'The moment she got pregnant she became enormous. And I saw her and I found it monstrous. She told me, "No, it's fine, I'm entitled to relax. I'm entitled to get fat. It's no big deal," et cetera. For us, the French, it's horrible to say that. We would *never* say that.' She adds a jab disguised as sociology: 'I think the Americans and the Northern Europeans are a lot more relaxed than us when it comes to aesthetics.'

Everyone in France takes for granted that pregnant women should battle to keep their figures intact. While my podiatrist is working on my feet, she suddenly announces that I should rub sweet almond oil on my belly, to avoid stretch marks (I do this dutifully, and get none). Parenting magazines run long features on how to minimize the damage that pregnancy does to your breasts (don't gain too much weight, and take a daily jet of cold water to the chest).

French doctors treat the weight-gain limits like holy edicts. Anglophones in Paris are routinely shocked when their obstetricians scold them for going even slightly over. 'It's just the French men trying to keep their women slim,' a British woman married to a Frenchman huffed, recalling her pre-natal appointments in Paris. Paediatricians feel free to comment on a mother's post-pregnancy belly when she brings her baby for a check-up. (Mine will just cast a worried glance.)

The main reason that pregnant French women don't get fat is that they are very careful not to eat too much. In French pregnancy guides, there are no late-night binges on egg salad, or instructions to eat way past hunger in order to nourish the fetus. Women who are 'waiting for a child' are supposed to eat the same balanced meals as any healthy adult. One guide says that if a woman is still hungry, she should add an afternoon snack consisting of, for instance, 'a sixth of a baguette', a piece of cheese and a glass of water.

In the French view, a pregnant woman's food cravings are a nuisance to be vanquished. French women don't let themselves believe – as I've heard Anglophone women claim – that the fetus wants cheesecake. The French *Guidebook for Mothers to Be* says that instead of giving in to a craving, women should distract their bodies by eating an apple or a raw carrot.

This isn't all as austere as it sounds. French women don't see pregnancy as a free pass to overeat, in part because they haven't been denying themselves the foods they love – or secretly bingeing on those foods – for most of their adult lives. 'Too often, American women eat on the sly, and the result is much more guilt than pleasure,' Mireille Guiliano explains in her intelligent book *French Women Don't Get Fat*. 'Pretending such pleasures don't exist, or trying to eliminate them from your diet for an extended time, will probably lead to weight gain.'

About halfway through my pregnancy, I hear that there's a support group in Paris for English-speaking parents. I immediately recognize that these are my people. Members of the group, called Message, will tell you where to find an English-speaking therapist, or buy longed-for foods like English bacon, Marmite, and something called Frazzles.

Message members find a lot to like about France. In online forums, they marvel at the fresh bread, the cheap prescription drugs, and their toddlers' demands for Camembert after a meal. One member chuckles that her five-year-old plays 'going on strike' with his Playmobil figures.

But the group is also a bulwark against what are seen as the darker parts of French parenting. Members exchange the phone numbers of English-speaking birth assistants, sell each other breastfeeding pillows, and commiserate about French medicine's penchant for giving kids suppositories. One member I know was so reluctant to subject her daughter to a French state nursery school that she enrolled her in a brand-new Montessori, where the little girl was – for quite a while – the only student.

Like me, these women see being pregnant as an excuse to bond, worry, shop and eat. They fortify each other against the social pressure to lose their baby weight. 'At some point I'll get around to it,' one new mother writes. 'I'm not going to waste precious time weighing out lettuce leaves now.'

The salient dilemma, among pregnant Message members and other Anglophones I know, is *how* to give birth. I meet an American in Rome who delivered her baby in an Italian wine vat (filled with water, not Pinot Grigio). A friend in Miami read that the pain of childbirth is just a cultural construct, so she trained to birth her twins using only yoga breaths. In our Message-sponsored parenting class, there's a woman who plans to fly home to Sydney for an authentic Australian delivery.

Birth, like most everything else, is something we try to customize. My obstetrician says she once received a four-page birth plan from an English-speaking patient, instructing her to massage the woman's clitoris after the delivery. The uterine contractions from the woman's orgasm were supposed to help expel the placenta. Interestingly, this woman's birth plan also specified that both of her parents should be allowed in the delivery room. ('I said, "No way." I didn't want to be arrested,' my doctor recalls.)

Amid all this talk about giving birth, I don't hear anyone mention that the last time the World Health Organization ranked healthcare systems, France's was first, while Britain's was eighteenth (America's was thirty-seventh). Instead, we Anglos focus on how the French system is over-medicalized and hostile to the 'natural'. Pregnant Message members fret that French doctors will induce labour, force them to have epidurals, then secretly bottle-feed their newborns so they won't be able to breastfeed. We've all been reading the English-language pregnancy press, which emphasizes the most minute risks of epidurals.

Those among us who deliver 'naturally' strut around like war heroes. An English mother tells me that when she asked for an epidural back in Brighton, 'the midwife asked, "Why do you want an epidural? Are you afraid?" They treated me like a pansy.' A top British midwife has called for more women to experience the full pain of childbirth, in part to prepare them for looking after an infant.

Despite being the birthplace of natural-birth guru Dr Fernand Lamaze, epidurals are now extremely common in France. In Paris's top maternity hospitals and clinics, about 87 per cent of women have epidurals, on average (not counting C-sections). In some hospitals it's 98 or 99 per cent.

Very few women make a fuss about this. French mums often ask me where I plan to deliver, but never how. They don't seem to care. In France, the way you give birth doesn't situate you within a value system or define the sort of parent you'll be. It is, for the most part, a way of getting your baby safely from your uterus into your arms.

In France, giving birth without an epidural isn't called 'natural' childbirth. It's called 'giving birth without an epidural' (*accouchement sans péridurale*). A few French hospitals and maternity clinics now have birthing pools and giant rubber balls for labouring women to hug. But few French women choose to deliver this way. That 1 or 2 per cent of non-epidural births in Paris are, I'm told, mostly crazy Anglophones like me, or French women who didn't get to the hospital in time.

The earthiest French woman I know is Hélène. She takes her three kids on camping trips and breastfed them all past age two. Hélène also had an epidural at each delivery. For her, there's no contradiction. She likes some things *au naturel*, and some with a giant dose of drugs.

The difference between France and America crystallizes for me when, through mutual friends, I meet Jennifer and Éric. She's an American who works for a multinational company in Paris. He's a Frenchman who's in advertising. They live just outside Paris, with their two daughters. When Jennifer got pregnant for the first time, Éric just assumed that they would find a doctor, choose a hospital and have the baby. But Jennifer brought home a stack of baby books and pressed Éric to study them with her.

Éric still can't believe how Jennifer wanted to script the delivery. 'She wanted to give birth on a balloon, give birth in a bath,' he recalls. He says the doctor told her, 'It's not a zoo here, or a circus. Basically you will give birth like everyone else, on your back, legs open. And the reason is that if there is a problem, then I can do something.'

Jennifer also wanted to deliver without anaesthesia, so that she could feel what it was like to give birth. 'I've never heard of a woman wanting to suffer so much to have a kid,' Éric says.

What stands out for both Éric and Jennifer is what I've come to think of as the 'Croissant Story'. When Jennifer went into labour, it became clear that all her birthing plans were for naught: she needed a Caesarean. The doctor sent Éric into the waiting room. Eventually, Jennifer delivered a healthy baby girl.

Afterwards, Éric came into the recovery room, and happened to mention that he recently ate a croissant. Three years later, Jennifer's blood still boils when she thinks about that bread roll. 'Éric wasn't actually physically present [in the waiting room] during the whole thing. He went out and got a croissant! When they rolled me into the operating room, Éric walks out of the clinic, goes down the street, goes to the bakery, and buys a couple of croissants. He comes back, eats his croissant!'

This is not what Jennifer had envisioned. 'My husband needs to be sitting there biting his nails, thinking, "Oh, will it be a boy or a girl?"' she says. She mentions that there was a vending machine near the waiting room. He could have bought a bag of peanuts.

When Éric tells his own version of the Croissant Story, he gets mad too. Yes, there was a vending machine. But 'It was very stressful, I needed some sugar,' he says. 'I was sure there was a bakery just at the corner, and the bakery ended up being a bit far away. But they took her in at seven. I knew that they had one hour of preparation and things like that, and I think she came back out at eleven. So in all this time, yes, I spent at least fifteen minutes going to eat some food.'

At first, I see the Croissant Story as a classic Men-are-from-

Mars tale. But I eventually realize that it's an Anglo-French parable. For Jennifer, Éric's selfish pursuit of the croissant signalled that he wouldn't sacrifice his own comfort for the sake of his family, and the new baby. She worried that he wasn't sufficiently invested in the project of parenting.

For Éric, it signalled no such thing. He felt thoroughly invested in the birth, and is an extremely involved father. But at that moment, he was also calm, detached and self-interested enough to walk down the street. He wanted to be a dad, but he also wanted a croissant. 'In the US sometimes I have the feeling that if it's not difficult for you, you have to feel bad about that,' he says.

I'd like to think I'm the sort of wife who wouldn't be bothered by the croissant, or at least that Simon is the sort of husband who would hide the crumbs. I do submit a PG-rated birth plan, stating that under no circumstances should Simon be permitted to cut the umbilical cord (he can barely cut the chicken). But since I tend to scream when I get my legs waxed, I don't think I'm a great candidate for natural childbirth. I suspect I'll have trouble viewing the pain as a cultural construct.

I'm more concerned about getting to the hospital in time. Following a friend's advice, I've registered to give birth at a hospital all the way across town. If the baby makes a break for it during rush hour, there could be trouble.

And that's if I can get a taxi. The rumour among Paris's Anglophones (who, being here temporarily, tend not to have cars) is that French taxi drivers refuse to pick up women in labour, for fear that they'll end up scraping placenta off their seats. A back-seat delivery wouldn't be ideal for other reasons. Simon is too spooked to even read the instructions for emergency home deliveries in *What to Expect*.

My contractions begin around eight o'clock at night. That means I can't eat the steaming Thai food we've just picked up (I will fantasize about pad thai from my hospital bed), but at least the streets are clear. Simon calls a taxi, and I'm quiet while getting in. Let the driver – a moustachioed man in his fifties – try to pry me out.

I needn't have worried. As soon as we're on the road and he hears my yelps from the back seat, the driver becomes ecstatic. He says he's been waiting his whole career as a taxi driver for this cinematic event.

As we cross Paris in the dark, I open my seatbelt and slide to the floor of the taxi, moaning from the mounting pain. This is no leg wax. I ditch my *faux* fantasies of a natural childbirth. Simon opens the windows, either to give me some air or to drown out the unpleasant sounds I'm making.

Meanwhile, the driver speeds up. I can see the streetlights zipping past overhead. He begins loudly reciting the story of his own son's birth twenty-five years earlier. 'Slower, please!' I plead from the floor, between contractions. Simon is silent and pale, staring straight ahead.

'What are you thinking about?' I ask him.

'Dutch football,' he says.

When we arrive at the hospital, the driver pulls up at the

emergency entrance, jumps out of the car and sprints inside. It seems he may be planning to join us for the birth. Moments later he's back, sweaty and panting. 'They're expecting you!' he shouts.

I lurch into the building, leaving Simon to pay the fare and persuade the driver to leave. The moment I see a midwife, I declare in my clearest French: *'Je voudrais une péridurale!'* (I would like an epidural). If I'd had a wad of cash I would have waved it at her.

It turns out that despite the French passion for epidurals, they don't just perform them on demand. The midwife takes me into an examination room to check my cervix, then looks up at me with a bemused smile. I'm barely three centimetres dilated, out of a possible ten. Women don't usually ask for epidurals this early on, she says. She won't summon the anaesthetist from *his* pad thai for this.

She does put on the most soothing music I've ever heard – a sort of Tibetan lullaby – and rigs me up to a drip that softens the pain. Eventually, exhausted, I fall asleep.

I'll spare you the details of my very medicated, very pleasant birth. Thanks to the epidural, pushing the baby out has the precision and intensity of a yoga move, without the discomfort. I'm so focused that I don't even mind when my obstetrician's teenage daughter, who lives around the corner, pops in after the delivery to ask her mum for some cash.

As it happens, the anaesthetist, midwife and doctor are all women. (Simon, stationed far from the business end, is there too.) The baby comes out as the sun is rising.

I've read that babies look like their fathers when they're born, to assure the dads of their paternity and motivate them to go out hunting (or investment banking) for the family. My first thought when I see our daughter is that she doesn't merely resemble Simon; she has his face.

We cuddle with her for a while, then they dress her up in a chicly understated French outfit, supplied by the hospital, complete with an ecru-coloured beanie on her head. We do give her a proper name. But thanks to the hat, we mostly just call her Bean.

I stay in the hospital for six days. Staying this long is standard French practice for normal deliveries. (In public hospitals, the national insurance covers just about everything. Private hospitals charge more, so the national insurance only covers part of the total.) In any case, I see no reason to leave. We haven't yet ordered from the extensive room-service wine list, which includes champagne. There is fresh-baked bread with every meal (no need to go out for a croissant) and a sun-dappled garden where I steal away for walks. On day three, I can't stop telling Bean, 'You weren't born yesterday!' Simon doesn't even pretend this is funny.

As if to emphasize that there are universal parenting principles in France, babies born here come with instructions. Each newborn is issued a white paperback book called a *carnet de santé*, which follows the child until age eighteen. Doctors record every check-up and vaccination in this book, and plot the child's height, weight and head size. It also has common-sense basics on what to feed babies, how to bath them, when to go for check-ups, and how to spot medical problems.

The book doesn't prepare me for Bean's transformation. For the first month or so, she continues to look just like Simon, with dark brown eyes and hair. She even has his dimples. If anything's in doubt, it's her maternity. My fair-haired, light-eyed genes seem to have lost out to his swarthy Mediterranean ones in a first-round knockout.

But at about two months old, Bean undergoes a metamorphosis. Her hair turns blonde, and her brown eyes morph improbably into blue. Our little Mediterranean baby suddenly looks like a Swede.

Technically, Bean is American (she can request French citizenship when she's older. Simon wasn't born in Britain, so we can't immediately make her British either.) But I suspect that her French will surpass mine within a few months. I'm not sure whether we're going to raise a little Anglo-American girl, or a little French one. We might not have a choice.

# 3

# Doing Her Nights

A FEW WEEKS AFTER WE BRING BEAN HOME, NEIGHBOURS ON our little courtyard begin asking, 'Is she doing her nights?' ('*Elle fait ses nuits?*')

This is the first time I hear the French formulation of 'Is she sleeping through the night?' At first I find it comforting. If they're *her* nights, then she'll inevitably claim them. Whereas if they're just *the* nights, she might not.

But I soon find the question irritating. Of course she's not 'doing her nights'. She's two months old (and then three months, and then four). Everyone knows that tiny babies sleep badly. A few of my Anglophone friends have babies that age who go down at 9 pm and wake up at seven. But this seems to be sheer luck. Most parents I know don't get an uninterrupted night's sleep until their kids are around a year old. Heck, I know four-year-olds who still wander into their parents' rooms at night.

My Anglophone friends and family appreciate this. They tend to ask the more open-ended question: 'How is she sleeping?' And even that isn't really a request for information; it's a chance for us to vent.

For us, babies are automatically associated with sleep deprivation. A headline in the *Daily Mail* declares: 'Parents of newborns miss out on SIX MONTHS worth of sleep in their child's first two years,' citing a study commissioned by a bed company. The article seems credible to readers. 'Sadly this is true,' one comments. 'Our one-year-old daughter hasn't slept a single night in twelve months, and if we have four hours' sleep it's a good night.' A poll by the National Sleep Foundation in the US found that 46 *per cent of toddlers wake up during the night*, but just 11 per cent of parents believed that their child had a sleep problem. A toddler's T-shirt I see in Fort Lauderdale says simply, 'Party tonight at my crib 3 am.'

My English-speaking friends tend to view their kids as having unique sleep needs, which they just have to accommodate. I'm walking around Paris with a British artist one day when her toddler son climbs into her arms, reaches under her shirt to hold her breast, then falls asleep. She's clearly embarrassed that I've witnessed this ritual, but whispers that it's the only way he can nap. She carries him around in this position for the next forty-five minutes.

Simon and I had of course chosen a sleep strategy. Ours was premised on the idea that it's critical to keep a baby awake after she feeds. Once Bean is born, we go to enormous lengths to do this. As far as I can tell, it has no effect.

Eventually, we ditch this theory and try other ones. We keep Bean in the daylight all day and in the dark at night. We bath her at the same time each evening, and try to stretch out the time between her feeds. For a few days I eat almost nothing but crackers and Brie, after someone tells me that fatty food will thicken my breast milk. A New Yorker who stops by says she read that we should make loud whooshing sounds, to mimic the sounds in the womb. We whoosh obediently for hours.

Nothing seems to make a difference. At three months old, Bean still wakes up several times a night. We have a long ritual in which I nurse her back to sleep, then hold her for fifteen more minutes so that she doesn't wake up again when I put her back in her Moses basket. Simon's forward-looking view of the world suddenly seems like a curse: he's thrown into a nightly depression, convinced that this is going to last for ever. Whereas my myopia suddenly looks like a stroke of evolutionary brilliance. I don't think about whether this will last six more months (though it will); I just live night to night.

What's also consoling is that this is all to be expected. Parents of infants aren't supposed to get any sleep. Almost all the American and British parents I know say that their kids began sleeping through the night at eight or nine months, or much later. 'It was really early,' a friend of Simon's from Vermont says, consulting with his wife about when their son's 3 am wake-ups stopped. 'What was it, at one year old?' Kristin, a British lawyer in Paris, tells me that her sixteen-month-old sleeps through the night, then adds: 'Well, when I say "sleeps through the night", she gets up twice. But each time, only for five minutes.'

I take great comfort in hearing about parents who have it

much worse than we do. They're easy to find. My cousin, who shares a bed with her ten-month-old, hasn't gone back to her teaching job, in part because she's up feeding the baby much of the night.

The worst story I hear comes from Alison, a friend of a friend in Washington, DC, whose son is seven months old. Alison – a marketing expert with an Ivy League degree – explains that for the first six months of her son's life, she nursed him every two hours *around the clock*. At seven months old, he began sleeping four-hour stretches. Alison shrugs off her exhaustion, and the fact that her career is on pause. She feels that she has no choice but to cater to her baby's punishing, peculiar sleep schedule.

The alternative to all this night waking is supposedly 'sleep training', in which parents leave their babies alone for 'controlled crying'. I read up on this, too. It seems to be for babies who are at least six or seven months old. Alison tells me that she tried this one night, but gave up because it felt cruel. Online discussions about sleep training quickly dissolve into brawls, in which opponents claim the practice is at best selfish and at worst abusive. 'Babies are designed to cry when they need something and mothers are designed to respond,' a mother writes on mumsnet. Another, whose son was waking up every ninety minutes, feels she must justify having done controlled crying. 'I know that many people will think me intolerably cruel, but I was losing my sanity,' she writes.

Although sleep training sounds awful, Simon and I are theoretically in favour of it. But we're under the impression that Bean is too young for something so militaristic. Like our Anglophone friends and family, we think Bean wakes up at night because she's hungry, or because she needs something from us, or just because that's what babies do. She's very small. So we give in to her.

I talk to French parents about sleep too. They're neighbours, work acquaintances and friends of friends. They all claim that their own kids began sleeping through the night much earlier. Samia says her daughter, who's now two, started doing her nights at six weeks old; she wrote down the exact date. Stéphanie, a skinny tax inspector who lives on our courtyard, looks ashamed when I ask when her son, Nino, began doing his nights.

'Very late, late late!' Stéphanie says. 'He started doing his nights in November, so it was . . . four months old! For me it was very late.'

Some French sleep stories sound too good to be true. Alexandra, who works in a French nursery and lives in a suburb of Paris, tells me that both her daughters began sleeping through the night almost from birth. 'Already in the maternity ward, they woke up for their bottles around 6 am,' she says.

Many of these French babies are bottle-fed, or they drink a combination of breast milk and formula. But that doesn't seem to be a crucial difference. The French breastfed babies I meet do their nights early on too. Some French mums I meet tell me they stopped breastfeeding when they went back to work, at about three months. But by that time their babies were already doing their nights.

At first I think that I'm just meeting a few lucky French parents. But soon the evidence becomes overwhelming: having a baby who sleeps through the night early on seems to be the norm in France. Just as stories of terrible sleepers are easy to find in the Anglophone world, stories of spectacular sleepers are easy to find among the French. My neighbours suddenly seem less obnoxious. They weren't baiting me; they actually believed that my two-month-old might already be doing her nights.

French parents don't expect their babies to sleep well right after they're born. But by the time these broken nights start to seem unbearable – usually after two or three months – they end. Parents talk about night wake-ups as a short-term problem, not a chronic one. Everyone I speak to takes for granted that babies can and probably will do their nights by about six months, and often much sooner. 'Certain babies do their nights at six weeks, others need four months to find their rhythm,' an article in *Maman!* magazine says. *Le sommeil, le rêve et l'enfant* (*Sleep, Dreams and the Child*), a top-selling sleep guide, says that between three and six months, 'He's going to sleep complete nights, of eight or nine hours at a minimum. The parents will finally rediscover the pleasure of long un-interrupted nights.'

There are exceptions, of course. That's why France has baby sleep books and paediatric sleep specialists. Some babies who do their nights at two months start waking again a few months later. I do hear about French kids who take a year to start doing their nights. But the truth is, over many years in France, I don't meet them. Marion, the mother of a little girl who becomes one of Bean's close friends, says her baby boy did his nights at six months. That's the longest among any of my Parisian friends and acquaintances. Most of them are like Paul, another architect, who says that his 3½-month-old son sleeps a full twelve hours, from 8 pm to 8 am.

What's maddening is that while French parents can tell you exactly when their kids began sleeping through the night, they can't explain how this came about. They don't mention sleep training, 'Ferberizing' – a sleep technique promoted by Dr Richard Ferber – or any other branded method. And they claim that they never let their babies cry for long periods. In fact, most parents look a little queasy when I mention this.

Speaking to older parents isn't much help either. A French publicist in her fifties – who goes to work in pencil skirts and stilettos – is shocked to learn that I have any baby sleep issues. 'Can't you give her something to sleep? You know, some medicine or something like that?' she asks. At the very least, she says, I should leave the baby with someone and recover at a spa for a week or two.

None of the younger French parents I meet either drug their kids to sleep or hide in a sauna. Most insist that their babies learned to sleep long stretches all by themselves. Stéphanie, the tax inspector, claims she didn't have much to do with it. 'I think it's the child, he's the one who decides,' she said.

I hear this same idea from Fanny, thirty-three, the publisher of a group of financial magazines. Fanny says that at around three months old, her son Antoine spontaneously dropped his 3 am feed and slept through the night.

'He decided to sleep,' Fanny explains. 'I never forced anything. You give him food when he needs food. He just regulated it all by himself.'

Fanny's husband Vincent, who's listening to our conversation, points out that three months is exactly when Fanny went back to work. Like other French parents I speak to, he says this timing isn't a coincidence. He believes that Antoine understood that his mother needed to wake up early to go to the office. Vincent compares this understanding to the way ants communicate through chemical waves that pass between their antennae.

'We believe a lot in *le feeling*,' Vincent says, using the English word. 'We guess that children understand things.'

French parents do offer a few sleep tips. They almost all say that in the early months, they kept their babies with them in the light, during the day, even for naps, and put them to bed in the dark at night. And almost all say that, from birth, they carefully 'observed' their babies, and then followed the babies' own 'rhythms'. French parents talk so much about rhythm, you'd think they were starting rock bands, not raising kids.

'From zero to six months, the best is to respect the rhythms of their sleep,' explains Alexandra, the mother whose babies slept through the night practically from birth.

I observe Bean too, often at 3 am. So why is there no rhythm in our house? If sleeping through the night 'just happens', why hasn't it just happened to us?

When I pour out my frustration over coffee one day to Gabrielle, one of my new French acquaintances, she recommends that I look at a book called *L'enfant et son sommeil* (The Child and His Sleep). She says the author, Hélène de Leersnyder, is a well-known paediatrician in Paris who specializes in sleep. The book is baffling. I'm used to the straightforward self-help style of English-language baby books. De Leersnyder's book opens with a quotation from Marcel Proust, then launches into an ode to slumber.

'Sleep reveals the child and the life of the family,' De Leersnyder writes. 'To go to bed and fall asleep, to separate himself from his parents for a few hours, the child must trust his body to keep him alive, even when he's not in control of it. And he must be serene enough to approach the strangeness of the *"pensées de la nuit"* – thoughts that come in the night.'

*Sleep, Dreams and the Child* also says that a baby can only sleep well once he accepts his own separateness. 'The discovery of peaceful, long and serene nights, and an acceptance of solitude, is that not a sign that the child has recovered his inner peace, that he has moved beyond sorrow?'

Even the scientific sections of these books sound existential. What we call 'rapid-eye-movement sleep' the French call *'sommeil paradoxal'* – paradoxical sleep, so called because the body is still but the mind is extremely active. 'To learn to sleep, to learn to live, are these not synonyms?' De Leersnyder asks.

I'm still not sure what I'm supposed to do with this information. I'm not looking for a meta-theory on how to think about

Bean's sleep. I just want her to sleep. But how can I figure out why French babies sleep so well if their own parents can't explain it, and their sleep books read like cryptic poetry? What's a mother got to do for a good night's rest?

Oddly enough, my epiphany about the French sleep rules happens while I'm visiting New York. I've come to the US to visit family and friends, and also to get a hands-on feel for one corner of Anglophone parenting. For part of the trip I stay in Tribeca, the neighbourhood in lower Manhattan where industrial buildings have been converted into smart loft apartments. I hang out at a local playground, chatting with the other mothers there.

I thought I knew my parenting literature. But these women make it clear that I'm an amateur. Not only have they read everything, they've also assembled their own parenting styles like eclectic designer outfits, following separate gurus for sleep, discipline and food. When I naively mention 'attachment parenting' to one Tribeca mother, she quickly corrects me.

'I don't like that term, because who's not attached to their child?' she snaps.

When talk turns to how their kids sleep, I expect these women to cite lots of theories but then to complain that their one-year-olds wake up twice per night. But they don't. Instead, they say that lots of babies in Tribeca do their nights *à la française* at about two months old. One mother, a photographer, mentions that she and many others take their kids to a local paediatrician called Michel Cohen. She

pronounces his first name *me-shell*, like the Beatles' song.
'Is he French?' I venture.
'Yeah,' she says.
'French from France?' I ask.
'French from France,' she says.

I immediately make an appointment to meet him. When I walk into 'Michel's' waiting room, there's no doubt that I'm in Tribeca and not in Paris. There's an Eames lounge chair, retro seventies wallpaper, and a lesbian mother in a fedora. A receptionist in a black tank top is calling out the names of the next patients: 'Ella? Benjamin?'

When Cohen comes out, I immediately see why he's such a hit with mothers. He has tousled brown hair, doe-like eyes and a deep tan. He wears his designer shirts untucked, with sandals and Bermuda shorts. Despite two decades in the US, he has hung on to a charming French accent and parlance ('When I give my advices to parents . . .'). He's done for the day, so he suggests that we sit outside at a local café. I readily agree.

Cohen clearly loves America, in part because America venerates its mavericks and entrepreneurs. In the land of managed care, he's fashioned himself into a neighbourhood doctor (he greets a dozen passers-by by name as we sip our beers). His practice, Tribeca Paediatrics, has expanded to five locations. And he's published a pithy parenting book called *The New Basics* with his picture on the cover.

Cohen is reluctant to credit France for the innovations he's brought to lower Manhattan. He left France in the late 1980s, and remembers it as a country where newborn babies were left to cry it out in the hospital. Even now, he says, 'You can't go to a park without seeing a kid take a beating.' (Perhaps this used to be true. But in the scores of hours I've clocked in Parisian parks recently, I witnessed a spanking only once.)

But some of Cohen's 'advices' are exactly what today's Parisian parents do. Like the French, he starts babies off on vegetables and fruit rather than bland cereals. He's not obsessed with allergies. He talks about 'rhythm', and teaching kids to handle frustration. He values calm. And he gives real weight to the parent's own quality of life, not just to the child's welfare.

So how does Cohen get the babies of Tribeca to do their nights?

'My first intervention is to say, when your baby is born, just don't jump on your kid at night,' Cohen says. 'Give your baby a chance to self-soothe, don't automatically respond, even from birth.'

Maybe it's the beer (or Cohen's doe eyes), but I get a little jolt when he says this. I realize that I've seen French mothers and nannies pausing exactly this little bit before tending to their babies during the day. It hadn't occurred to me that this was deliberate, or a sleep strategy, or that it was at all significant. In fact, it had bothered me. I didn't think that you were supposed to make babies wait. Could this explain why French babies do their nights so early on, supposedly with few tears?

Cohen's advice to pause a little bit does seem like a natural extension of 'observing' a baby. A mother isn't strictly 'observing' if she jumps up and holds the baby the moment he cries.

For Cohen, this pause – I'm tempted to call it '*La Pause*' – is crucial. He says that using it very early on makes a big difference in how babies sleep. 'The parents who were a little less responsive to late-night fussing always had kids who were good sleepers, while the jumpy folks had kids who would wake up repeatedly at night until it became unbearable,' he writes. Most of the babies Cohen sees are breastfed. That doesn't seem to make a difference.

One reason for pausing is that young babies make a lot of movements and noise while they're sleeping. This is normal and fine. If parents rush in and pick the baby up every time he makes a peep, they'll sometimes wake him up.

Another reason for pausing is that babies wake up between their sleep cycles, which last about two hours. It's also normal for them to cry a bit when they're first learning to connect these cycles. If parents automatically interpret this cry as a demand for food or a sign of distress, and rush in to soothe the baby, he'll have a hard time learning to connect the cycles on his own. That is, he'll need an adult to come in and soothe him back to sleep at the end of each cycle.

Newborns usually can't connect sleep cycles on their own. But from about two or three months they often can, if given a chance to learn how. And according to Cohen, connecting sleep cycles is like riding a bike: if a baby manages to fall back asleep on his own even once, he'll find it easier to do it again the next time. (Adults wake up between sleep cycles too, but we typically don't remember this because we've learned to plunge right into the next one.)

Cohen says that sometimes babies do need to be fed or picked up at night. But unless we pause and observe them, we can't be sure. 'Of course, if [the baby's] requests become more persistent, you'll have to feed her,' Cohen writes. 'I'm not saying let your baby wail.' What he's saying is, just give your baby a chance to learn.

This idea isn't entirely new to me. It sounds familiar from some of my English-language sleep books. But it's usually mentioned among lots of other advice. I may have tried it once or twice with Bean, but never with particular conviction. No one has ever pointed it out to me as the one crucial thing to do, and to stick with.

Cohen's singular instruction could solve the mystery of why French parents claim they never let their babies cry for long periods. If they do the Pause in the baby's first two months, their babies can learn to fall back asleep on their own. That means parents don't have to resort to 'crying it out' later on.

The Pause doesn't have the brutal feeling of sleep training. It's more like sleep teaching. But the window for it is pretty small. According to Cohen, it's only until the baby is four months old. After that, bad sleep habits are formed.

Cohen says his sleep methods are an easy sell for the results-oriented parents in his Tribeca practice. But elsewhere, he says parents often need more coaxing. They're opposed to letting their babies cry even a little. But Cohen says he eventually convinces almost all the parents of newborns in his practice to try his methods. 'I try to explain the roots of things,' he says. That is, he teaches them about sleep.

\* \* \*

When I get back to Paris, I immediately ask French mothers whether they do the Pause. Every single one says that, yes, of course they do. They say this is so obvious they hadn't thought to mention it. Most say they started doing the Pause when their babies were a few weeks old.

Alexandra, whose daughters slept through the night while they were still in the hospital, says that of course she didn't rush over to them the second they cried. She sometimes waited five or ten minutes before picking them up. She wanted to see whether they needed to fall back asleep between sleep cycles or whether something else was bothering them: hunger, a dirty nappy, or just anxiety.

Alexandra is extremely warm. She wasn't ignoring her newborn babies. To the contrary, she was carefully *observing* them. She trusted that when they cried, they were telling her something. During the Pause, she watched and listened. (She adds that there's another reason for the Pause: 'to teach them patience'.)

French parents don't have a name for the Pause; they just consider it common sense. (It's the American in me who needs to brand it.) But they all seem to do it, and to remind each other that it's critical. It's such a simple thing. It strikes me that the French genius isn't coming up with a novel, mind-blowing sleep trick. It's clearing out the clutter of competing ideas and focusing on one thing that truly makes a difference.

Now that I'm attuned to the Pause, I start to notice that it's mentioned a lot in France. 'Before responding to an interrogation, common sense tells us to listen to the question,' says an article on doctissimo.fr, a popular French website. 'It's exactly the same thing with a crying baby: the first thing to do is to listen to him.'

I notice that once you get past the philosophical sections, the authors of *Sleep, Dreams and the Child* write that intervening in between sleep cycles 'indisputably' leads to sleep problems, such as a baby who fully wakes up after every ninety-minute or two-hour cycle.

It's suddenly clear to me that Alison, the businesswoman in Miami whose son fed every two hours for six months, hasn't just been handed a baby with weird sleep needs. Much more likely, she has unwittingly taught the baby to need a feed at the end of every two-hour sleep cycle. Alison thought she was merely catering to her son's demands. In fact, despite the best intentions, she was creating those demands. What seems like an act of maternal devotion and self-sacrifice starts to seem like a giant misunderstanding.

I never hear of a single case like Alison's in France. The French treat the Pause as sleep solution number one, and something to wheel out when the baby is only a few weeks old. An article in *Maman!* magazine points out that in the first six months of a baby's life, 50 per cent to 60 per cent of his sleep is *sommeil agité* – agitated sleep. In this state, a sleeping baby suddenly yawns, stretches, and even opens and closes his eyes. 'The error would be to interpret this as a call, and thus derail our baby's sleep train by picking him up,' the article says.

The Pause isn't the only thing that French parents do. But

it's a critical ingredient. When I visit Hélène de Leersnyder, the Proust-quoting sleep doctor, she mentions the Pause right away. 'Sometimes when babies sleep their eyes move, they make noise, they suck, they move around a bit. But in reality, they're sleeping. So you mustn't go in all the time and disturb him while he's sleeping. You have to learn how the baby sleeps.'

'What if he wakes up?' I ask.

'If he wakes up completely, you pick him up, of course.'

French parents don't just know about the Pause. They know why they're doing it. Once I get them talking, they mention sleep cycles, circadian rhythms and *sommeil paradoxal*. They know that one reason babies cry in the night is that they're in between sleep cycles, or they're in *sommeil agité*. When these parents 'observed' their babies, they were trying to train themselves to recognize these stages.

When I talk to Anglophone parents about sleep, science rarely comes up. Faced with so many different and seemingly valid sleep philosophies, the one they ultimately choose seems like a matter of taste.

When French parents pause, they do it consistently and confidently. They're making informed decisions based on their understanding of how babies sleep.

Behind this is an important philosophical assumption. French parents believe it's their job to gently teach babies how to sleep well, the same way they'll later teach them to have good hygiene, eat balanced meals and ride a bike. They don't view being up half the night with an eight-month-old as a sign of parental commitment. They view it as a sign that the child has a sleep problem, and that his family is wildly out of balance. When I describe Alison's case to French women, they say it's *impossible* – both for the child and for his mother.

The French believe, as we do, that each baby is beautiful and special. But they also realize that some things about babies are just biological. Before we assume that our own children sleep like no others, we should probably think about science.

Armed with my revelation about the Pause, I decide to look at some of the scientific literature on babies and sleep. Much of what's been written is published in English-language journals. What I find really surprises me: Anglophone parents are fighting the 'baby sleep wars', but Anglophone sleep researchers aren't. They mostly agree about the best way to get kids to sleep. And their recommendations sound remarkably French.

Sleep researchers, like French parents, believe that, beginning very early on, parents should play an active role in teaching their babies to sleep well. They say it's possible to begin teaching a healthy baby to sleep through the night when he's just a few weeks old, without the baby ever 'crying it out'.

A meta-study of dozens of peer-reviewed sleep papers concludes that what's critical is something called 'parent education/prevention'. That involves teaching pregnant women and parents of newborns about the science of sleep, and giving them a few basic sleep rules. Parents are supposed to start following these rules from their babies' birth, or when their babies are just a few weeks old.

What are these rules? The authors of the meta-study point to a paper in which pregnant women who planned to breast-feed were given a two-page handout. One instruction on the handout was not to hold, rock or nurse the baby to sleep in the evenings, to help him learn the difference between day and night. An additional instruction for week-old babies was that if he cried between midnight and 5 am, parents should re-swaddle, pat, change the nappy or walk the baby around, but that the mother should only offer the breast if the baby continued crying after that.

And from birth, mothers were instructed to distinguish between when their babies were crying and when they were just whimpering in their sleep. In other words, before picking up a crying baby, they should pause to make sure he's awake. The researchers explained the scientific basis for these instructions. A 'control group' of breastfeeding mothers got no instructions.

The results are remarkable: from birth to three weeks old, babies in the treatment and control groups had nearly identical sleep patterns. But at four weeks old, 38 per cent of the treatment-group babies were sleeping through the night, versus 7 per cent of the control-group babies. At eight weeks, all of the treatment babies were sleeping through the night, compared to 23 per cent of the control babies. The authors' conclusion is resounding: 'The results of this study show that breastfeeding need not be associated with night waking.'

The Pause isn't just some French folk wisdom. Neither is the belief that sleeping well, early on, is better for everyone. 'In general, night wakings fall within the diagnostic category of behavioural insomnia of childhood,' the meta-study explains.

It says there's growing evidence that young children who don't sleep enough, or who have disturbed sleep, can suffer from irritability, aggression, hyperactivity and poor impulse control, and can have trouble learning and remembering things. They're more prone to accidents, their metabolic and immune functions are weakened, and their overall quality of life diminishes. And sleep problems that begin in infancy can persist for many years. In the study of breastfeeding mothers, the treatment-group infants were afterwards rated more secure, more predictable and less fussy.

The studies I read point out that when children sleep badly there's spillover to the rest of the family, including maternal depression and lower overall family functioning. Conversely, when babies slept better, their parents reported that their marriages improved, and that they became better and less-stressed parents.

Of course, some French babies miss the four-month window for sleepteaching. When this happens, French experts usually recommend some version of crying it out.

Sleep researchers aren't ambivalent about this either. The meta-study found that letting kids do controlled crying, either by going cold turkey (known by the unfortunate scientific term 'extinction') or in stages ('graduated extinction') both work extremely well, and usually succeed in just a few days.

'The biggest obstacle associated with extinction is lack of parental consistency,' the study says.

Michel Cohen, the French doctor in Tribeca, recommends a rather extreme version of this. He says parents should make the baby feel cosy with his usual night-time bath and songs. Then they should put him in bed at a reasonable hour, preferably while he's still awake. Then they should come back at 7 am.

In Paris, crying it out has a French twist. I start to realize this when I meet Laurence, a nanny from Normandy who's working for a French family in Montparnasse. Laurence has been looking after babies for two decades. She tells me that before letting a baby do controlled crying it's crucial to explain to him what you're about to do.

Laurence walks me through this: 'In the evening, you speak to him. You tell him that, if he wakes up once, you're going to give him his dummy once. But after that, you're not going to get up. It's time to sleep. You're not far away, and you're going to come in and reassure him once. But not all night long.'

Laurence says that a crucial part of getting a baby to do his nights, at any age, is to truly believe that he's going to do it. 'If you don't believe it, it's not going to work,' she says. 'Me, I always think that the child is going to sleep better the next night. I always have hope, even if he wakes up three hours later. You have to believe.'

It does seem possible that French babies rise to meet their parents' and carers' expectations. Perhaps we all get the sleepers we expect, and the simple fact of believing that babies have a rhythm helps us to find it.

To believe in the Pause, or in letting an older baby do controlled crying, you also have to believe that a baby is a person who's capable of learning things (in this case, how to sleep) and coping with some frustration. Michel Cohen spends a lot of time converting parents to this French idea. To the common worry that a four-month-old is hungry at night, he writes: 'She is hungry. But she does not need to eat. You're hungry in the middle of the night too; it's just that you learn not to eat because it's good for your belly to take a rest. Well, it's good for hers too.'

The French don't believe that babies should withstand biblical-sized trials. But they also don't think that a bit of frustration will crush kids. On the contrary, they believe it will make children more secure. According to *Sleep, Dreams and the Child*, 'To always respond to his demands, and never tell him "no", is dangerous for the construction of his personality. Because the child won't have any barrier to push up against, to know what's expected of him.'

For the French, teaching a small baby to sleep isn't a self-serving strategy for lazy parents. It's a first, crucial lesson for children in self-reliance and in how to enjoy one's own company. A psychologist quoted in *Maman!* magazine says that babies who learn to play by themselves during the day – even in the first few months – are less worried when they're put into their beds alone at night.

De Leersnyder writes that even babies need some privacy.

'The little baby learns in his cradle that he can be alone from time to time, without being hungry, without being thirsty, without sleeping, just being calmly awake. At a very young age, he needs time alone, and he needs to go to sleep and wake up without being immediately watched by his mother.'

De Leersnyder even devotes a portion of her book to what a mother should do while her baby sleeps. 'She forgets about her baby, to think about herself. She now takes her own shower, gets dressed, puts on make-up, becomes beautiful for her own pleasure, that of her husband and of others. Evening comes, and she prepares herself for the night, for love.'

As an Anglophone parent, this film-noir scene – with its suggestion of kohl eyeliner and silk stockings – is hard to imagine in anything but the movies. Simon and I just assumed that, for quite a while, we'd rearrange our lives around Bean's whims.

The French don't think that's good for anyone. They view learning to sleep as an aspect of learning to be part of the family, and adapting to what other members of the family need too. De Leersnyder tells me: 'If he wakes up ten times at night, [the mother] can't go to work the next day. So that makes the baby understand that – voilà – he can't wake up ten times a night.'

'The baby understands that?' I ask.

'Of course he understands that,' she says.

'How can he understand that?'

'Because babies understand everything.'

\* \* \*

French parents think the Pause is essential. But they don't hold it up as a panacea. Instead, they have a bundle of beliefs and habits which, when applied patiently and lovingly, put babies in the mood to sleep well. The Pause works in part because parents believe that tiny babies aren't helpless blobs. They can learn things. This learning, done gently and at a baby's own pace, isn't damaging. To the contrary, parents believe it gives the babies confidence and serenity, and makes them aware of other people. And it sets the tone for the respectful relationship between parents and children that I see later on.

If only I had known all this when Bean was born. We definitely miss the four-month window for painlessly teaching her to sleep through the night. At nine months old, she still wakes up every night at around 2 am. We brace ourselves to let her do controlled crying. On the first night, she cries for twelve minutes. (I clutch Simon and cry too.) Then she goes back to sleep. The next night she cries for five minutes.

On the third night, Simon and I both wake up to silence at 2 am. 'I think she was waking up for us,' Simon says. 'She thought that we needed her to do it.' Then we go back to sleep. Bean has been doing her nights ever since.

# 4

# Wait!

I'M GETTING MORE USED TO FRANCE. ONE DAY, I'M FEELING SO worldly I announce to Simon that we've joined the global elite.

'We're global, but we're not elite,' he replies.

The truth is, I miss America. I miss grocery shopping in tracksuit bottoms, smiling at strangers, and being able to banter. Mostly, I miss my parents. I can't believe I'm raising a child while they're 4,500 miles away.

Neither can my mother. My meeting and marrying a handsome foreigner was the thing she most dreaded when I was growing up. She discussed this fear so extensively that it's probably what planted the idea. On one visit to Paris, she takes me and Simon out to dinner, and breaks down in tears at the table. 'What do they have here that they don't have in America?' she demands to know. (Had she been eating *escargots*, I could have pointed at her plate. Unfortunately she had ordered the chicken.)

Although living in France is easier now, I haven't really assimilated. On the contrary, having a baby – and speaking better French – makes me realize just how foreign I am. Soon after Bean begins sleeping through the night, we arrive for her first day at France's state-run day nursery, the crèche. During the intake interview, we sail through questions about her dummy use and favourite sleeping positions. We're ready with her inoculation records and emergency-contact numbers. But one question stumps us: what time does she have her milk?

On the matter of when to feed babies, Anglophone parents are once again in sparring camps. You could call it a food fight: one camp believes in feeding babies at fixed times, another says to feed them on demand.

We've drifted into a hybrid. Bean always has milk when she wakes up, and again before bedtime. In between, we just feed her whenever she seems hungry. Simon thinks there isn't a problem that a bottle or a boob can't solve. We'll both do anything to keep her from yowling.

When I finish explaining our feeding system to the crèche lady, she looks at me like I've just said that we let our baby drive the family car. We don't know when our child eats? This is a problem she will soon solve. Her look says that although we're living in Paris, we're raising a child who eats and sleeps – and yes, probably poos – like a foreigner.

The crèche lady's look also reveals that on this, too, there are no sparring camps in France. Parents don't anguish about how often their children should eat. From the age of about four months, most French babies eat at regular times. As with sleep techniques, French parents see this as common sense, not as part of a parenting philosophy or as the dictate of some parenting guru.

What's even stranger is that these French babies all eat at roughly the same times. With slight variations, mothers tell me that their babies eat at about 8 am, 12 pm, 4 pm and 8 pm. *Votre Enfant* (*Your Child*), a respected French parenting guide, has just one sample menu for four- or five-month-olds. It's this same sequence of feeds.

In French these aren't even called 'feeds', which after all sounds like you're pitching hay at cows. They're called 'meals'. And their sequence resembles a schedule I'm quite familiar with: breakfast, lunch and dinner, plus an afternoon snack. In other words, by about four months old, French babies are already on the same eating schedule that they'll be on for the rest of their lives (grown-ups usually drop the snack).

You'd think the existence of this national baby meal plan would be obvious. Instead, it feels like a state secret. If you merely ask French parents if their babies eat on a schedule, they almost always say no. As with sleep, they insist that they're merely following their babies' 'rhythms'. When I point out that French babies all seem to eat at roughly the same times, parents shrug it off as a coincidence.

The deeper mystery to me is how all these French babies are capable of waiting four hours from one meal to the next. Bean gets anxious if she has to wait even a few minutes for a feed. We get anxious too. But I'm beginning to sense that there's a lot of waiting going on all around me in France. First there was the Pause, in which French babies wait after they wake up.

Now there's the baby meal plan, in which they wait long stretches from one feed to the next. And of course there are all those toddlers waiting contentedly in restaurants until their food arrives.

The French seem collectively to have achieved the miracle of getting babies and toddlers not just to wait, but to do so happily. Could this ability to wait explain the difference between French and Anglophone kids?

To get my head around these questions, I email Walter Mischel, the world's expert on how children delay gratification. He's eighty years old, and holds a chair in psychology at Columbia University. I've read all about him, and read some of his many published papers on the topic. I explain that I'm in Paris researching French parenting, and ask if he might have time to talk on the phone.

Mischel replies a few hours later. To my surprise, he says that he's in Paris too. Would I like to come by for a coffee? Two days later we're at the kitchen table in his girlfriend's apartment in the Latin Quarter, just down the hill from the Panthéon.

Mischel hardly looks seventy, and certainly not eighty. He has a shaved head and the coiled energy of a boxer, but with a sweet, almost childlike face. It's not hard to envision him as the eight-year-old boy from Vienna who fled Austria with his family after the Nazis annexed the country.

The family eventually landed in Brooklyn, where adapting to America was a trial. When Walter entered school at age nine, he was assigned to kindergarten to learn English, and remembers 'trying to walk on my knees to not stick out from the five-year-olds when our class marched through the corridors'. Mischel's parents – who were cultured and comfortably middle class in Vienna – opened a struggling five-and-dime. His mother, who'd been mildly depressed in Vienna, was energized by America. But his father never recovered from his fall in status.

This early experience gave Mischel a permanent outsider's perspective, and helped frame the questions that he has spent his career answering. In his thirties, he upended the whole science of personality by arguing that people's 'traits' aren't fixed; they depend on context. Despite marrying an American and bringing up three daughters in California, Mischel began making annual pilgrimages to Paris. 'I always felt myself to be European and felt Paris was the capital of Europe,' he tells me. Mischel, who divorced in 1996, has lived with a Frenchwoman for the past decade. They divide their time between New York and Paris.

Mischel is most famous for devising the 'marshmallow test' in the late 1960s, when he was at Stanford. In it, an experimenter leads a four- or five-year-old into a room where there's a marshmallow on a table. The experimenter tells the child he's going to leave the room for a little while. If the child manages not to eat the marshmallow until he comes back, he'll be rewarded with two marshmallows. If he eats the marshmallow, he'll only get that one.

It's a very hard test. Of the 653 kids who took it back in the 1960s and '70s, only one in three managed to resist eating the marshmallow for the full fifteen minutes that the experimenter was away. Some ate it as soon as they were alone. Most could only wait about thirty seconds. In the mid-1980s, Mischel revisited the kids from the original experiment, to see if there was a difference between how good and bad delayers were faring as teenagers. He and his colleagues found a remarkable correlation: the longer children had resisted eating the marshmallow as four-year-olds, the higher Mischel and his colleagues assessed them in all sorts of other categories. Among other skills, the good delayers were better at concentrating and reasoning. And according to a report that Mischel and his colleagues published in 1988, they 'do not tend to go to pieces under stress'.

Could it be that making children delay gratification – as French parents do – actually makes them calmer and more resilient? Whereas Anglophone children, who are in general more used to getting what they want right away, go to pieces under stress? Are French parents once again doing – by tradition and instinct – exactly what scientists recommend?

Bean, who expects immediate gratification, can go from calm to hysterical in seconds. Whenever I go to Britain or the US, I realize that miserable, screaming toddlers are just part of the scenery of daily life. One day in Muswell Hill, London, I see an angry toddler pitch himself on to the pavement in front of a chemist's, where he lay face down and refused to budge. We pedestrians just parted round him.

I rarely see such scenes in Paris. French babies and toddlers, who are used to waiting longer, seem oddly calm about not getting what they want right away. When I visit French families and hang out with their kids, there's a conspicuous lack of whining and complaining. Often – or at least much more often than in my house – everyone's calm and absorbed in what they're doing.

In France I regularly see what amounts to a minor miracle: adults in the company of small children at home having entire cups of coffee and full-length adult conversations. And instead of telling eager kids 'quiet' or 'stop', French parents often just say a sharp *attend* – wait. Mischel hasn't performed the marshmallow test on any French children (he'd probably have to do a version with *pain au chocolat*). But as a long-time observer of France, he says he's struck by the difference between French and American kids.

In America, he says, 'Certainly the impression one has is that self-control has gotten increasingly difficult for kids.' That's sometimes true even with his own grandchildren. 'I don't like it when I call a daughter, if she tells me that she can't talk now because a child is pulling on her, and she can't say, "Hold on, I'm talking to papa."'

Having kids who can wait does make family life a lot more pleasant. Children in France 'seem much more disciplined and more raised the way I was', Mischel says. 'With French friends coming over with small children, you can still have a French dinner . . . the expectation with French kids is that they'll behave themselves in an appropriate, quiet way and enjoy the dinner.'

'Enjoy' is an important word here. For the most part, French parents don't expect their kids to be joylessly compliant.

Parents just don't see how their kids can enjoy themselves if they can't control themselves.

I often hear French parents telling their kids to 'be *sage*'. Saying 'be *sage*' is a bit like saying, as we would in English, 'be good'. But it implies more than that. When I tell Bean to 'be good' before we walk into someone's house, it's as if she's a wild animal who must act tame for an hour, but who could go wild again at any moment. There's some fear in my telling her to 'be good', as if that goes contrary to what a child really is.

When I tell Bean to 'be *sage*', I'm also telling her to behave appropriately. But I'm asking her to use good judgement, and to be aware and respectful of other people. I'm implying that she has a certain wisdom about the situation, and that she's in command of herself. Underlying all of this is the idea that I trust her.

I hope I'm not making French kids sound grim. The ones I know have a lot of fun. On weekends, Bean and her friends run shouting and laughing through the park for hours. Breaktime at her nursery, and later at her school, are free-for-alls. There's also plenty of controlled fun in Paris, like children's film festivals, theatres and cooking classes, which require patience and attention. The French parents I meet want their kids to have rich experiences and to be exposed to art and music.

But they believe that kids need patience in order to absorb these experiences fully. In the French view, having the self-control to be calmly present, rather than anxious, irritable and demanding, is what allows kids to have fun.

French parents and carers don't think that kids have infinite patience. They don't expect toddlers to sit through symphonies or formal banquets. They usually talk about waiting in terms of minutes or seconds.

But even these small delays seem to make a big difference. I'm now convinced that the secret of why French kids don't whine (well, hardly ever) and don't often collapse into tantrums is that they've developed the internal resources to cope with frustration. They don't expect to get what they want instantly. When French parents talk about the '*éducation*' of their children, they are talking, in large part, about teaching them how not to eat the marshmallow.

So how exactly do the French turn ordinary children into expert delayers? And can we teach Bean how to wait too?

Walter Mischel watched videotapes of hundreds of squirming four-year-olds taking the marshmallow test. He eventually figured out that the bad delayers focused on the marshmallow. The good delayers distracted themselves. 'The kids who manage to wait very easily are the ones who learn during the wait to sing little songs to themselves, or pick their ears in an interesting way, or play with their toes and make a game of it,' he tells me. The ones who didn't know how to distract themselves, and just stared at the marshmallow, ended up eating it.

Mischel concludes that having the will power to wait isn't about being a stoic. It's about knowing techniques that make waiting less frustrating. 'There are many many ways of doing that, of which the most direct and the simplest . . . is to self-distract,' he says.

Parents don't have to specifically teach their kids 'distraction strategies'. Mischel says kids learn these skills intuitively, if parents just allow them to practise. 'I think what's often underestimated in parenting is how extraordinary . . . the cognitive faculties of very young kids are, if you engage them,' he says.

This is exactly what I've been seeing French parents doing. They don't explicitly teach their kids distraction techniques. Mostly, they just seem to give them lots of opportunities to practise waiting.

On a grey Saturday afternoon, I take a commuter train to Fontenay-sous-Bois, a suburb just east of Paris. A friend of mine has arranged for me to visit a family that lives there. Martine, the mother, is a pretty lawyer in her mid-thirties. She lives with her husband, an A&E doctor, and their two kids in a modern low-rise building set amid a patch of trees.

I'm immediately struck by how much Martine's apartment resembles my own. Toys line the perimeter of the living room, which is attached to an open kitchen (known in French as a 'cuisine américaine'). We have the same stainless-steel appliances.

But the similarities end there. Despite having two young kids, Martine's house has a calm that we could only wish for. When I arrive, her husband is working on his laptop in the living room, while one-year-old Auguste naps nearby. Paulette, their three-year-old, who has a pixie haircut, is sitting at the kitchen table plopping cupcake batter into little wrappers. When each wrapper is full, she tops it with coloured sprinkles and fresh red gooseberries.

Martine and I sit down to chat at the other end of the table. But I'm transfixed by little Paulette and her cupcakes. Paulette is completely absorbed in her task. She somehow resists the temptation to eat the batter. When she's done she asks her mother if she can lick the spoon.

'No, but you can have some sprinkles,' Martine says, prompting Paulette to shake out several tablespoons of sprinkles on to the table.

My daughter Bean is the same age as Paulette, but it wouldn't have occurred to me to let her do a complicated task like this all on her own. I'd be supervising, and she'd be resisting my supervision. There would be much stress and whining (mine and hers). Bean would probably grab batter, berries and sprinkles each time I turned away. I certainly wouldn't be chatting calmly with a visitor.

The whole scene definitely wouldn't be something I'd want to repeat a week later. Yet baking seems to be a weekly ritual in France. Practically every time I visit a French family on a weekend, they're either making a cake or serving the one they made earlier that day.

At first I think it must be because I'm visiting. But I soon realize that it has nothing to do with me. There's a national bake-off in Paris every weekend. Practically from the time kids can sit up, their mums begin leading them in weekly or bi-weekly baking projects. These kids don't just spill some flour and mash a few bananas. They crack eggs, pour in cups of sugar, and mix with preternatural confidence. They make the whole cake.

The first cake that most French kids learn to bake is *gâteau au yaourt* – yogurt cake – in which the empty yogurt tubs are used to measure out the other ingredients. It's a light, not-too-sweet cake to which they can add berries, chocolate chips, lemon or a tablespoon of rum. It's pretty hard to screw up.

All this baking doesn't just make lots of cakes. It also teaches kids how to control themselves. With its orderly measuring and sequencing of ingredients, baking is a perfect lesson in patience. So is the fact that French families don't devour the cake as soon as it comes out of the oven, as I would do. They typically bake in the morning or early afternoon, then wait and eat the cake or muffins as a *goûter* – the French afternoon snack.

It's hard for me to imagine a world in which mums don't walk around with packets of Cheerios in their bags, to patch over the inevitable moments of angst. Jennifer, a mother and a reporter for the *New York Times*, complains that every activity her daughter attends, no matter how brief or at what time of day, now includes snacks. 'Apparently we have collectively decided as a culture that it is impossible for children to take part in any activity without simultaneously shoving something into their pie holes,' she writes.

In France the *goûter* is the official and only snack time. It's usually at 4 or 4:30 pm, when kids get out of school. It has the same fixed status as other mealtimes, and is universally observed for kids.

The *goûter* helps explain why those French kids I saw at the restaurant were eating so well. They were actually hungry, because they hadn't been snacking all day. (Adults might have a coffee, but rarely a snack. A friend of mine who was visiting France complained that he had a hard time finding any adult snack food.)

Martine, the mother in the suburbs, says she never set out specifically to teach her kids patience. But her family's daily rituals – which I see re-enacted in many other homes – are an ongoing apprenticeship in how to delay gratification. Martine says she often buys Paulette sweets (*bonbons* are on display in most bakeries). But Paulette doesn't eat the sweets until that day's *goûter*, even if that means waiting many hours. Paulette is used to this. Martine sometimes has to remind her of the rule, but Paulette doesn't protest.

Even the *goûter* isn't a free-for-all. 'The great thing is that there was cake to eat,' recalls Clotilde Dusoulier, a French food writer. 'But the flip side of the coin was that my mum would say, "That's enough." It was also teaching kids restraint.' Clotilde, who's now in her early thirties, says that as a kid she baked with her mother 'pretty much every weekend'.

It's not just what and when French families eat that makes their meals little capsules of patience training. It's also how they eat, and with whom. From a very young age, French kids get used to eating meals in courses, with – at a minimum – a starter, a main course and a dessert. They also get used to eating with their parents, which has to be better for learning patience. According to Unicef, 90 per cent of French fifteen-year-olds eat the main meal of the day with their parents 'several times per week'. In the US and UK, it's about 67 per cent.

At these meals, there's no devouring everything at once. In that study of women in Rennes and Ohio, the French women spent more than twice as much time eating each day. They surely pass on this pace to their kids.

Fortunately it's *goûter* time when the cupcakes come out of the oven at Martine's. Paulette happily eats two of them. But Martine doesn't even taste one. She seems to have tricked herself into thinking of cupcakes as 'children's food' in order not to eat them. (Sadly, I think she assumes I'm doing the same tricks, and doesn't even offer me one.)

This is yet another way that French parents teach their kids to wait. They model waiting themselves. Little girls who grow up in homes where the mother doesn't eat the cupcake surely grow up to be women who don't eat the cupcake either. (My own mother has many wonderful qualities, but she always eats the cupcake.)

It strikes me that Martine doesn't expect her daughter to be perfectly patient. She assumes that Paulette will sometimes grab stuff and make mistakes. But Martine doesn't overreact to these mistakes, the way that I tend to. She understands that all this baking and waiting is practice in building a skill.

In other words, Martine is even patient about teaching patience. When Paulette tries to interrupt our conversation,

Martine says, 'Just wait two minutes, my little one. I'm in the middle of talking.' It's both very polite and very firm. I'm struck both by how sweetly Martine says it, and by how certain she seems that Paulette will obey her.

Martine has been teaching her children patience since they were tiny. When Paulette was a baby, Martine usually waited five minutes before picking her up when she cried (and, of course, Paulette did her nights at two and a half months). Martine also teaches her kids a related skill: learning to play by themselves. 'The most important thing is that he learns to be happy by himself,' she says of Auguste, her eighteen-month-old son.

A child who can play by himself can draw upon this skill when his mother is on the phone. And it's a skill that French mothers explicitly try to cultivate in their kids, more than Anglophone mothers do. In a study of university-educated mothers in the US and France, the American mums said that encouraging one's child to play alone was of average importance. But the French mums said it was very important.

Parents who value this ability are probably more apt to leave a child alone when he's playing well by himself. When French mothers say that it's important to take cues from a child's own rhythm, what they mean is that when the child is playing, they leave him alone.

This seems to be another example of French mothers and caregivers intuitively following the best science. Walter Mischel says the worst-case scenario for a kid from eighteen to twenty-four months is 'the child is busy and the child is happy, and the mother comes along with a fork full of spinach'.

'The mothers who really foul it up are the ones who are coming in when the child is busy and doesn't want or need them, and are not there when the child is eager to have them. So becoming alert to that is absolutely critical,' Mischel says.

Indeed, an enormous US government study of the effects of childcare found that what's especially crucial is the mother or caregiver's 'sensitivity' – how attuned she is to her child's experience of the world. 'The sensitive mother is aware of the child's needs, moods, interests, and capabilities,' a researcher explains. 'She allows this awareness to guide her interactions with her child.' Conversely, having a depressed mother is very bad, because the depression stops the mother from tuning in to her child.

Mischel's conviction about the importance of sensitivity doesn't just come from research. He says that his own mother was alternately smothering and absent. Mischel still can't ride a bike, because she was too afraid of head injuries to let him learn. But neither of his parents came to hear him give the valedictory address at his secondary school.

Of course we Anglophone parents want our children to be patient. We believe that 'patience is a virtue'. We encourage our kids to share, to wait their turn, to set the table, and to practise the piano. But patience isn't a skill that we hone quite as assiduously as French parents do. As with sleep, we tend to view whether kids are good at waiting as a matter of temperament. Parents are either lucky, and get a child who waits well, or they aren't.

French parents and carers can't believe that we're so *laissez-faire* about this crucial ability. For them, having kids who need instant gratification would make life unbearable. When I mention the topic of this book at a dinner party in Paris, my host – a French journalist – launches into a story about the year he lived in Southern California. He and his wife, a judge, had made friends with an American couple, and decided to spend a weekend away with them in Santa Barbara. It was the first time they'd met each other's kids, who ranged in age from about seven to fifteen.

From my hosts' perspective, the weekend quickly became maddening. Years later, they still remember how the kids frequently interrupted the adults mid-sentence. And they recall that there were no fixed mealtimes; the kids went to the refrigerator and took food whenever they wanted.

More than any one detail, it just seemed like the kids were in charge. 'What struck us, and bothered us, was that the parents never said no,' the journalist said. 'They did *n'importe quoi*' – whatever – his wife added. This was apparently contagious. 'The worst part is, our kids started doing *n'importe quoi* too,' she says.

After a while, I realize that most French descriptions of Anglophone kids (I seem to trigger more stories about Americans) include this phrase '*n'importe quoi*'. It means 'whatever' or 'anything they like'." It suggests that the children in the story don't have firm boundaries, that their parents lack authority, and that anything goes. It's the antithesis of the French ideal of the *cadre*, or framework, that French parents talk about. In the *cadre*, kids have very firm limits – that's the framework. But they also have a lot of freedom within those limits.

Anglophone parents impose limits too, of course. But often they're different from the French ones. In fact, French people often don't see them as limits at all. Laurence, the nanny from Normandy, tells me she won't work for American families any more, and that several of her nanny friends won't either. She says she left her last job with Americans after just a few months, mostly over the issue of limits.

'It was difficult because it was *n'importe quoi*, the child does what he wants, when he wants,' Laurence says.

Laurence is tall with short hair and a gentle, no-nonsense manner. She's been a nanny in Paris for twenty years. She's reluctant to offend me. But she says that compared to French families she's worked for, in the American homes there was much more crying and whining (this is the first time I hear the onomatopoeic French verb *chouiner* – to whine).

The last American family she worked for had three kids, aged eight, five and eighteen months. For the five-year-old girl, whining 'was her national sport. She whined all the time, with tears that could fall at a moment's notice.' Laurence believed that it was best to ignore the girl, so as not to reinforce the whining. But the girl's mother – who was often home, in another room – usually rushed in and capitulated to whatever the girl was asking for.

Laurence says the eight-year-old son was worse. 'He always wanted a little bit more, and a little bit more,' she says. And when his escalating demands weren't met, he became hysterical.

Laurence's conclusion is that, in such a situation, 'the child is less happy. He's a little bit lost . . . in the families where there is more structure, not a rigid family but a bit more *cadre*, everything goes much more smoothly.'

Laurence's breaking point came when the mother insisted that Laurence put the two older kids on a diet. Laurence refused, and said she would simply feed them balanced meals. Then she discovered that after she put the kids to bed and left, at about 8:30 pm, the mother would feed them cookies and cake.

'They were stout,' Laurence says of the three children.

'Stout?' I ask.

'I say "stout" so I don't say "fat",' she says.

I'd like to write off this story as a stereotype. Obviously not all American or other Anglophone kids behave this way. And French kids do plenty of *n'importe quoi* too. (Bean will later say sternly to her eight-month-old brother, in imitation of her own teachers, '*Tu ne peux pas faire n'importe quoi*' – you can't do whatever you fancy.)

But the truth is, in my own home, I've witnessed Anglophone kids doing quite a lot of *n'importe quoi*. When their families come over, the grown-ups spend much of the time chasing after or otherwise tending to their kids. 'Maybe in about five years we'll be able to have a conversation,' jokes

a friend from California, who's visiting Paris with her husband
and two daughters, aged seven and four. We've been trying for
an hour just to finish our cups of tea.

She and her family arrived at our house after spending the
day touring Paris, during which the younger daughter threw a
series of spectacular tantrums. When the dinner I'm preparing
isn't ready, both parents come into the kitchen and say that
their girls probably can't wait much longer. When we finally
sit down, they let the younger girl crawl under the table while
the rest of us (Bean included) eat dinner. The parents explain
that the girl is tired, so she can't control herself. Then they
wax lyrical about her prodigious reading skills and her possible
admission to a gifted kindergarten.

During the meal, I feel something stroking my foot.

'Rachel is tickling me,' I tell her parents, nervously. A
moment later, I yelp. The gifted child has bitten me.

Setting limits for kids isn't a French invention, of course.
Plenty of Anglophone parents and experts also think limits are
very important. But in the US and Britain, this runs up against
the competing idea that children need to express themselves.
I sometimes feel that the things Bean wants – apple juice
instead of water, to be sprung from her buggy every twenty feet
– are immutable and primordial. I don't concede to everything. But repeatedly blocking her urges feels wrong, and
possibly even damaging.

It's also hard for me to conceive of Bean as someone who
can sit through a four-course meal, or play quietly when I'm on

the phone. I'm not even sure I want her to do those things. Will it crush her spirit? Am I stifling her self-expression, and her possibility of starting the next Facebook? With all these anxieties, I often capitulate.

I'm not the only one. At Bean's fourth birthday party, one of her English-speaking friends walks in carrying a wrapped present for Bean, and another one for himself. His mother says he got upset at the shop because he wasn't getting a present too. My friend Nancy tells me about a new parenting philosophy in which you never let your child hear the word no, so that he can't say it back to you.

In France, there's no such ambivalence about *non*. 'You must teach your child frustration' is a French parenting maxim. In my favourite series of French children's books, *The Perfect Princess*, the heroine, Zoé, is pictured pulling her mother towards a crêpe stand. The text explains, 'While walking past the *crêperie*, Zoé made a scene. She wanted a *crêpe* with blackberry jam. Her mother refused, because it was just after lunch.'

On the next page, Zoé is in a bakery, dressed as the Perfect Princess of the title. This time she's covering her eyes so she won't see the piles of fresh *brioche*. She's being *sage*. 'As [Zoé] knows, to avoid being tempted, she turns her head away,' the text says.

It's worth noting that in the first scene, where Zoé isn't getting what she wants, she's crying. But in the second one, where she's distracting herself, she's smiling. The message is that children will always have the impulse to give in to their vices. But they're happier when they're *sage*, and in command of themselves.

In the book A *Happy Child*, French psychologist Didier Pleux argues that the best way to make a child happy is to frustrate him. 'That doesn't mean that you prevent him from playing, or that you avoid hugging him,' Pleux says. 'One must of course respect his tastes, his rhythms and his individuality. It's simply that the child must learn, from a very young age, that he's not alone in the world, and that there's a time for everything.'

I'm struck by how different the French expectations are when – on that same seaside holiday when I witnessed all the French kids happily eating in restaurants – I take Bean into a shop filled with perfectly aligned stacks of striped 'mariner' T-shirts in bright colours. Bean immediately begins pulling them down. She barely pauses when I scold her.

To me, Bean's bad behaviour seems predictable for a toddler. So I'm surprised when the saleswoman says, without malice, 'I've never seen a child do that before.' I apologize and head for the door.

Walter Mischel says that capitulating to kids starts a dangerous cycle: 'If kids have the experience that, when they're told to wait, if they scream Mummy will come and the wait will be over, they will very quickly learn not to wait. Non-waiting and screaming and carrying on and whining are being rewarded.'

French parents delight in the fact that each child has his own temperament. But they take for granted that any healthy child is capable of not whining, not collapsing after he's told no, and generally not nagging or grabbing things.

French parents are more inclined to view a child's somewhat random demands as *caprices* – impulsive fancies or whims. They have no problem saying no to these. 'I think [French women] understand earlier than American women that kids can have demands and those demands are unrealistic,' a paediatrician who treats French and Anglophone children tells me.

A French psychologist writes that when a child has a *caprice* – for instance, his mother is in a shop with him and he suddenly demands a toy – the mother should remain extremely calm, and gently explain that buying the toy isn't in the day's plan. Then she should try to 'bypass' the *caprice* by redirecting the child's attention, for example by telling a story about her own life. ('Stories about parents are always interesting to children,' the psychologist says. After reading this, in every crisis I shout to Simon: 'Tell a story about your life!').

The psychologist says that, throughout, the mother should stay in close communication with the child, embracing him or looking him in the eye. But she must also make him understand that 'he can't have everything right away. It's essential not to leave him thinking that he is all-powerful, and that he can do everything and have everything.'

French parents don't worry that they're going to damage their kids by frustrating them. On the contrary, they think their kids will be damaged if they can't cope with frustration. They treat coping with frustration as a core life skill. Their kids simply have to learn it. The parents would be remiss if they didn't teach it.

Laurence, the nanny, says that if a child wants her to pick him up while she's cooking, 'It's enough to explain to him, "I can't pick you up right now," and then tell him why.'

Laurence says her charges don't always take this well. But she stays firm, and lets the child express his disappointment. 'I don't let him cry eight hours, but I let him cry,' she explains. 'I explain to him that I can't do otherwise.'

This happens a lot when she's watching several children at once. 'If you are busy with one child and another child wants you, if you can pick him up obviously you do. But if not, I let him cry.'

The French expectation that even little kids should be able to wait comes in part from the darker days of French parenting, when children were expected to be quiet and obedient. But it also comes from the belief that even babies are rational people who can learn things. According to this view, when we rush to feed Bean whenever she whimpers, we're treating her like an addict. Seen in this light, expecting kids to have patience is a way of respecting them.

But mostly, as with teaching kids to sleep, French experts view learning to cope with 'no' as a crucial step in a child's evolution. It forces them to understand that there are other people in the world, with needs as powerful as their own. A French child psychiatrist writes that this *éducation* should begin when a baby is three to six months old. 'His mother begins to make him wait a bit sometimes, thus introducing a temporal dimension into his spirit. It's these little frustrations that his parents impose on him day after day, along with their love, that let him withstand, and allow him to renounce, between ages two and four, his all-powerfulness, in order to humanize him. This renunciation is not always verbalized but it's an obligatory rite of passage.'

In the French view, I'm doing Bean no service by catering to her every whim. French experts and parents believe that hearing 'no' rescues children from the tyranny of their own desires. 'As small children you have needs and desires that basically have no ending. This is a very basic thing. The parents are there – that's why you have frustration – to stop that [process],' says Caroline Thompson, a family psychologist who runs a bilingual practice in Paris.

Thompson, who has a French mother and an English father, points out that kids often get very angry at their parents for blocking them. She says English-speaking parents often interpret this anger as a sign that the parents are doing something wrong. But she warns that parents shouldn't mistake angering a child for bad parenting.

On the contrary, 'If the parent can't stand the fact of being hated, then he won't frustrate the child, and then the child will be in a situation where he will be the object of his own tyranny, where basically he has to deal with his own greed and his own need for things. If the parent isn't there to stop him, then he's the one who's going to have to stop himself or not stop himself, and that's much more anxiety-provoking.'

Thompson's view reflects what seems to be the consensus in

France: making kids face up to limitations and deal with frustration turns them into happier, more resilient people. And one of the main ways to gently induce frustration, on a daily basis, is to make children wait a bit. As with the Pause as a sleep strategy, French parents have homed in on this one thing. They treat waiting not just as one important quality among many, but as a cornerstone of raising kids.

I'm still mystified by France's national baby-feeding schedule. How do French babies all end up eating at the same times, if their mothers don't make them do it? When I point this out, mothers continue to wax eloquent about rhythms and flexibility, and about how each child is different.

But after a while, I realize that they also take a few principles for granted, even if they don't always mention them. The first principle is that, after the first few months, a baby should eat at roughly the same time each day. The second is that babies should have a few big feeds rather than a lot of small ones. And the third is that the baby should fit into the rhythm of the family.

So while it's true that they don't force their babies on to a schedule, they do nudge them towards it by observing these three principles. *Votre Enfant* says the ideal is to breastfeed on demand for the first few months, and then bring the baby 'progressively and flexibly, to regular hours that are more compatible with daily life'.

If parents follow these principles and the baby wakes up at seven or eight, and you think he should wait about four hours between meals, he is going to be routed on to the national meal plan. He'll eat in the morning. He'll eat again around noon. He'll have an afternoon feed around four, and then eat again at about 8 pm, before bed. When he cries at 10:30 am, you're going to assume that what's best for him is to wait until lunchtime and have a big feed then. It might take a while for him to ease into this rhythm. Parents do this gradually, not abruptly. But eventually the baby gets used to it, the same way that grown-ups do. The parents get used to it too.

Martine says that for the first few months she nursed Paulette on demand. Around the third month, to get her to wait three hours between feeds, she took her for walks or put her in a sling, where Paulette would usually quickly stop crying. Martine then did the same when she wanted to space out the feeding times to four hours. Martine says she never let either of her kids cry for very long. Gradually, she says, they just fell into the rhythm of eating four times a day. 'I was really flexible, I'm just like that,' she says.

The critical assumption is that while the baby has his own rhythm, the family and the parents have rhythms too. The ideal, in France, is to find a balance between these two. The parenting book *Your Child* explains, 'You and your baby each have your rights, and every decision is a compromise.'

Bean's regular paediatrician never mentioned this four-meal-a-day plan to me. But he's away at Bean's next appointment. His replacement is a young French woman who has a daughter about Bean's age. When I ask her about the schedule, she says that – *bien sûr* – Bean should only be eating four times a day. Then the doctor grabs some Post-its and scribbles down the Schedule. It's the same one again: morning, noon, 4 pm and 8 pm. When I later ask Bean's regular doctor why he never mentioned this, he says he prefers not to suggest schedules to Anglophone parents, because they become too doctrinaire about them.

It takes a few weeks, but we gradually nudge Bean on to this schedule. It turns out that she can take the wait. She just needed a bit of practice.

## Gâteau au Yaourt (Yogurt Cake)

*2 tubs plain whole-milk yogurt (the individual portion-sized tubs, about 175g/6 oz)*

*2 eggs*

*2 tubs sugar (or just one, depending on how sweet you like it)*

*1 teaspoon vanilla essence*

*just under 1 tub vegetable oil*

*4 tubs plain flour*

*1½ tsp baking powder*

Preheat oven to 190 degrees Celcius. Use vegetable oil to grease a 9-inch round pan (or a loaf tin).

Gently combine the yogurt, eggs, sugar, vanilla and oil. In a separate bowl, mix the flour and baking powder. Add the dry ingredients to the wet ingredients; mix gently until the ingredients are combined, but don't over-mix. You can add

2 tubs frozen berries, a tub of chocolate chips, or any flavouring you like. Cook for 35 minutes, then 5 minutes more if it doesn't pass the knife test. It should be almost crispy on the outside, but springy on the inside. Let it cool. The cake is delicious served with tea and a dollop of crème fraîche.

# 5

# Tiny Little Humans

WHEN BEAN IS A YEAR AND A HALF, WE REGISTER HER AT the Centre for the Adaptation of the Young Child to the Aquatic Milieu, known as 'babies in the water' – *bébés dans l'eau*. It's a weekly swimming class organized by our local town hall, and held every Saturday at one of the public pools in our neighbourhood. A month before the first class, the organizers summon parents to a meeting. The other parents seem a lot like us: university-educated, and willing to push buggies in the cold on Saturday mornings in order to teach their kids to swim. Each family is assigned a forty-five-minute swimming slot and reminded that – as in all public pools in Paris – men must wear tight swimming trunks, not shorts. (This is supposedly for hygiene. Swimming shorts could be worn elsewhere, and thus carry dirt into the pool.)

The three of us arrive at the pool, get undressed and put on our swimming gear as discreetly as possible in the unisex changing room. Then we slip into the pool alongside the other kids and their parents. Bean throws around some plastic balls, goes down the slide and jumps off the rafts. At one point an instructor paddles up to us and introduces himself, then swims away. Before we know it, our time is up and the next shift of parents and kids is climbing into the pool.

I figure that this must be an introductory class, and that the lessons will begin the following week. But at the next class it's the same thing: lots of splashing around, no one teaching anyone how to kick, blow bubbles or otherwise begin to swim. In fact, there's no organized instruction at all. Every so often the same instructor paddles by and makes sure we're happy.

This time, I corner him in the pool: when is he going to start teaching my daughter how to swim? He smiles indulgently. 'Children don't learn how to swim in "babies in the water",' he says, as if this is completely obvious. (I find out later that Parisian kids typically don't learn to swim until they're six. In the US, they often learn much younger.)

So what are we all doing here? He says the point of these sessions is for children to *discover* the water, and to *awaken* to the sensations of being in it.

Huh? My daughter has already 'discovered' water in the bath. I want her to swim! And I want her to swim as early as possible, preferably by age two. That's what I thought I'd paid for, and why I dragged my family out of bed on a frigid Saturday morning.

I suddenly look around and realize that all those parents at the meeting knew that they were signing up for their kid to merely 'discover' and 'awaken' to the water, not to learn how to swim. Do their kids 'discover' the piano too, instead of learning how to play it?

French parents aren't just doing a few things differently. They have a whole different view of how kids learn, and of who they are. I don't just have a swimming-class problem; I seem to have a philosophical problem too.

In the 1960s, the Swiss psychologist Jean Piaget came to America to share his theories on the stages of children's development. After each talk, someone in the audience typically asked him what he began calling the American Question. It was: 'How can we speed these stages up?'

Piaget's answer was: 'Why would you want to do that?' He didn't think that pushing kids to acquire skills ahead of schedule was either possible or desirable. He believed that children reach these milestones at their own speeds, driven by their own inner motors.

The American question (I think it's fair to assume that these days it's a British question too) sums up an essential difference between French and Anglophone parents. We assign ourselves the job of pushing, stimulating and urging our kids from one developmental stage to the next. The better we are at parenting, we think, the faster our kids will move up. In my Anglophone playgroup in Paris, some of the mothers flaunt the fact that their kids take music classes, or that they go to a separate Portuguese-speaking playgroup. But often they don't reveal too many details about these activities, so that no one else's child can do them. These mothers would never admit that there's competition between us, but it is palpable.

'When every other helicopter parent is hovering anxiously over their offspring – encouraging them, guiding them and, yes, occasionally pushing them – it feels like a dereliction of duty not to do the same,' a mother writes in the *Telegraph*.

French parents just don't seem so anxious for their kids to get ahead. They don't push them to read, swim or do maths ahead of schedule. They aren't trying to prod them into becoming prodigies. I don't get the feeling that – surreptitiously or otherwise – we're all in a race for some unnamed prize. They do sign their kids up for tennis, fencing and English lessons. But they don't parade these activities as proof of what good parents they are. Nor do they hide the classes, like they're some sort of secret weapon. In France, the point of enrolling a child in Saturday-morning music class isn't to activate some neural network. It's to have fun. Like that swimming instructor, French parents believe in 'awakening' and 'discovery'.

French parents have a different view of what the nature of a child is. When I start to read about this view, I keep coming across two people who lived 200 years apart: the philosopher Jean-Jacques Rousseau, and a French woman I had never previously heard of called Françoise Dolto. They're the two great influences on French parenting. And their spirits are very much alive in France today.

The modern French idea of how to parent starts with Rousseau. The philosopher wasn't much of a parent himself (or, like Piaget, even born French). He was born in Geneva in 1712, and didn't have an ideal childhood. His mother died ten days after he was born. His only sibling, an older brother, ran away from home. Later his father, a watchmaker, fled Geneva because of a business dispute, leaving Jean-Jacques behind with an uncle. Rousseau abandoned his own children to orphanages soon after they were born. He said this was to protect the honour of their mother, a former seamstress whom he'd hired as a servant in Paris.

None of this stopped Rousseau from publishing *Émile, or On Education*, in 1762. It describes the education of a fictional boy named Émile (who will, after puberty, meet the lovely and equally fictional Sophie). The German philosopher Immanuel Kant later compared the book's significance to that of the French Revolution. It remains a classic; French friends tell me they read it in high school. *Émile*'s impact is so enduring that passages and catchphrases from it are modern-day parenting clichés, like the importance of 'awakening'. And French parents still take many of its precepts for granted.

*Émile* was published during a dire time for French parenting. A Parisian police official estimated that of the 21,000 babies born in Paris in 1780, 19,000 were sent to live with wet nurses as far away as Normandy or Burgundy. Some of these newborns died en route, bouncing around in the back of cold wagons. Many others died in the care of the poorly paid, overburdened wet nurses, who took on too many babies and often kept them tightly swaddled for long periods, supposedly to keep them from hurting themselves.

For working parents, wet nurses were an economic choice; it was cheaper to pay a nurse than to hire someone to replace the mother in the family shop. For upper-class mothers, however, it was a lifestyle choice. There was social pressure to be free to enjoy a sophisticated social life. The child 'interferes not just in his mother's married life, but also in her pleasures', writes a French social historian. 'Taking care of a child was neither amusing, nor *chic*.'

Rousseau tried to upend all of this with *Émile*. He urged mothers to breastfeed their own babies. He decried swaddling, 'padded bonnets' and 'leading strings', the child-safety devices of his day. 'Far from being attentive to protecting Émile from injury, I would be most distressed if he were never hurt and grew up without knowing pain,' Rousseau wrote. 'If he grabs a knife he will hardly tighten his grip and will not cut himself very deeply.'

Rousseau thought children should be given space to let their development unfold naturally. He said Émile should be 'taken daily to the middle of a field; there let him run and frisk about; let him fall a hundred times a day'. He imagined a child who is free to explore and discover the world, and let his senses gradually 'awaken'. 'In the morning let Émile run barefoot in all seasons,' he wrote. He allows the fictional boy to read just a single book: *Robinson Crusoe*.

Until I read *Émile*, I was mystified by all the talk among French parents and educators about letting children 'awaken' and 'discover'. One of the teachers at Bean's crèche gushed at the parents' meeting that the kids go to a local gymnasium on Thursday mornings not to exercise but to 'discover' their bodies. The nursery's mission statement says that kids should 'discover the world, in pleasure and gaiety . . .' Another centre near by is simply called Enfance et Découverte – Childhood and Discovery. The highest compliment anyone seems to pay a baby in France is that he is '*éveillé*' – alert and awakened. Unlike in America, this isn't a euphemism for 'ugly'.

Awakening is about introducing a child to sensory experiences, including tastes. It doesn't always require the parent's active involvement. It can come from staring at the sky, smelling dinner as it's being prepared, or letting him play alone on a blanket. It's a way of sharpening the child's senses and preparing him to discern between different experiences. It's the first step towards teaching him to be a cultivated, discerning adult.

I'm in favour of all this awakening, of course. Who wouldn't be? I'm just puzzled by the emphasis. We Anglophone parents – as Piaget discovered – tend to be more interested in having kids acquire concrete skills and reach developmental milestones.

And we tend to think that how well and how quickly kids advance depends on what their parents do. That means that parents' choices and the quality of their intervention are crucial. In this light, baby sign language, pre-reading strategies, and picking the right nursery understandably seem critically important. So does the never-ending search for parenting experts and advice.

I see this cultural difference in my little Parisian courtyard. Bean's room is filled with black-and-white flash cards, baby blocks with the ABC printed on them, and the Baby Einstein

DVDs that we've gladly received as gifts from English-speaking friends and family. We play Mozart as background music constantly, because we've heard it will make her smarter.

But my French neighbour Anne, the architect, had never heard of Baby Einstein. She wasn't interested when I told her about it. Anne liked to let her little girl sit and play with old toys bought at jumble sales, or meander around our shared courtyard.

I later mention to Anne that there is an opening at our local nursery school. Bean could start a year early. This would mean taking her out of her crèche, where she is one of the oldest kids, and where I fear she isn't being sufficiently challenged.

'Why would you want to do that?' Anne asks. 'There are so few years to just be a child.'

The University of Texas study found that with all this awakening, French mothers aren't trying to help their kids' cognitive development or make them advance in school. Rather, they believe that awakening will help their kids forge 'inner psychological qualities such as self-assurance and tolerance of difference'. Others believed in exposing children to a variety of tastes, colours and sights, simply because doing so gives the children pleasure.

This pleasure is 'the motivation for life', one of the mothers said. 'If we didn't have pleasure, we wouldn't have any reason to live.'

In the twenty-first-century Paris of parents and children that I inhabit, Rousseau's legacy takes two apparently contradictory forms. On the one hand, there's the frolicking in the fields (or the pool). But on the other hand, there's quite strict discipline. Rousseau says the child's freedom should be bound by firm limits and strong parental authority.

'Do you know the surest means of making your child miserable?' he writes. 'It is to accustom him to getting everything. Since his desires grow constantly due to the ease of satisfying them, sooner or later powerlessness will force you, in spite of yourself, to end up with a refusal. And this unaccustomed refusal will give him more torment than being deprived of what he desires.'

Rousseau says the biggest parenting trap is to think that because a child can argue well, his argument deserves the same weight as your own. 'The worst education is to leave him floating between his will and yours and to dispute endlessly between you and him as to which of the two will be the master.'

For him, the only possible master is the parent. It seems clear that Rousseau is the inspiration behind the *cadre* – or framework – that is the model for today's French parents. The ideal of the *cadre* is that parents are very strict about certain things, but very relaxed about almost everything else.

Fanny, the publisher with two young children, tells me that before she even had kids, she heard a well-known French actor on the radio talking about being a parent. He put her ideas about the *cadre* – and the way she herself was brought up – into words.

'He said, "Education is a firm *cadre*, and inside is liberty." I really like that. I think the kid is reassured. He knows he can do what he wants, but some limits will always be there.'

Almost all the French parents I meet describe themselves as 'strict'. This doesn't mean that they're constantly ogres. It means that, like Fanny, they are very strict about a few key areas. These things are the backbone of the *cadre*.

'I tend to be severe all of the time, a little bit,' Fanny says. 'There are some rules I found that if you let go, you tend to take two steps back. I rarely let these go.'

For Fanny, these areas are eating, sleeping and watching TV. 'For all the rest she can do what she wants,' she tells me. Even within these key areas, Fanny tries to give her daughter some freedom and choices. 'With the TV, it's no TV, just DVDs. But she chooses which DVD. I just try to do that for everything . . . Dressing up in the morning, I tell her, "At home, you can dress however you want. If you want to wear a summer shirt in wintertime, OK. But when we go out, we decide." It works for the moment. We'll see what happens when she's thirteen.'

The point of the *cadre* isn't to hem the child in; it's to create a world that's predictable and coherent to her. 'You need that *cadre* or I think you get lost,' Fanny says. 'It gives you confidence. You have confidence in your kid, and your kid feels it.'

The *cadre* feels enlightened and empowering for kids. But Rousseau's legacy has a darker side too. When I take Bean to get her first inoculations, I cradle her in my arms and apologize to her for the pain she's about to experience. The French paediatrician scolds me.

'You don't say, "I'm sorry,"' he says. 'Getting injections, and experiencing pain, is part of life. There's no reason to apologize for that.' He seems to be channelling Rousseau, who said, 'If by too much care you spare them every kind of discomfort, you are preparing great miseries for them.' (I'm not sure what Rousseau thought about suppositories.)

Rousseau wasn't sentimental about children. He wanted to make good citizens out of impressionable lumps of clay. Many thinkers continued to view babies as *tabulae rasae* – blank slates – for hundreds of years. Near the end of the nineteenth century, the American psychologist and philosopher William James said that to an infant, the world is 'one great blooming, buzzing confusion'. Well into the twentieth century, it was taken for granted that children only slowly begin understanding the world and the fact of their own presence in it.

In France, the idea that kids are second-class beings and only gradually gain status persisted into the 1960s. I've met French men and women now in their forties who, as children, weren't allowed to speak at the dinner table unless they were first addressed by an adult. Children were often expected to be '*sage comme une image*' – quiet as a picture, the equivalent of the old English dictum that children should be 'seen but not heard'.

This conception of children began changing in France in the late 1960s, and came to a head after the 1968 student protests, which led to a general strike. What many people really wanted was a whole different way of life. France's religious, socially conservative, male-dominated society, in place for centuries, suddenly seemed dated. The protesters envisioned a kind of personal liberation that included different life options for women, less of a rigid class hierarchy, and a daily existence that wasn't just about '*Métro, boulot, dodo*' – commute, work, sleep. Eventually the French government broke up the protests, sometimes violently. But the revolt had a profound impact on French society. (France is now, for example, one of the least religious countries in Europe.)

The authoritarian model of parenting was a casualty of 1968 too. If everyone was equal, why couldn't children speak at dinner? The pure Rousseauian model – children as blank slates and obedient subjects – didn't suit France's newly emancipated society. And the French were fascinated by psychoanalysis. It suddenly seemed that by shutting kids up, parents might be screwing them up too.

French kids were still expected to be well behaved and to control themselves, but gradually after 1968 they were encouraged to express themselves too. The young French parents I know often use *sage* to mean self-controlled, but also happily absorbed in an activity. 'Before it was "*sage* like a picture". Now it's "*sage* and awakened", explained the French psychologist and writer Maryse Vaillant, herself a member of the famous 'Generation of '68'.

Into this generational upheaval walked Françoise Dolto. Dolto is the other titan of French parenting. French people I speak to – even those without kids – can't believe that Anglophones haven't heard of Françoise Dolto, or that only one of her books has ever been translated into English (it's long out of print).

In France, Dolto is a household name, a bit like Dr Spock used to be in America. The centenary of her birth was celebrated in 2008 with a flood of articles, tributes, and even a made-for-TV movie about her life. UNESCO convened a three-day conference in Paris on Dolto. Her books are for sale in practically every French bookshop.

In the mid-1970s, Dolto was in her mid-sixties and already the most famous psychoanalyst and paediatrician in France. Then, in 1976, a French radio station began broadcasting daily twelve-minute programmes in which Dolto responded to listeners' letters about parenting. 'Nobody imagined the immediate and lasting success of the programme,' recalled Jacques Pradel, then the programme's 27-year-old host. He describes her responses to readers' questions as 'brilliance bordering on premonition'. 'I don't know where she got her answers,' he says.

When I watch film clips of Dolto from that period, I can see why she appealed to anxious parents. With her thick glasses and matronly outfits, she had the bearing of a wise grand-mother. (The famous person she most resembles is Golda Meir.) And like her American counterpart Dr Spock, Dolto had the gift of making everything she said – even her more outrageous claims – sound like common sense.

Dolto may have looked like everyone's *grand-mère*, but her message about how to treat kids was deliciously radical, and fitting for the new times. In a sort of emancipation of babies, she claimed that children are rational, and indeed that even babies understand language as soon as they're born. It's an intuitive, almost mystical message. And it's a message that ordinary French people still embrace, even if they don't all articulate it. Once I read Dolto, I realize that so many of the most curious claims that I've heard French parents make, like the one that you're supposed to talk to babies about their sleep troubles, come straight from her.

The radio broadcasts made Dolto into an almost mythic figure in France. Well into the 1980s, books containing transcripts of her broadcasts, and other conversations, were stacked like produce in French supermarkets. A whole cohort of children were known as Génération Dolto. A psychoanalyst quoted in a special Dolto-themed edition of *Télérama* magazine in 2008 recalled riding in a taxi whose driver said he never missed a broadcast. 'He was dumbfounded. He said, "She talks to children like they are human beings!"'

Dolto's core message isn't a 'parenting philosophy'. It doesn't come with a lot of specific instructions. But if you accept as a first principle that children are rational – as French society does – then many things begin to shift. If babies understand what you're saying to them, then you can teach them quite a lot, even while they're very young. That includes, for example, how to eat in a restaurant.

The future Françoise Dolto was born Françoise Marette in 1908, into a large, well-off Catholic family in Paris. On the surface she had a charmed life: violin lessons, a cook in the kitchen, and peacocks prancing around the back yard. She was groomed to marry well.

But Françoise wasn't the discreet and obedient daughter that her parents expected. She wasn't '*sage comme une image*'. She was wilful, outspoken, and passionately curious about the people around her. In her early letters, the young Dolto seems preternaturally aware of the troubling gap of understanding between herself and her parents. She studied both psycho-analysis and paediatrics, and trained in hospitals around France.

Unusually for a parenting expert, Dolto was apparently an excellent parent to her own three children. Her daughter Catherine writes of her parents: 'They never made us do our homework, for example. However we did get bawled out, like everyone else, when we had bad grades. I got detention every Thursday for bad behaviour. Mum said to me, "It's too bad for you, it's you who has the detention. When you get tired of it, you'll be able to hold your tongue."'

Dolto always maintained an unusually lucid memory of how she had seen the world as a child. She rejected the prevailing view that doctors should treat children as merely a collection of physical symptoms. (At the time, bed wetters were still attached to 'peepee-stops' that released electric shocks.) Instead, she spoke to children about their lives, and assumed that many of their physical symptoms had psychological origins. 'And you, what do you think?' she would ask her young patients.

Dolto famously insisted that older children 'pay' her at the end of each session, with an object like a stone, to emphasize their independence and accountability. This respect for children resonated strongly with Dolto's students. 'She changed everything, and we, the students, wanted things to change,' the psychoanalyst Myriam Szejer recalls.

Dolto's respect extended even to babies. A former student described her dealing with an upset baby who was several months old: 'All of her senses were on alert, totally receptive to the emotions that the baby aroused in her. It was not to console [the baby], but to understand what the baby was telling her. Or more precisely, what the baby saw.' There are legendary stories about Dolto approaching previously inconsolable infants in the hospital and simply explaining to them why they were there, and where their parents were. According to legend, the babies suddenly calmed.

This isn't Anglo-style talking to babies, where you believe that babies recognize the mother's voice, or are soothed by a calming sound. Nor is it a method to teach a child to speak, or to prime him to become the next Jonathan Franzen.

Rather, Dolto insisted that the content of what you say to a baby matters tremendously. She said it was crucial that parents tell their babies the truth, in order to gently affirm what the babies already know.

In fact, she thought that babies begin eavesdropping on adult conversations – and intuiting the problems and conflicts swirling around them – from the womb. She envisioned (in the pre-ultrasound days) a conversation between a mother and her minutes-old baby going something like this: 'You see, we were waiting for you. You're a little boy. Maybe you heard us saying that we wanted a little girl. But we're very happy that you're a little boy.'

Dolto wrote that a child should be included in conversations about his parents' divorce from the age of six months. When a grandparent dies, she believed that even a young child should briefly attend the funeral. 'Someone in the family goes with him to say, "*Voilà*, it's the burial of your grandfather." It's something that happens in a society.' For Dolto, 'The child's best interest is not always what will make him or her happy, but rational understanding,' wrote MIT sociologist Sherry Turkle, in an introduction to Dolto's *When Parents Separate*. Turkle writes that what a child most needs, according to Dolto, is 'a structured inner life able to support autonomy and further growth'.

Dolto was criticized by some foreign psychoanalysts for relying too much on her own intuitions. But inside France, parents seemed to take both an intellectual and an aesthetic pleasure in her imaginative leaps.

If Dolto's ideas ever reached English-speaking parents, they probably just sounded strange. American and (to a slightly lesser extent) British parents were under the sway of Dr Benjamin Spock, who was born five years before Dolto and also trained as a psychoanalyst. Spock wrote that a child can only understand that he's soon to have a baby brother or sister from the age of about eighteen months. His forte was listening carefully to parents, not to babies. 'Trust yourself. You know more than you think you do,' is the famous opening salvo of his parenting guide, *Baby and Child Care*.

For Dolto, it was children who knew more than anyone thought. Even into old age, when she was hooked up to an oxygen tank, Dolto would get down on the floor with her young patients to see the world as they did. Her view from there was appealingly blunt.

'. . . If there's no jealousy when the baby comes . . . it's a very bad sign. The older child *should* show signs of jealousy, because for him it *is* a problem, the first time that he sees everyone admiring someone younger than him,' she said.

Dolto insisted that children have rational motives, even when they misbehave, and she said that it's the job of parents to listen and grasp these motives. 'The child who has an unusual reaction always has a reason for having it . . . when a child suddenly has an unusual, troubling reaction, our task is to *understand* what has happened,' Dolto says.

She gives the example of a small child who suddenly refuses to continue walking down the street. To the parent, it seems like stubbornness. But to the child, there's a reason. 'We should try to understand him, and say, "There's a reason. I don't understand, but let's think about it." Above all, don't suddenly make a drama out of it.' In one of the centennial tributes to Dolto, a French psychoanalyst summed up her teachings this way: 'Human beings speak to other human beings. Some of them are big, some of them are small. But they communicate.'

Whereas Spock's giant tome *Baby and Child Care* seems like it's straining to contain every possible scenario involving children, from obstructed tear ducts to (in posthumous editions) gay parenting, Dolto's books are pocket-sized. Instead of giving lots of specific instructions, she keeps returning to a few basic principles, and seems to expect that parents will think things through on their own.

Dolto agreed to do the radio broadcasts on the condition that she could answer letters from parents rather than phone calls. She thought that parents would begin to see solutions simply by writing out their problems. Pradel, the radio host, remembers: 'She told me, "You'll see, one day we'll get a letter from a person who's going to say to us, 'I'm sending you these pages, but I think I already understand.'"' And we received one, exactly like she predicted.'

Like Spock in the US, Dolto has been blamed in France for unleashing a wave of overly permissive parenting, especially in the 1970s and '80s. It's easy to see how Dolto's advice could be interpreted this way. Some parents surely thought that if they listened to what a child said, they then had to do what he said too.

This wasn't what Dolto advocated. She thought that parents should listen carefully to their kids, and explain the world to them. But she thought that this world would of course include many limits, and that the child, being rational, could absorb and handle these limits. Dolto didn't want to upend Rousseau's *cadre* model. She wanted to preserve it. She just added a huge measure of empathy and respect for the child – something that may have been lacking in France pre-1968.

The parents I see in Paris today really do seem to have found a balance between paying close attention to their kids and being clear that it's the parents who are in charge (even if they sometimes have to remind themselves of this). French parents listen to their kids all the time. But if little Agathe says she wants *pain au chocolat* for lunch, she isn't going to get it.

French parents have made Dolto (standing on the shoulders of Rousseau) part of their parenting firmament. When a baby has a nightmare, 'You always reassure him by speaking to him,' says Alexandra, who works in the Parisian nursery. 'I'm very much in favour of speech and language with children, even the smallest ones. They understand. For me, they understand.'

The French magazine *Parents* says that if a baby is scared of strangers, his mother should warn him that a visitor will be coming over soon. Then, when the doorbell rings, 'Tell him that the guest is here. Take a few seconds before opening the door . . . if he doesn't cry when he sees the stranger, don't forget to congratulate him.'

I hear of several cases where, upon bringing a baby home from the maternity hospital, the parents give the baby a tour of the house. French parents often tell babies what they're doing to them: I'm picking you up, I'm changing your nappy, I'm going to give you a bath. This isn't just to make soothing sounds; it's to convey information. And since the baby is a person like any other, parents are often quite polite about all this. (Plus it's apparently never too early to start instilling good manners.)

The practical implications of believing that a baby or toddler understands what you say, and can act on it, are considerable. It means you can teach him to sleep through the night early on, not to barge into your room every morning, to sit properly at the table, to eat only at mealtimes, and not to interrupt his parents. You can expect him to accommodate – at least a little bit – what his parents need, too.

I get a strong taste of this when Bean is about ten months old. She begins pulling herself up in front of a bookcase in our living room, and pulling down all the books she can reach.

This is irritating, of course. But I don't think I can stop her. Often I just pick up the books and put them back. But one morning, Simon's French friend Lara is visiting. When Lara sees Bean pulling the books down, she immediately kneels next to Bean and explains, patiently but firmly, 'We don't do that.' Then she shows Bean how to put the books back on the shelf, and tells her to leave them there. Lara keeps using the word *doucement* – gently. (After this, I start to notice that French parents say *doucement* all the time.) I'm shocked when Bean listens and obeys.

This incident revealed the enormous cultural gap between Lara and me, as parents. I had assumed that Bean was a very cute, very wild creature with a lot of potential but almost no self-control. If she occasionally behaved well, it was because of a kind of animalistic training, or just luck. After all, she couldn't talk, and didn't even have hair yet.

But Lara (who at the time was childless, but now has two well-behaved daughters) assumed that, even at ten months old, Bean could understand language and learn to control herself. She believed that Bean could do things *doucement* if she wanted to. And as a result, Bean did.

\* \* \*

Françoise Dolto died in 1988. Some of her intuitions about babies are now being confirmed by scientific experiments. Scientists have figured out that you can tell what babies know by measuring how long they look at one thing versus another. Like adults, babies look longer at things that surprise them. Beginning in the early 1990s, research using this method has shown that 'babies can do rudimentary maths with objects' and that 'babies have an actual understanding of mental life: they have some grasp of how people think and why they act as they do', writes Yale psychologist Paul Bloom. A study at the University of British Columbia found that eight-month-olds understand probabilities.

There's also evidence that babies have a moral sense. Bloom and other researchers showed six- and ten-month-old babies a sort of puppet show in which a circle was trying to roll up a hill. A 'helper' character helped the circle go up, while a 'hinderer' pushed it down. After the show, the babies were offered the helper and the hinderer on a tray. Almost all of them reached for the helper. 'Babies are drawn to the nice guy and repelled by the mean guy,' Paul Bloom explains.

Of course, these experiments don't prove that – as Dolto claims – babies understand speech. But they do seem to prove her point that, from a very young age, babies are rational. Their minds aren't a 'blooming, buzzing confusion'. At the very least, we should watch what we say to them.

# 6

# Daycare?

WHEN I CALL MY MOTHER IN AMERICA TO TELL HER THAT Bean has been accepted into a state nursery – we call it 'daycare' – there's a long pause on her end of the line.

'Daycare?' she asks, finally.

Friends back home are sceptical too.

'It's just not a situation I want,' sniffs a marketing consultant whose son is nine months old, about the same age Bean will be when she starts. 'I want him to have a little more individual attention.'

But when I tell my French neighbours that Bean has been accepted at the crèche, as the full-time state nurseries are known here, they congratulate me and practically crack open the champagne.

In America, the word 'daycare' conjures images of paedophiles and howling babies in dirty, dimly lit rooms. 'I want him to have a little more individual attention' is a euphemism for 'Unlike you, I actually love my child and don't want to institutionalize him.' American parents who can afford it tend to hire full-time nannies, then start easing kids into preschool when they're two or three. Those who must send their babies to nurseries do so warily and often full of guilt.

British mothers don't have the same negative associations. They generally accept that nurseries are necessary, and that they are regulated and OK for kids. But most British nurseries are private. And many mothers hesitate to put their kids in nurseries until they're at least a year old.

And British parents' acceptance of nurseries doesn't compare with the enthusiasm of the French. Middle-class French parents – architects, doctors, fellow journalists – are clawing past each other to get a spot in their neighbourhood crèche. And it's not just for a few tentative hours a day. The crèche is open five days a week, usually from eight to six. Mothers apply when they're pregnant, then harangue, cajole and beg for a spot for a year after that. The monthly fees are subsidized by the state, and parents are charged sliding rates based on their incomes.

'I felt that it was a perfect system, absolutely perfect,' gushes my friend Esther, a French lawyer, whose daughter started at the crèche when she was nine months old. Even friends of mine who don't work try to enrol their kids in the crèche. As a distant second choice, they consider shared nannies, or childminders who look after up to three kids in the childminder's own home. These are subsidized too, through tax credits. Sleek government websites lay out all the childcare options.

All this gives me a kind of cultural vertigo. Will nursery

make my child aggressive, neglected and insecurely attached, as the scary English-language headlines say? Or will she be socialized, 'awakened' and skilfully looked after, as French parents proclaim?

For the first time, I worry that we're taking our little inter-cultural experiment too far. It's one thing to start holding a fork in my left hand, and giving blank looks to strangers. It's quite another to subject my child to a potentially weird and damaging experience for the bulk of her toddlerhood. Are we going a bit too native? She can try *foie gras*, but should she try the crèche?

I decide to calm myself by reading up on the French crèche. Its story begins in the 1840s. Jean-Baptiste-Firmin Marbeau, an ambitious young lawyer in search of a cause to champion, was deputy mayor of Paris's first district. It was the middle of the industrial revolution, and cities like Paris were teeming with women who'd arrived from the provinces to work as seamstresses and in factories. Marbeau was charged with writing a study of the *salles d'asile*, free nursery schools for kids aged two to six.

He was impressed. 'How carefully, I said to myself, society watches over the children of the poor!' he wrote.

But Marbeau wondered who looked after poor children between birth and age two, while their mothers worked. He consulted the district's 'poor list' and set off to visit several mothers. 'At the far end of a filthy backyard, I call out for Madame Gérard, a washerwoman. She comes down, not wanting me to enter her home, *too dirty to be seen* (those are her words). She holds a new-born baby on her arm, and a child of eighteen months by the hand.'

Marbeau discovered that when Madame Gérard went off to wash laundry, she left the children with a babysitter. This cost her 70 centimes a day, about a third of her daily wages. And the babysitter was an equally poor woman who, when Marbeau visited, was 'at her post, watching over three young children on the floor in a shabby room'.

That wasn't bad childcare by the day's standards for the poor. Some mothers locked kids alone in apartments or tied them to bedposts for the day. Slightly older kids were often left to watch their siblings while their mothers worked. Many very young babies still lived at the homes of wet nurses, where conditions could be life-threatening.

Marbeau was seized with an idea: the crèche! (The name was meant to invoke the cosy manger in the Nativity story.) It would be all-day care for poor children from birth to age two. Funding would come from donations by wealthy patrons, some of whom would also help oversee crèches. Marbeau envisioned spartan but spotless buildings, where women called nurses would look after babies and counsel mothers on hygiene and morals. Mothers would pay just 50 centimes a day. Those with unweaned infants would return twice a day to breastfeed.

The middle and upper classes felt a strong sense of *noblesse oblige* towards the working classes, and especially towards their children. They also worried that these kids would grow up into unruly adolescents. The crèche was meant to be a cheerful, clean oasis for them.

Marbeau's idea struck a chord. There was soon a crèche commission to study the matter, and Marbeau set out to woo potential donors. Like any good fundraiser, he appealed both to their sense of charity and to their economic self-interest.

'These children are your fellow citizens, your brothers. They are poor, unhappy and weak: you should rescue them,' he wrote in a crèche manual published in 1845. Then he added, 'If you can save the lives of 10,000 children, make haste: 20,000 extra arms a year are not to be disdained. Arms are work and work creates wealth.'

In his manual, Marbeau instructs crèches to open from 5:30 am to 8:30 pm, to wrap around the typical workday for labourers. The life Marbeau describes for mothers isn't too different from that of a lot of working mothers I know today:

'She gets up before 5 o'clock, dresses her child, does some housework, runs to the Crèche, runs to work . . . at 8 o'clock she hastens back, fetches her child with the day's dirty linen, rushes home to put the poor little creature to bed, and to wash his linen so it will be dry the next day, and every day the whole process is repeated! . . . how on earth does she manage!' From the start, the crèche was also supposed to give a mother peace of mind, so she could 'devote herself to her work with an easy conscience'.

Evidently Marbeau was quite persuasive. The first crèche opened in a donated building on the rue de Chaillot in Paris.

Two years later there were thirteen crèches. The number continued to grow, especially in Paris.

Crèches never became as ubiquitous as the *salles d'asile*, which eventually became the *école maternelle* (Bean will attend this too). But crèches were tightly regulated. After the Second World War, the French government put them under the control of the newly formed Mother and Infant Protection service (PMI) and created an official degree programme for the job of '*puéricultrice*', a person trained in caring for babies and young children.

By the beginning of the 1960s, the French poor were less desperate, and there were fewer of them. And more middle-class mothers were working. The crèche began attracting these women's families too. The number of spots nearly doubled in ten years, reaching 32,000 in 1971. Suddenly middle-class mothers got sulky if they couldn't get a place in a crèche. It started to seem like an entitlement for working mothers.

All kinds of variants on the crèche opened too. There were part-time nurseries, 'family' crèches where parents pitched in, and 'company' crèches for employees. Guided by Françoise Dolto's insistence that babies are people too, there was a new interest in childcare that didn't merely keep kids from getting ill, or treat them like potential delinquents.

Soon crèches were spouting middle-class values like 'socialization' and 'awakening', and mothers became convinced that the crèche was good for kids. In Paris, about a third of kids under three now go to the crèche, and half are in some kind of collective care. (There are fewer crèches outside Paris.)

French mothers do worry about paedophiles, but not at the crèche. They believe that kids are safer in settings with lots of trained adults looking after them, rather than being 'alone with a stranger', according to a report by a national parenting group. 'If she's going to be *tête-à-tête* with someone, I want it to be me,' the mother of an eighteen-month old at Bean's crèche tells me. This mother says that if her daughter hadn't got a place in the crèche, she would have given up her job to look after her.

French parents take it for granted that crèches are of universally high quality, and that their staff are caring and highly skilled. In French parenting chat rooms, the most serious complaint I can find about a crèche is from a mother whose child was served ravioli along with moussaka, a similarly heavy dish.

'I sent a letter to the crèche, and they responded by saying their regular chef was not there,' she explains. She adds, darkly: 'Let's see what happens the rest of the week.'

I first hear about the crèche when I'm pregnant, from my friend Dietlind. She's a Chicagoan who's lived in Europe since she graduated from university. (In Paris there's a whole caste of expatriates who studied abroad and married their foreign boyfriends or just never got around to leaving.) Dietlind is energetic and warm, and speaks effortless French. She's one of the few people I know who's actually striving to make the world a better place. About the only thing wrong with Dietlind is that she can't cook. Her family subsists almost entirely on food from Picard, the French frozen-food chain. She once tried to serve me defrosted sushi, rice and all.

Despite this, Dietlind is a model mother. So when she tells me that her two sons, aged five and eight, attended the crèche around the corner from me, I take note. She says the crèche was excellent. Years later, she still stops by to greet the *directrice* and her sons' old teachers. The boys still talk about their crèche days with joyful nostalgia. Their favourite care-giver used to give them haircuts.

What's more, Dietlind offers to put in a good word with the *directrice*. She also keeps repeating that the crèche isn't *fancy*. I'm not sure what this means. Does she think that I require Philippe Starck playpens? Is 'not fancy' code for 'dirty'?

Though I've put up a brave multicultural front for my mother, the truth is that I share some of her doubts. The fact that the crèche is run by the city of Paris seems kind of creepy. It feels like I'll be dropping my baby off at the post office. I have visions of faceless bureaucrats rushing past Bean's Moses basket. Maybe I do want 'fancy', whatever that means. Or maybe I just want to look after Bean myself.

Unfortunately, I can't. I'm midway through writing the book that I was supposed to hand in before Bean was born. I took a few months off after her birth. But now my (already once-extended) deadline looms. We've hired a lovely nanny, Adelyn, from the Philippines, who arrives in the morning and looks after Bean all day. The problem is, I work from home in a little alcove office. The temptation to micromanage them both – to the irritation of everyone – is irresistible.

Bean does seem to be developing a decent passive understanding of Tagalog, the main language of the Philippines. But I suspect she often ends up speaking Tagalog at our local McDonald's, since each time we pass by it, she points and shouts. Perhaps the non-fancy crèche is a better option.

I'm also amazed that, thanks to Dietlind, we have an 'in' somewhere. I'm used to being out of synch with the rest of the country. Sometimes I don't know it's a national holiday until I walk outside and find that all the shops are closed. Having Bean in crèche would connect us more to France.

The crèche is also tantalizingly convenient. There's one across the street from our house. Dietlind's is a five-minute walk. Like those nineteenth-century washerwomen, I could pop in to breastfeed Bean, and wipe her snot.

Mostly, though, it's hard to resist all the French adult peer pressure (I'm glad they're not trying to get me to smoke). Anne and the other French mothers in our courtyard chime in about the wonders of the crèche too. Simon and I figure that even with our contact, our odds of actually getting in are small. So we go to our local town hall and apply for a place.

Competition for the existing spots in crèches is – as the French say – *énergique*. A committee of bureaucrats and crèche directors in each of Paris's twenty *arrondissements* convenes to dole out their available places. In the well-heeled 16th *arrondissement* there are 4,000 applicants for 500 places. In our less rarified area of eastern Paris, the odds are one in three.

Scrambling for a spot in a crèche is one of the initiation rituals of new parenting. In Paris, women can officially begin petitioning the town hall when they're six months pregnant. But magazines urge women to schedule a meeting with the director of their preferred crèche as soon as they have a positive pregnancy test.

Priority goes to single parents, multiple births, adoptees, families with three or more kids, or those with 'particular difficulties'. How to fit into this last, ambiguous category is the topic of furious speculation in online forums. One mother advises writing to town-hall officials about your urgent need to return to work and your epic but ultimately failed efforts to find any other form of childcare. She suggests copying this letter to the regional governor and the President of France, then requesting a private audience with the district mayor. 'You go there with the baby in your arms, looking desperate, and you retell the same story as in the letter,' she says. 'I can assure you that this will succeed.'

Simon and I decide to work our only angle: being foreign. In a letter attached to our crèche application, we extol Bean's budding multilingualism (she doesn't actually speak yet) and describe how her Anglo-Americanism will enrich the crèche. As promised, Dietlind talks us up to the director of the crèche that her sons went to. I meet this woman, and try to project a mix of desperation and charm. I call the town hall once a month (for some reason, as with French couples, most of the crèche-courting falls to me) to remind them of our 'enormous interest and need for a spot'. Since I'm not French and can't vote here, I decide not to bother the President.

Amazingly, these attempts to massage the process actually

work. A congratulatory letter arrives from our town hall explaining that Bean has been assigned a spot in crèche for mid-September, when she'll be nine months old. I call Simon, triumphant: we foreigners have beaten the natives at their own game! We're amazed, and giddy from the victory. But we also have the feeling that we've won a prize that we don't quite deserve, and aren't even sure we want.

The main question people in France ask about nurseries is how to get more kids into them. Thanks to France's current baby boom, you can't run for public office in France – on the right or the left – without promising to build more crèches or expand existing ones. There's a new proposal to turn disused baggage areas in railway stations into crèches for the children of commuters (much of the construction cost would go towards sound-proofing).

French mothers do worry about the anguish they'll feel when they drop their children off at crèche for the first time. But they view this as their own separation issue. 'In France parents are not afraid of sending their children to the crèche,' explains Marie Wierink, a sociologist with France's Ministry of Labour. '*Au contraire*, they fear that if they cannot find a place in the crèche their child will be missing out on something.'

Kids don't learn to read in crèche. They don't learn letters, or other 'pre-literacy' skills. What they do is socialize with other kids. In America, some parents mention this to me as a benefit of nurseries. In France, all parents do. 'I knew that it was very good, it was an opening to social life,' says my friend

Esther, the lawyer, whose daughter entered crèche at nine months old.

My friend Hélène, an engineer, didn't work in the first few years after her youngest daughter was born. But she was never remotely apologetic about sending the little girl to the crèche five days a week. This was in part so that Hélène would have time to herself, but also because she didn't want her daughter to miss out on the communal experience.

I still have my doubts when we bring Bean to her first day of crèche. It's at the end of a dead-end street, in a three-storey concrete building with a little Astroturf courtyard in front of it. It looks like a state school in America, but with everything in miniature. I recognize some of the kids' furniture from the Ikea catalogue. It's not fancy, but it's cheerful and clean.

The kids are divided by age into sections called small, medium and large. Bean's class is in a sunlit room with play kitchens, tiny furniture, and cubbyholes full of age-appropriate toys. Attached to the room is a glassed-in sleeping area where each child has his own cot, stocked with his dummies and the ubiquitous stuffed-animal companions called *doudous*.

Anne-Marie greets us. She'll be Bean's main caregiver and she's the one who gave haircuts to Dietlind's sons. Anne-Marie is a grandmother in her sixties, with short blonde hair and a rotating collection of printed T-shirts from places her charges have travelled to (we'll eventually bring her a T-shirt attesting to her love of Brooklyn). Employees have worked at the crèche for an average of thirteen years. Anne-Marie has been there much longer. She and many of the other caregivers are trained as *auxiliaires de puériculture*, or childcare assistants.

A paediatrician and a psychologist each visit the crèche regularly. The caregivers chart Bean's daily naps and poos, and report to me about how she's eaten. They feed the kids Bean's age one at a time, with the child either on someone's lap or in a bouncy seat. They put the kids down to sleep at roughly the same time each day, and claim not to wake them up. For this initial adaptation period, Anne-Marie asks me to bring in a shirt that I've worn, so that Bean can sleep with it. This feels a bit canine, but I do it.

I'm struck by the confidence of Anne-Marie and the other caregivers. They're quite certain about what children of each age need, and they're equally confident in their abilities to provide it. They convey this without being smug or impatient. My one gripe is that Anne-Marie insists on calling me 'mother of Bean' rather than 'Pamela'; she says it's too difficult to learn the names of all the parents.

Given our doubts about sending Bean to a crèche, we've compromised by enrolling her just four days a week, from about 9:30 to 3:30. Plenty of her classmates will be there five days a week, for much longer each day (the crèche is open from 7:30 to 6 pm).

As in Marbeau's day, Bean is supposed to arrive with a clean nappy. This becomes an almost Talmudic point of discussion between Simon and me. What constitutes 'arrival'? If Bean poos on her way in the door, or while we're saying goodbye, who changes the offending nappy? Is it us, or the *auxiliaires*?

The first two weeks are an adaptation period, in which she

stays for increasingly long periods at the crèche, with and without us. She cries a bit each time I leave, but Anne-Marie assures me that she quiets down soon after I go. Often one of the caregivers holds her up at the window facing the street, so I can wave when I get outside.

If the crèche is damaging Bean, we can't tell. Pretty soon she's cheerful when we drop her off, and happy when we pick her up. Once Bean has been at the crèche for a while, I begin to notice that the place is a microcosm of French parenting. That includes the bad stuff. Anne-Marie and the other caregivers are mystified that I'm still breastfeeding Bean when she's nine months old and especially when I feed her on the premises. They're not thrilled with my short-lived plan to drop off pumped breast milk before lunch each day, but they don't try to stop me.

All the big, positive French parenting ideas are in evidence too. Since there's so much agreement anyway on the best way to do things, the caregivers reinforce the things that French parents do – or at least would like to be doing – at home. They talk to even very young children all the time at the crèche, with what seems like perfect conviction that the children understand.

There's a lot of talk about the *cadre*, or framework. At a parents' meeting, one of the teachers speaks almost poetically about it: 'Everything is very *encadré* – built into a framework – the hour that they arrive and leave, for example. But inside this framework we try to introduce flexibility, fluidity and spontaneity, for the children and also for the [teaching] team.'

Bean spends a lot of the day just ambling around the room, playing with whatever she wants. I'm concerned about this. Where are the music circles? What about organized activities? But I soon realize that all this freedom is by design. It's the French *cadre* model yet again: kids get firm boundaries, but lots of freedom within those boundaries. And they're supposed to learn to cope with boredom and to play by themselves. 'When the child plays, he constructs himself,' explains Sylvie, one of Bean's caregivers when she moves up to *grande section*.

A mayor's report on Parisian crèches calls for a spirit of 'energetic discovery' in which the children are 'left to exercise their appetite for experimentation of their five senses, of using their muscles, of sensations, and of physical space.' As kids get older they do have some organized activities, but no one is obliged to participate.

'We propose, we don't force,' another of Bean's teachers explains. There's soothing background music to launch the kids into their naps, and a pile of books that they can read in bed. The kids gradually wake up to their *goûter*, the afternoon snack. The crèche isn't the post office. It's more like a spa holiday, but with better food.

In the playground there are no rules or structure, also by design. The idea is to give kids as much freedom as possible. 'When they're outside, we intervene very little,' says Mehrie, another of Bean's caregivers. 'If we intervene all the time, they go a little nuts.'

The crèche also teaches kids patience. I watch as a two-year-old demands that Mehrie pick her up. But Mehrie is cleaning the table where the children have just had lunch. 'For the moment I'm not free. You wait two seconds,' Mehrie says gently to the little girl. Then she turns to me and explains: 'We try to teach them to wait, it's very important. They can't have everything right away.'

The caregivers speak calmly and respectfully to the kids, using the language of rights: you have the right to do this, you don't have the right to do that. They say it with the same utter conviction that I've heard in the voices of French parents. Everyone believes that for the *cadre* to seem immutable, the rules have to be consistent. 'The prohibitions are always the same, and we always give a reason for them,' Sylvie tells me.

I know the crèche is strict about certain things because, after a while, Bean repeats phrases she's learned. We know they're crèche phrases because the teachers there are her only source of French. It's like she's been wearing a wire all day, and we get to listen to the tape. Most of what Bean repeats is in the command form, like 'On *va pas crier!*' – we're not going to shout. My rhyming favourites, which I immediately begin using at home, are '*Couche-toi!*' (go to sleep) and '*Mouche-toi!*' (blow your nose), said when you're holding a tissue up to a child's face.

For a while Bean speaks French *only* in the command form, or in these declarations of what's permissible and what isn't. When she plays 'teacher' at home, she stands on a chair, wags her finger and shouts instructions to imaginary children, or occasionally to our surprised lunch guests.

Soon, in addition to commands, Bean is coming home with songs. She often sings one that we know only as '*Tomola tomola, vatovi!*' in which she sings more and more loudly with each line, while making a spinning motion with her arms. It's only later that I learn this is one of the most popular French children's songs, which actually goes '*Ton moulin, ton moulin va trop vite*' – about a windmill that's going too quickly.

What really wins us over about the crèche is the food or, more specifically, the dining experience. Each Monday, the crèche posts its menu for the week on a giant white board near the entrance.

I sometimes photograph these menus and email them to my mother. They read like the chalkboard menus at Parisian brasseries. Every day, lunch is served in four courses: a cold vegetable starter; a main dish with a side dish of grains or cooked vegetables; a different cheese each day and a dessert of fresh fruit or fruit purée. There's a slightly modified version for each age group. The youngest kids have the same foods, but puréed.

A typical menu starts with hearts of palm and tomato salad. This is followed by sliced turkey *au basilic* accompanied by rice in a *provençal* cream sauce. The third course is a portion of St Nectaire cheese with a slice of fresh baguette. Dessert is fresh kiwi.

A van arrives several times a week with seasonal, fresh, sometimes even organic ingredients. Aside from the occasional tin of tomato purée, nothing is processed or pre-cooked. A few vegetables are frozen, but never pre-cooked. Using these ingredients, an in-house cook prepares lunch from scratch each day.

I have trouble imagining two-year-olds sitting through a meal like this, so the crèche lets me sit in on lunch one Wednesday, when Bean is at home with a babysitter. I'm stunned when I realize how my daughter eats lunch most days. I sit quietly with my reporter's notebook while her classmates assemble, in groups of four, at a series of square toddler-sized tables. One of her caregivers wheels up a cart filled with covered serving plates, and bread wrapped in plastic to keep it fresh. There's an adult at each table.

First, the teacher uncovers and displays each dish. There's a bright-red tomato salad in vinaigrette, and a side dish of peas, carrots and onions in a tomato sauce. 'This is followed by *le poisson*,' she says, to approving glances, as she reveals a flaky white fish in a light butter sauce. Next she previews the cheese course: 'Today it's *le bleu*,' she says, showing the kids a crumbly blue cheese. Then she displays dessert: whole apples, which she'll slice at the table.

The food looks simple, fresh and appetizing. The children eat with gusto. Except for the melamine plates, the bite-size pieces and the fact that some of the diners have to be prodded to say '*merci*', I might be in a high-end restaurant.

Just who are the people taking care of Bean? To find out, one windy autumn morning I turn up for the annual entrance examination for ABC Puériculture, one of the schools that trains crèche workers. There are hundreds of nervous women (and a few men) in their twenties, who are looking shyly at each other or doing last-minute practice questions in thick workbooks.

They're understandably anxious. Of the more than 500 people who sit the annual entrance test, just thirty are admitted to the training school. Applicants are grilled on reasoning, reading comprehension, maths and human biology. Those who advance to the second round face a psychological exam, an oral presentation and interrogation by a panel of experts.

The thirty winners then do a year of coursework and internships, following a curriculum set by the government. They learn the basics of child nutrition, sleep and hygiene. They practise mixing baby formula and changing nappies. They'll have additional week-long training sessions throughout their careers.

In France, working in a crèche is a career. There are schools all over the country with similarly rigorous entrance standards, creating an army of skilled workers. Just half of the carers at a crèche must be *auxiliaires* or have a similar degree. A quarter must have degrees related to health, leisure or social work. Another quarter are exempt from any qualifications, but must be trained in-house. At Bean's crèche, thirteen of the sixteen carers are *auxiliaires* or similar.

I start to see Anne-Marie and other caregivers at Bean's crèche as the Rhodes Scholars of babycare. And I understand their confidence. They've mastered their subject and earned the respect of parents. And I'm indebted to them. During nearly three years that Bean is at the crèche, they potty-train her, teach her table manners, and give her a French immersion course.

By Bean's third year at the crèche, I suspect that the days are starting to feel long, and that perhaps she's not being stimulated enough. I'm ready for her to move on to nursery. But Bean still seems perfectly content. She chatters all the time about Maky and Lila (pronounced 'Lee-lah'), her two best friends. (Interestingly, she's gravitated to other children of foreigners: Lila's parents are Moroccan and Japanese. Maky's dad is from Senegal.) She has definitely been socialized. When Simon and I take Bean to Barcelona for a long weekend, she keeps asking where the other children are.

The kids in Bean's section spend a lot of time running around and shouting in the Astroturf courtyard, which is stocked with little scooters and carts. Bean is usually out there when I pick her up. As soon as she spots me, she bolts over and throws herself happily into my arms, shouting the news of the day.

On Bean's last day at the crèche, after the goodbye party and the clearing out of her locker, Bean gives a big hug and kiss goodbye to Sylvie, who's recently been her main caregiver. Sylvie has been the model of professionalism all year. But when Bean embraces her, Sylvie begins to cry. I cry too.

By the end of crèche, Simon and I feel that she's had a good experience. But we did often feel guilty dropping her off each day. And we can't help but notice all the alarming headlines in the American press, on how nurseries affect kids.

Continental Europeans aren't really asking about that any more. Sheila Kamerman at Columbia University says they generally believe that high-quality nurseries, with small groups and warm, well-trained caregivers who have made the job a career, are good for kids. And conversely, they assume that bad nurseries are bad for kids.

Americans have too many misgivings about nurseries to take this for granted. So the US government has funded the largest-ever study of how early childcare arrangements correlate with the way kids develop and behave later in life.

Many of the headlines on nurseries in America come out of data from this giant study. These headlines often ignore one of the study's principal findings: that early childcare arrangements just aren't very significant. 'Parenting quality is a much more important predictor of child development than type, quantity or quality of childcare,' explains a press release. Children fared better when their parents were more educated and wealthier, when they had books and play materials at home, and when they had 'enhancing experiences' like going to the library. This was the same whether the child went to a nursery for thirty or more hours a week, or had a stay-at-home mother. And as I mentioned earlier, the study found that what's especially crucial is the mother's 'sensitivity' – how attuned she is to her child's experience of the world.

This is also true at a nursery. One of the study's researchers writes that kids get 'high-quality' care when the caregiver is 'attentive to [the child's] needs, responsive to her verbal and non-verbal signals and cues, stimulating of her curiosity and desire to learn about the world, and emotionally warm, supportive and caring'.

Kids fared better with a caregiver who was sensitive, whether it was a nanny, a grandparent or a nursery worker. 'It would not be possible to go into a classroom and, with no additional information, pick out which children had been in center care,' the researcher writes.

What we should be fretting about isn't just whether bad nurseries have bad outcomes (of course they do), but how unpleasant it is for kids to spend their days in bad nurseries. We're so concerned about cognitive development that we're forgetting to ask whether children in nurseries are happy, and whether it's a positive experience for them while it's happening. That's what French parents are talking about.

Even my mother gets used to the crèche. She starts calling it 'the crèche' instead of 'daycare', which probably helps. The crèche certainly has benefits for us. We do feel more a part of France, or at least a part of our neighbourhood. Thankfully, we put our ongoing 'to stay or not to stay in Paris' conversation on pause. We can't really imagine moving somewhere where we'd struggle to find decent, affordable childcare. And we can see the next excuse for staying in France coming up soon: the école maternelle, free state nursery school, with places for just about everyone.

Mostly, we like the French crèche because Bean likes it. She eats blue cheese, shares her toys, and plays '*tomate ketchup*' (the French version of 'duck, duck, goose'). Also, she has mastered the command form of French. She is a bit too aggressive: she likes to kick me in the shins. But I suspect she'll outgrow this. I don't think I can blame the crèche for her faults.

Maky and Lila are still Bean's dear friends. Occasionally we even take Bean back to the crèche to stare through the railings at the children who are now playing in the courtyard. And every once in a while, out of nowhere, Bean turns to me and says: 'Sylvie cried.' This was a place where she mattered.

# 7

# Bébé au Lait

WARMING UP TO THE CRÈCHE TURNED OUT TO BE EASY. Warming up to the other mothers there isn't. I'm aware that Anglo-American-style instant bonding between women doesn't happen in France. I've heard that female friendships here start out slowly, and can take years to ramp up. (Though once you're finally 'in' with a French woman, you're supposedly stuck with her for life. Whereas your English-speaking insta-friends can drop you at any time.)

I have managed to make friends with a few French women in the time I've now lived in Paris. But most either don't have kids or they live across town. The ones in my courtyard are barely around, or their kids are older. I'd just assumed that I'd also meet other mums in my neighbourhood, with kids the same age as Bean. In my fantasy, we'd swap recipes, organize picnics, and complain about our husbands. That's how it's supposed to happen. My own mother is still close to women she met in the playground when I was small.

So I'm unprepared when the French mothers at the crèche – who all live in my neighbourhood and have age-appropriate kids – barely say *bonjour* to me when we plop our toddlers down next to each other in the morning. I eventually learn the names of most of the kids in Bean's classes. But even after a year or so, I don't think any of the mothers knows Bean's name. They certainly don't know mine.

This initial stage, if that's what it is, doesn't feel like progress. Mothers I see several days a week at the crèche seem not to recognize me when we pass each other in the supermarket. Perhaps, as the cross-cultural books claim, they're giving me privacy; to speak would be to forge a relationship, and thus create obligations. Or perhaps they're just stuck up.

It's the same at the playground. The Canadian and Australian mothers I occasionally meet there treat the playground like I do: as a place to mingle, and perhaps make friends for life. Within minutes of spotting each other, we've revealed our hometowns, marital status and views on bilingual schooling. Soon we're mirroring like nobody's business: 'You trek to Concorde to buy Grape-Nuts cereal? Me too!'

But usually it's just me and the French mothers. And they don't do me too's. In fact, they barely exchange glances with me, even when our kids are sparring over sandbox toys. When I try icebreakers like 'How old is he?' they usually mutter a number, then eye me like I'm a stalker. They rarely ask any questions back. When they do, they turn out to be Italian.

Granted, I'm in the middle of Paris, surely one of the world's least friendly places. The sneer was probably invented here. Even people from the rest of France tell me that they find Parisians cold and distant.

I should probably just ignore these women. But I can't help it: they intrigue me. For starters, many of them look so much better than we Anglophones do. I drop Bean off at crèche in the morning wearing a ponytail and whatever was on the floor next to my bed. They arrive fully coiffed, perfumed and looking like they have early-rising personal stylists. I don't even gawk any more when French mothers prance into the park dressed in high-heeled boots and skinny jeans, while pushing buggies with tiny newborns in them. (Mums do get a bit fatter as you get further from central Paris.)

These mothers aren't just chic; they're also strangely collected. They don't shout the names of their children across the park, or rush out with a howling toddler strapped into a pram. They have good posture. They don't radiate that famous combination of fatigue, worry and on-the-vergeness that's bursting out of most Anglophone mums I know (myself included). Except for the actual child, you wouldn't know that they're mothers.

Part of me just wants to force-feed these women some spoonfuls of fatty pâté. But another part of me is dying to know their secrets. Having kids who sleep well, wait and don't whine surely helps them stay so calm. But there's got to be more to it. Are they secretly struggling with anything? Where's their belly fat? If this is all a façade, what's behind it? Are French mothers really perfect? And if so, are they happy?

After the baby is born, the first obvious difference between French and Anglophone mums is breastfeeding. For us, the length of time that we breastfeed – like the size of a Wall Street bonus – is a measure of performance. One former businesswoman in my Anglophone playgroup used to sidle up to me and ask, *faux* innocently, 'Oh, are you still nursing?'

It's *faux* because we all know that our breastfeeding 'number' is a concrete way to compete. A mother's score is reduced if she mixes in formula, relies too heavily on a breast-milk pump, or actually breastfeeds too long (at which point she starts to seem like a crazed hippie).

In Britain and the US, many mothers treat infant formula as practically a form of child abuse. The fact that breastfeeding requires endurance, inconvenience and in some cases physical suffering adds to its status.

You get bonus points from Anglophone mums for nursing in France, where breastfeeding isn't encouraged and many people find it disturbing. 'The breastfeeding mother is regarded, if not as an interesting oddity, then as someone who is performing above and beyond the call of duty,' explains the parenting guide published by Message, the organization for Anglophone mothers in Paris.

We expatriates exchange horror stories about French doctors who – when confronted with the occasional cracked nipple or blocked duct – blithely tell mothers to switch to formula. To combat this, Message has its own army of volunteer 'breastfeeding supporters'. Before I delivered Bean, one of them warned me never to hand my baby over to the hospital staff while I slept, lest they defy my instructions and give her a bottle when she cried. This woman made 'nipple confusion' sound scarier than autism.

All this adversity makes Anglophone mothers in Paris feel like lactating superheroes, battling the evil doctors and strangers who would like to steal antibodies from our babies. In chat rooms, mothers list the strangest places they've nursed in Paris: inside Sacré Coeur basilica, on a tomb at the Père Lachaise cemetery, and at a cocktail party at the Four Seasons Hotel George V. One mother says she breastfed her baby 'while standing and complaining at the easyJet desk in Charles de Gaulle Airport. I sort of laid him on the counter.' I pity the poor clerk.

Given our zeal, we can't fathom why French mothers barely breastfeed. About 63 per cent of French mothers do some breastfeeding, compared to 76 per cent of mothers in the UK (and 90 per cent of mothers in London). Long-term breast-feeding is rare in France. A bit more than half of French mothers are still nursing when they leave the maternity hospital, but most abandon it soon after that.

It's harder still for us Anglos to understand why even a certain type of middle-class French mother – the ones who steam and purée organic leeks for their seven-month-olds and send their older children to the same African drumming classes that we do – don't breastfeed much either.

'Don't they have the same medical information we have?' one incredulous American mother asks me. Among Anglophones, the reigning theories about why French women don't nurse include: they can't be bothered; they care more about their boobs than about their babies (though apparently it's pregnancy, not breastfeeding, that stretches out breasts); and they just don't know how important it is.

Locals tell me that breastfeeding still has a 'peasant' image, from the days when babies were farmed out to rural wet nurses. Others say that artificial-milk companies pay off hospitals, give away free samples in maternity wards, and advertise mercilessly. Olivier, who's married to my journalist friend Christine, theorizes that breastfeeding demystifies the female breast, turning it into something utilitarian and animalistic. Just as French fathers steer clear of a woman's business end during the birth, they avoid viewing the female breast when it's used for unsexy purposes. 'Men prefer not to see breast-feeding,' Olivier says.

There are small pockets of breastfeeding enthusiasts in France. But mostly, there's little peer pressure to nurse for a long time. My friend Alison, who's from Brighton and teaches English in Paris, innocently told her doctor that she was still nursing her thirteen-month-old. Alison says the doctor immediately asked her, 'What does your husband say? And your shrink?' *Enfant* magazine acknowledges that 'Breastfeeding after three months is always viewed badly by one's entourage.'

Alexandra, the mother of two girls who works in a crèche, tells me that she didn't give a drop of breast milk to either of her daughters. She says this without a trace of apology or guilt. She says she was thrilled that her husband, who's a fireman, wanted to help care for the girls, and that bottle-feeding them was a great way to do this. She points out that both of her daughters are now perfectly healthy.

Alexandra adds: 'It was good practice for the father to give a bottle at night. And I could sleep, and drink wine in restaurants. It wasn't so bad for *maman*.'

Pierre Bitoun, a French paediatrician and long-time proponent of breastfeeding in France, says many French women think they don't have enough milk. Dr Bitoun says the real problem is that French maternity hospitals often don't encourage mothers to feed their newborns every few hours. That's critical at the beginning to stimulate mothers to produce enough milk. If they don't nurse very frequently, a recourse to formula starts to seem inevitable. 'By day three the kid has lost 200 grams, and they say, "Oh you don't have enough milk, let's give him some formula, the kid is starving." That's what happens. It's crazy.'

Dr Bitoun speaks often at French hospitals, to explain the science and the benefits of breastfeeding. 'The culture is stronger than the science,' he says. 'Three-quarters of the people I work with in hospitals don't believe that breast milk is healthier than formula. They think there's no difference. They think artificial milk is fine, or at least that's what they say to mothers.'

In fact, even though French children consume enormous amounts of formula, they beat American kids on nearly all measures of health. France ranks about six points *above* the developed-country average in Unicef's overall health-and-safety ranking, which includes infant mortality, immunization rates until age two, and deaths from accidents and injury up to age nineteen. The United States ranks about eighteen points *below* the average, the UK ranks about two points below.

French parents see no reason to believe that artificial milk is terrible, or to treat breastfeeding as a holy rite. They assume that breast milk is far more critical for a baby born to a poor mother in sub-Saharan Africa than it is for one born to middle-class Parisians. 'We look around and see that all the babies who drink formula are fine,' says Christine, the journalist, who has two young kids. 'We all drank formula too.'

I'm not so calm about it. In fact, I'm so panicked by my conversation with the breastfeeding consultant that, when I'm in the maternity hospital after Bean is born, I insist that she stays in the room with me round the clock. I wake up each time she whimpers, and barely get any rest.

This suffering and self-sacrifice just seems like the natural order to me. But after a few days, I realize I'm probably the only mother in the maternity ward who's subjecting herself to this torture. The others, even the ones who are breastfeeding, hand their babies over to the nursery down the hall at night. They feel entitled to a few hours' sleep.

I'm finally shattered enough to give this a try too, even though it feels enormously indulgent. I'm immediately won over by the system. And Bean doesn't seem any the worse for it. Contrary to the rumours, the nurses and *puéricultrices* who work in the nursery are more than happy to wheel her to my room whenever she needs a feed, then take her away again.

France is probably never going to be ground-zero for breast-feeding. But it does have the Protection Maternelle et Infantile, the same agency that oversees the crèche. This government health service has offices all over Paris that give free check-ups and injections to all children until age six, even those who are in France illegally. Middle-class parents rarely use the PMI, because the government insurance plan covers much of the cost of their visits to private paediatricians. (The French government is the main insurer, but most French doctors are in private practice.)

I'm reluctant to use a public clinic. Will it be impersonal? Will it be clean? One crucial fact convinces me: it will be completely free. Our local PMI office is a ten-minute walk from our house. It turns out that we can see the same doctor each time we go. There's a giant indoor playground in the immaculate waiting area. The PMI will send a *puéricultrice* to your house, to check on you and your baby when you get back from the hospital. If you get *le baby blues*, they've got an in-house shrink. All of this is free. It's worth weighing that against an ounce of breast milk.

I'm not taking any chances about breastfeeding. The American Academy of Paediatrics says I should nurse for twelve months, so I do, practically to the day. I give Bean a final, valedictory feed on her first birthday. Sometimes I enjoy nursing. But often I find it irritating to interrupt whatever I'm doing to rush back home for feeds or – increasingly – for a date with my electric breast pump. Mostly I forge on because of everything I've read about the health benefits, and because I want to stick it to that lady in my playgroup.

All the peer pressure among Anglophones to breastfeed does serve a public-health purpose: it gets breast milk into our babies' mouths. But it also makes us a little crazy. French women can see that steamroller of anxiety and guilt coming from a few kilometres away, and they're at least trying to resist it.

Dr Bitoun says that in his years of campaigning for breast-feeding, he's found that French mothers generally aren't won over by the health arguments, involving IQ points and secretory IgA, which boosts immunity. What does persuade them to nurse, he says, is the claim that both they and the baby will enjoy it, because of the physical closeness, the emotional connection, or the physical sensation. 'It's the pleasure of breastfeeding and the nice comfort that comes from breastfeeding, that's what convinces mothers,' Dr Bitoun says. 'We know that the pleasure argument is the best – the mother's pleasure and the baby's pleasure.'

Many French mothers would surely like to breastfeed longer than they do. But they don't want to do it under moral duress; and they don't flaunt it to each other. Powdered milk may be worse for babies, but it no doubt makes the early months of motherhood a lot more relaxing for French mums.

French mothers may be relaxed about not breastfeeding, but they aren't relaxed about getting back in shape after they give birth. I'm shocked when I find out that the skinny waitress at the café where I go to write most days has a six-year-old. I had taken her for a 23-year-old hipster.

When I tell her about the expression 'MILF' ('Mother I'd Like to Fuck') she thinks it's hilarious. There's no French-language equivalent. In France, there's no *a priori* reason why a woman wouldn't be sexy just because she happens to have children. It's not uncommon to hear a French man say that being a mother gives a woman an appealing air of *plénitude* – happiness and fullness of spirit (not of body).

Of course some British and American mums quickly shed their baby weight too. But it's easy to find role models urging women in the other direction. I happen upon a depressing 'New Mum Makeover' fashion spread in one English-language magazine. It shows three embarrassed, still slightly chubby women smiling uncomfortably in loose-fitting dresses. They've strategically positioned their toddlers in front of their hips. The text is unapologetic: 'Giving birth changes your body, and becoming a mum changes your life,' it says, before singing the praises of drawstring trousers.

For some Anglophone mums, there's something morally righteous about committing to motherhood at the expense of their bodies. It's like giving yourself over to a higher cause. 'Why is it that when so many women become mothers they turn into boring frumps with one-track conversational minds that rarely stray from the oh-so-fascinating subjects of nurseries, nappies and (lactating) nipples,' a columnist writes in the *Daily Mail*.

Among Anglophones, there can actually be peer pressure to stay frumpy. A mother in Cambridge says that when she told the women in her mums' group that she was on a diet, they got angry. If she lost her baby weight, the rest of them would look fat.

A sports-marketing consultant from Connecticut, who has a six-month-old, tells me that when a French woman showed up at her local playgroup, the woman immediately asked the group, in what I imagine to be a charming Gallic accent, 'OK, *zo* how *eez* everyone losing *ze* weight?' According to the consultant, she and the other American mothers fell silent. This wasn't something they usually discussed. It seemed selfish to take time away from their babies to tend to their fat, or even to talk too much about it.

You won't silence any rooms in Paris by asking how new mothers lose their baby weight. Just as there's enormous social pressure for women not to gain too much weight while they're pregnant, there's similar pressure to shed the weight soon after they give birth.

The sister of that sports-marketing consultant is an American named Nancy who lives in Paris, and has a son with her French boyfriend. The two sisters, who even look alike, are a kind of social experiment. Just by virtue of where they live and who their partners are, they're facing opposite social pressures. Nancy tells me that a few months after she gave birth, her French boyfriend began needling her to stop wearing tracksuit bottoms and shed her spare tyre. As an incentive, he offered to take her shopping for new clothes.

Nancy says she was both surprised and offended. Like her sister in Connecticut, she had imagined herself to be in a protected 'mum zone' where she got a pass on her appearance for a while so she could devote herself to looking after the baby. But Nancy's boyfriend was working from a different script. He still viewed her fully as a woman, and felt entitled to the aesthetic benefits that go with that. He was equally surprised and bothered that she was willing to just give that up.

In France, three months seems to be the magic number: French women of all ages keep telling me they 'got back their *ligne*' – their figure – by three months post-partum. Audrey, a French journalist, tells me over coffee that she got her figure back right away after both of her pregnancies – one of which was with twins. 'Of course. It was natural,' she says. 'You too, no?' (I was already sitting down when she arrived at the café.)

As a foreigner who's not married to a Frenchman, I've excused myself from the three-month rule. I'm not sure I even heard about it until Bean was six months old. My body has charmingly decided to store its extra bulk around my belly and hips, giving the impression that I might be holding on to at least the placenta.

I'd surely be skinnier if I had French in-laws to needle me. It seems that just as obesity spreads through social networks, so does thinness. If everyone around you assumes that they're going to drop the extra pounds, you're more likely to actually do it. (It's also easier to lose weight if you haven't gained too much.)

To lose their baby weight, French women seem to do a slightly more intensified version of what they do the rest of the time.

'I pay a lot of attention,' is how my friend Virginie, a svelte mother of three, explains it to me over lunch one day, as I gorge on a giant bowl of Cambodian noodle soup. Virginie says she never goes on a diet, known in French as a *régime*. She just pays a lot of attention, some of the time.

'What do you mean?' I ask Virginie between slurps.

'No bread,' she says, firmly.

'No bread?' I repeat, incredulous.

'No bread,' Virginie says, with steely, calm conviction.

Virginie doesn't mean 'no bread' ever. She means 'no bread' during the week, from Monday to Friday. On the weekends, and on the occasional night out during the week, she says she eats whatever she wants.

'You mean whatever you want in moderation, right?' I ask.

'No, I eat whatever I want,' she says, with that conviction again.

This is similar to what Mireille Guiliano prescribes in *French Women Don't Get Fat*. (Guiliano suggests taking just one day off, and even then not overdoing it too much.) But it's inspiring to see someone who's actually implementing this, evidently with great success. I also like the neutral, pragmatic formulation 'paying attention' rather than the guilt-laden English 'being good' (and its opposites: 'cheating' and 'being bad').

Virginie says this way of eating is an open secret among women in Paris. 'Everyone you see who is thin' – she draws an imaginary line down her small frame – 'pays very close attention'. When Virginie feels like she's put on a few pounds, she pays closer attention still. (My friend Christine, the French journalist, later sums up this system very succinctly: 'Women in Paris don't eat very much.')

Over lunch, Virginie looks me up and down, and evidently decides that I have not been paying attention.

'You drink *café crème*, don't you?' she asks. '*Café crème*' is a cup of steaming milk poured on to a shot of espresso, without the foam that would make it a cappuccino.

'Yes, but I use fat-free milk,' I say, weakly. I do this when I'm at home. Virginie says that even fat-free milk is hard to digest. She drinks *café allongé* – lengthened coffee – which is espresso diluted with boiling water. (Filtered coffee or tea is fine too.) I scribble down Virginie's suggestions – Drink more water! Climb the stairs! Go for walks! – like I'm receiving revelation.

I'm not obese. Like my friend Nancy, I'm just sort of motherly. There's no risk of Bean getting jabbed by a hipbone when I bounce her on my lap. I have skinny aspirations, though. I've promised myself that I won't think of getting pregnant again until I finish my book and reach my target number of kilos. (After years in France, I still don't know whether to wear a sweater when I hear the temperature in Celsius, or how tall someone is when they give their height in centimetres. But I immediately know whether my weight in kilos means I'll fit into my jeans or not.)

Of course, the secret of French mothers isn't simply being thin. Not all of them are, anyway. And I meet Brits and Australians who fit back in their pre-pregnancy jeans by the three-month mark too. But I can still spot them from a distance in the park, just by their body language. Like me they're hunched over their kids, setting out toys on the grass while scanning the ground for choking hazards. They're transparently given over to the service of their children.

What's also different about French mums is that they get back their pre-baby identities too. For starters, they are more physically separate from their children. I've never seen a French mother climb a jungle gym, go down a slide with her child, or sit on a see-saw – all regular sights back in the US, and among Anglos visiting France. For the most part, except when toddlers are just learning to walk, French parents park themselves on the perimeter of the playground or the sandbox and chat with each other (though not with me).

In Anglophone homes, every room in the house is liable to be overrun with toys. In one home I visit in London, the parents have taken all the books off the shelves in their living room, and replaced them with stacks of kids' toys and games.

Some French parents store toys in their living room. But plenty don't. The children in these families have loads of toys and games, but these playthings don't engulf the common spaces. At a minimum, the toys are put away at night. Parents see this as a healthy separation, and a chance to clear their minds when the kids go to bed. Samia, my neighbour who during the day is the doting mother of a two-year-old, tells me that when her daughter goes to bed, 'I don't want to see any toys . . . Her universe is in her room.'

It's not just the physical space that's different in France. I'm also struck by the nearly universal assumption that even good mothers aren't at the constant service of their children, and that there's no reason to feel badly about that.

English-language parenting books typically tack on reminders for mothers to have lives of their own. But I frequently hear Anglophone stay-at-home mothers say they never use babysitters, since they consider all childcare to be *their* job.

In Paris, even mothers who don't work take it for granted that they'll enrol their toddlers in part-time childcare, even for just a few hours a week, in order to have some time alone. They grant themselves guilt-free windows to go to yoga class and get their highlights retouched. As a result, even the most harried stay-at-home mums don't show up at the park looking frazzled and dishevelled, as if they're part of a separate tribe.

French women don't just permit themselves physical time off; they allow themselves to mentally detach from their kids. In Hollywood films, you know instantly if a female character has children. That's often what the film is about. But in the French romantic dramas and comedies I occasionally sneak out to watch, the fact that the protagonist has kids is often irrelevant to the plot. In one typical French film, *Les Regrets*, a small-town schoolteacher rekindles a love affair with her former boyfriend, who comes back to town when his mother is taken ill. During the film, we're vaguely aware that the schoolteacher has a daughter. But the little girl only appears briefly. Mostly, the movie is a love story, complete with steamy scenes in bed. The protagonist isn't supposed to be a bad mother; it's just that being a mother isn't part of the story.

In France, the dominant social message is that while being a parent is very important, it shouldn't subsume one's other roles. Women I know in Paris express this by saying that mothers shouldn't become 'enslaved' to their children. When

Bean is born, one of the main television channels runs a talk show most mornings called *Les Maternelles*, in which experts and parents dissect all aspects of parenting. Right afterwards there's another programme, *We're Not Just Parents*, which covers work, sex, hobbies and relationships.

Of course some French women lose themselves in motherhood, just as some American mothers manage not to. But the ideals in each place are very different. I'm struck by a fashion spread in a French mothers' magazine, featuring the French actress Géraldine Pailhas. Pailhas, thirty-nine, is a real-life mother of two. In one photograph she's smoking a cigarette, pushing a buggy and gazing into the distance. In another she's wearing a blonde wig and reading a biography of Yves Saint Laurent. In a third, she's wearing a black evening gown and impossibly high feathered stilettos, while pushing an old-fashioned pram.

The text describes Pailhas as an ideal of French motherhood: 'She is fundamentally the simplest expression of female liberty: happy in her role as mother, avid and curious about new experiences, perfect in crisis situations and always attentive to her children, but not chained to the concept of perfect mother, who, she assures us, "does not exist".'

There's something in this text, and in Pailhas's bearing, that reminds me of those French mothers who snub me in the park. In real life, they mostly aren't prancing around in Christian Louboutin heels. But like Pailhas, they signal that while they are devoted mothers, they also think about stuff that has nothing to do with their kids, and enjoy moments of guilt-free *liberté*.

Pailhas of course shed her baby weight the instant her kids came out. But that inner life, which we glimpse in the photos, and which I see in those French mums in the crèche and the park, is also required to keep her looking and feeling seductive. Pailhas doesn't look like a cartoonish MILF. She just looks like a sexy, relaxed woman. I can't imagine her telling me that she's only as happy as her least-happy child.

I consult my friend Sharon, who's a Francophone Belgian literary agent married to a handsome French man. She's lived all over the world with him and their two kids. Sharon immediately homes in on another thing I'm seeing in the Pailhas pictures, and in the mothers all around me in Paris.

'For Anglophone women, the role of mum is very segmented, very absolute,' Sharon says. 'When they wear the mum "hat", they wear the mum clothes. When they're sexy they're totally sexy. And the kids can only see the mum part.'

In France (and apparently in Belgium, too) the 'mum' and 'woman' roles ideally are fused. At any given time, you can see both.

# 8

# The Perfect Mother Doesn't Exist

HERE'S SOMETHING YOU MIGHT NOT KNOW: SPENDING twelve hours a day at the computer, stress-eating chocolate M&Ms, does not promote weight loss.

It does, however, enable me to finish my book. And the mere presence of this book on Amazon.com jolts awake the 'woman' in me. So does the book tour. I travel to New York, *sans* husband and child, to talk about the book to anyone who'll listen, and stare lovingly at it in bookstores. (One salesman has seen this behaviour before. He approaches me and asks, 'Are you the author?')

My real transformation happens when the book comes out in French. After years of having a 'semi-detached' presence in Paris, I'm suddenly thrust into the national conversation. The book is a journalistic study of how different cultures treat infidelity. (This was as far as I could get from financial writing, and had seemed like a salient topic to research from France.) Americans treated the book as a serious moral enquiry. The French assume that the book is meant to be amusing.

A talk show called *Le Grand Journal* invites me to come on

and discuss it, live and in French. I'd vaguely noticed *Le Grand Journal*, which is broadcast five nights a week at 7:05 pm. My French publisher – a wizened woman in her fifties with a solid-gold Rolex – explains that the show is a French institution. Host Michel Denisot is a legendary journalist. He and a panel of interviewers grill each guest. Everyone is witty but a bit savage. It's like a posh French dinner party, but broadcast on live TV.

My publisher is thrilled for the publicity, but she's panicked about my French. She arranges for me to spend hours fielding practice questions in French from a businessman she knows. He seems nervous too. He keeps reminding me that *affaire* in French doesn't mean anything extramarital; for that I need to say *aventure* or *liaison*.

By the night of the show, I'm feeling immersed and ready. I have three cups of espresso, and sit for hair and make-up. Then suddenly I'm standing behind two giant curtains. Michel Denisot says my name, and the curtains open. I descend the glossy white steps, Miss America-style, then walk to a large table where Denisot and the three-person panel are waiting for me.

I'm concentrating so hard on understanding the questions that I'm not even nervous. Fortunately, they're mostly questions I've practised. How did I get the idea for the book? How does France compare with the US? When one of the interviewers asks me if I was unfaithful myself while writing the book, I bat my eyelids coquettishly and say that I'm a journalist, so of course I was *très professionnelle*. The interviewers – and the studio audience – love it. On this high note, Denisot starts to wrap up the interview. He seems to be summing up. I stop paying close attention. My brother, who watches a replay on the internet, says at this point I look visibly relieved.

Then, suddenly, I hear my name again. Denisot is formulating another question for me. He can't let it rest. It's something about *Moïse* – French for Moses – and a blog. Moses had a blog? My brother says that when the camera cuts back to me, I look petrified. I have no idea what he's asking me.

All at once I get it: Denisot isn't saying 'blog', he's saying '*blague*', the French word for 'joke'. He wants me to retell a joke from my book. It's the one where Moses comes down from the mount and says, 'I have good news and bad news. The good news is that I got him down to ten commandments. The bad news is adultery is still in there.'

This isn't one of the questions I have practised. On the spot, I can't think of exactly how the joke goes, and certainly not how it goes in French. How do you say 'mount'? How do you say 'commandment'? All I manage to say is: 'Adultery's still in there!' The audience, I'm thankful to hear, is still in a good enough mood to laugh. And Denisot wisely moves on to the next guest.

Despite this incident, I'm grateful to be in the working world again. It puts me in synch with French society. That's because, after boldly not breastfeeding, then reconditioning their minds and bodies, French mothers go back to work. University-educated mothers rarely ditch their careers, temporarily or permanently, to do childcare. When I tell

Britons and Americans that I have a child, they usually ask, 'Are you working?' Whereas French people just ask, 'What do you do?'

I know lots of Anglophone professional women who've stopped working to raise their kids. In France, I know exactly one. I have a vision of what my life as a stay-at-home mum would have been in France, when I ditch work one morning and take Bean to the park. Our local park was built in the nineteenth century, on the site of the former palace of the Knights Templar (take that, Central Park). This may sound like something out of *The Da Vinci Code*, but really it's quite bourgeois. You're more likely to dig up an abandoned dummy there than a medieval relic. There's a little lake, a wrought-iron gazebo, and a playground that fills up as soon as school finishes for the day.

Bean and I are in the gazebo when I'm jolted by the sound of American English, coming from a woman with two little kids. She and I are soon exchanging life stories. She tells me that she left her job as a magazine fact-checker to accompany her husband on his year-long sabbatical in Paris. They agreed that he would do his research while she soaked up the city and looked after the children.

Nine months into the sabbatical, she doesn't look like someone who's been relishing the City of Light. She looks like someone who's been schlepping two toddlers back and forth to the park. She stumbles over her words a bit, then apologizes, explaining that she doesn't often speak to adults. She's heard about the playgroups organized by

English-speaking mums, but says she didn't want to spend her precious time in France with other Anglophones (I try not to take this personally). She speaks excellent French, and had assumed that she'd meet some French mums and befriend them.

'Where are all the mothers?' she asks.

The answer, of course, is that they're at work. French mothers go back to work, in part, because they can. The high-quality crèches, subsidized shared nannies and childminders all make the transition logistically possible. It's no accident that French women are supposed to get their figures back in three months. That's roughly when they go back to the office.

French mothers also go back to work because they want to. In a 2010 survey by the Pew Research Center, 91 per cent of French adults said the most satisfying kind of marriage is one in which both husband and wife have jobs (just 71 per cent of Americans and Britons said this).

Some university-educated women I know do 'four-fifths', which means they stay home with their kids on Wednesday, when there's no nursery or primary school. But these mothers say they hardly know any women who stay home full-time by choice. 'I know one, and she is about to divorce,' says my friend Esther, the lawyer. Esther recounts this woman's story as a cautionary tale: she gave up her job as a saleswoman to look after the kids. But then she was financially dependent on her husband, and thus less entitled to voice her opinions.

'She was withholding her feelings and complaints, and therefore after a while the misunderstandings got worse and worse,' Esther explains. She says that there are circumstances when mothers really can't work, such as when a third child arrives. But she says any break from work should be for a limited time, say until the youngest is two.

French professional women tell me that giving up work for even a few years is a precarious choice. 'If tomorrow your husband is unemployed, what will you do?' says my friend Danièle. Hélène, the engineer with three kids, says that she'd really prefer not to work and to rely on her husband's salary. But she won't do it. 'Husbands can disappear,' she explains.

French women work not just for financial security, but also for status. Stay-at-home mums don't have much, at least not in Paris. There's a recurring French image of a housewife sitting sullenly at a dinner party, because no one wants to talk to her. 'I have two friends who don't work, I feel like nobody is interested in them,' Danièle tells me. She's a journalist in her early fifties, with a teenage daughter. 'When the kids are grown up, what is your social usefulness?'

French women also openly question what their own quality of life would be if they looked after children all day. The French media have no problem describing this experience with cold-eyed ambivalence. One article I read says that for mothers 'without a professional activity ... the principal advantage is to see their kids grow up. But the fact of being an at-home mother brings inconveniences, notably isolation and solitude.'

Since there aren't many middle-class stay-at-home mums in Paris, there also aren't many weekday playgroups, story-telling hours or mummy-and-me classes. The ones that do exist are mostly by and for Anglophones. There's one fully French kid in our neighbourhood playgroup, but he comes with his nanny. His mother, a lawyer, apparently wants the boy to be exposed to English (I don't hear him actually speak it). The mother shows up once, when it's her turn to host. She has raced back from the office, wearing high heels and a business suit. She looks at us Anglophone mothers, with our sneakers and bulging nappy bags, like we're a bunch of exotic animals.

Anglophone parenting and its accoutrements – the baby flash cards and competition to get into nurseries – are by now clichés. There's been both a backlash and a backlash to the backlash. So I'm stunned by what I see at a playground in New York City. It's a special toddler playground, with a low-rise slide and some bouncy animals, separated from the rest of the park by a high metal gate. The playground is designed so that toddlers can safely climb around and fall. A few nannies are sitting French-style on benches around the perimeter, chatting and watching their charges play.

Then a white, upper-middle-class mother walks in with her toddler. While she follows him around the miniature equipment, she keeps up a non-stop monologue. 'Do you want to go on the froggy, Caleb? Do you want to go on the swing?'

Caleb ignores these questions. He evidently plans to just bumble around. But his mother tracks him, continuing to narrate his every move. 'You're stepping, Caleb!' she says at one point.

I assume that Caleb just landed a particularly zealous mother. But then the next upper-middle-class woman walks through the gate, pushing a blond toddler in a black T-shirt. She immediately begins narrating all of her child's actions too. When the boy wanders over to the gate to stare out at the lawn, the mother evidently decides this isn't stimulating enough. She rushes over and holds him upside down.

'You're upside down!' she shouts. Moments later, she lifts up her shirt to offer the boy a nip of milk. 'We came to the park! We came to the park!' she chirps while he's drinking.

This scene keeps repeating itself with other mums and their kids. After about an hour I can predict with total accuracy whether a mother is going to do this 'narrated play' simply by the price of her handbag. What's most surprising to me is that these mothers aren't ashamed of how batty they sound. They're not whispering their commentaries; they're broadcasting them.

When I describe this scene to Michel Cohen, the French paediatrician in New York, he knows immediately what I'm talking about. He says these mothers are speaking loudly to flaunt what good parents they are. This practice of narrated play is so common that Cohen included a section in his parenting book called 'stimulation', which essentially tells mothers to cut it out. 'Periods of playing and laughing should alternate naturally with periods of peace and quiet,' Cohen writes. 'You don't have to talk, sing or entertain constantly.'

Whatever your view on whether this intensive supervision is good for kids, it seems to make childcare less pleasant for mothers. Just watching it is exhausting. And it continues outside the playground. 'We might not stay up nights worried about how to keep our whites whiter, but you can bet we're losing sleep over why little Jasper isn't yet out of diapers,' Katie Allison Granju writes on Babble.com. She describes a mother she knows with an MA in biology who spent the previous week – the *whole* week – teaching her child to use a spoon.

That biologist surely questioned her own sanity too. We Anglophone mothers know that parenting this intensively has its costs (but we keep going). Like the parents who asked Piaget the American Question – how can we speed up the stages of a child's development? – we believe that the pace at which our kids advance hinges on the choices we make, and on how actively we engage with them. So the cost of not spoon training or narrating a trip down the slide seems unacceptably high, especially when others are doing it.

The standard for how much mothers should engage with their kids seems to have risen. Narrated play – and intensive spoon training – are expressions of the 'concerted cultivation' that the sociologist Annette Lareau observed among white and African-American middle-class parents.

'Middle-class parents . . . see their children as a project,' Lareau explains. 'They seek to develop their talents and skills through a series of organized activities, through an intensive process of reasoning and language development, and through close supervision of their experiences in school.'

My decision to live in France is arguably one giant act of concerted cultivation. My project is to make my kids bilingual, international, and lovers of fine cheese. But at least in France I have other role models, and there are no special kinder-gartens for gifted children. In America – and to a slightly lesser extent in Britain – doing 'concerted cultivation' doesn't feel like a choice. On the contrary, its demands seem to have crept upward. A friend of mine, who works full-time, complained to me that she's not just expected to go to her daughter's football games any more; she's also supposed to attend *the practices*.

The push to excel often begin before kids can walk. I hear about a mother in New York whose one-year-old twins had at-home tutors in French, Spanish and Mandarin Chinese. At two years old the mother dropped the French but added lessons in art, music, swimming and – according to my source, who's a family member – some sort of maths. Meanwhile the mother, who'd given up her job as a corporate executive to raise the twins, was spending most of her time applying to two dozen nursery schools.

Such stories aren't just the province of a few extreme New Yorkers. On a trip to Miami I have lunch with a particularly sane American mother I know, named Danielle. I had thought that if anyone could resist the lure of the frenetic family, she could. She's level-headed, warm and – in a city where people tend to closely follow trends in jewellery – decidedly non-materialistic.

Danielle dislikes overzealous parenting. She's horrified by a mother in her neighbourhood whose four-year-old son already takes tennis, football, French and piano lessons. Danielle says this mother is extreme, but simply having her around makes everyone anxious.

'You start getting nervous, you start thinking: this kid's doing all that stuff. How is my kid going to compete? And then you have to check yourself and say: that's not the point. We don't want him competing with someone like that.'

Nevertheless, Danielle has found herself sliding into a practically non-stop schedule with her own four kids (the youngest are twins). In a typical week her seven-year-old, Juliana, has football on Tuesday and Thursday afternoons, Communion class on Wednesday, Brownies every other Thursday (after football) and a play date on Fridays. Once Juliana gets home, she has two hours of homework.

'Last night she had to write a folk tale, she had to write a mini-essay on how Martin Luther King changed America, and she had to study for a Spanish test,' Danielle says.

Recently Juliana said she wanted to do an after-school ceramics class too. 'And I, feeling guilty because there's no art at the school, said, "OK, let's do ceramics." The only day she had free was Monday.' Juliana's whole week is now booked. And Danielle has three more kids.

'The logistics of making sure everyone gets to where they need to be at the correct time has been the best use of the skills I acquired in Operations Management class in business school,' she says.

Danielle acknowledges that she could simply cut out all these activities, except for football (her husband is the coach). But what would her kids do at home? She says there'd be no other children around in the neighbourhood, since they're all out doing activities too.

The net result is that Danielle hasn't gone back to work. 'I always thought that when my kids got to elementary school I could get a full-time job again,' she says. Then she apologizes and rushes off to her car.

The fact that the French state provides and subsidizes child-care certainly makes life easier for French mothers. But when I get back to France, I'm struck by how French mothers make their own lives a lot easier too. The French equivalent of a 'play date' is that I drop off Bean at her friend's house, then I leave. (My Anglophone friends assume I'll stay the whole time.) French parents aren't curt, they're practical. They correctly assume that I have other stuff to do. I sometimes stay for a cup of coffee when I return to pick Bean up.

It's the same at birthday parties. American and British mothers expect me to stick around and socialize, often for several hours. No one ever says it, but I think part of why we're there is to make sure our kids are comforted and OK.

But from about three, French birthday parties are drop-offs. We're supposed to trust that our kids will be OK without us. Parents are usually invited to come back at the end for a glass of champagne and some hobnobbing with the other mums and dads. Simon and I are thrilled whenever we get invitations: it's free babysitting, followed by a cocktail party.

In France, there's an expression for mothers who spend all their free time schlepping their kids around: 'maman-taxi'. This isn't a compliment. Nathalie, a Parisian architect, tells me that she hires a babysitter to take her three kids to all their activities on Saturday mornings. Then she and her husband go out to lunch. 'When I'm there I give them 100 per cent, but when I'm off, I'm off,' Nathalie tells me.

Virginie, my diet guru, gets together most mornings after school drop-offs with a group of mums from her son's elementary school. I join the group at their café one morning, and mention extracurricular activities. The temperature at the table immediately rises. Virginie sits up and speaks for the group. 'You have to leave kids alone, they need to be a bit bored at home, they must have time to play,' she says.

Virginie and her friends aren't slackers. They all have university degrees and good CVs. They're devoted mothers. Their homes are full of books. Their kids take lessons in fencing, guitar, tennis, piano and wrestling (the latter is weirdly called '*catch*' in French). But they don't do all of these activities at once. Most choose just one per school term.

One of the mums at the café, a pretty, zaftig publicist (like me, she's trying to 'pay more attention'), says she stopped sending her kids to tennis lessons, or anything else, because she found the lessons 'constraining'.

'Constraining for whom?' I ask.

'Constraining for me,' she says.

She explains: 'You bring them, and you wait for an hour, then you have to go back and pick them up. For music you have to make them practise in the evenings . . . It's a waste of time for me. And the children don't need it. They have a lot

174

of homework, they have the house, they have other games at the house, and there are two of them so they can't get bored. They're together. And we go away every weekend.'

I'm struck by how these small decisions and assumptions make daily life so different for French mothers. When they have moments to spare, French mothers pride themselves on being able to detach and relax. At the hairdresser, I tear out an article from an issue of French *Elle* in which a mother says that she loves taking her two boys to the old-fashioned merry-go-round near the Eiffel Tower.

'While Oscar and Léon try to catch the wooden rings . . . I spend thirty minutes in pure relaxation. I usually turn off my cellphone and just space out while I'm waiting for them . . . it's like a deluxe babysitter!' I know that merry-go-round well. I usually spend my half-hour there waiting to wave at Bean each time she comes round.

It's no coincidence that so many French mothers seem to parent this way. The let-him-be principle comes straight from Françoise Dolto, the patron saint of French parenting. Dolto very clearly argued for leaving a child alone, safely, to muddle about and figure things out for himself.

'Why does a mother do everything for her child?' Dolto asks in *The Major Stages of Childhood*, a collection of her remarks. 'He's so content to deal with things himself, to pass the morning getting dressed by himself, to put on his shoes, so happy to put on his sweater backwards, to get tangled up in his pants, to play, to rummage around in his corner. So he doesn't go to the market with his mother? Well too bad, or even better!'

On Bastille Day, I take Bean for a picnic in the grassy field in our neighbourhood park. It's filled with parents and their young kids. I'm not narrating Bean's play but I don't really expect to have a chance to read the three-week-old magazine that I've brought along for myself, along with a giant sack of books and toys for her. I spend a lot of the day helping her play with the toys and reading to her.

On the next blanket over is a French mother. She's a thin, auburn-haired woman who's chatting with a girlfriend while her year-old daughter plays with, well, not much of anything. The mother seems to have brought just one ball to amuse her daughter for the entire afternoon. They have lunch, and then the little girl plays with the grass, rolls around a bit, and checks out the scene. Meanwhile her mother, from the look of it, is having a full adult conversation with her friend.

It's the same sun, and the same grass. But I'm having an Anglo picnic and – *voilà* – she's having a French one. Not unlike those mothers back in New York, I'm trying to cheer Bean on to the next stage of development. And I'm willing to sacrifice my own pleasure to do that. The French mum – who looks like she could buy a fancy handbag if she wanted to – seems content to let her daughter 'awaken' all by herself. And her little girl evidently doesn't mind at all.

All this goes a long way towards explaining the mysteriously calm air of the French mothers I see all around me. But it still doesn't tell the whole story. There's a crucial missing piece.

That ghost in the French mothering machine is, I think, how French mothers cope with guilt.

Today's Anglophone mothers spend much more time on childcare than parents did in 1965. To do this, they have cut back on housework, relaxing and even sleeping. Even so, today's Anglophone parents believe they should be spending even more time with their kids.

The result is enormous guilt. I see this when I visit Emily, who lives in Atlanta with her husband and their eighteen-month-old daughter. After I've been with Emily for a few hours, it dawns on me that she has said 'I'm a bad mother' a half-dozen times. She says it when she caves in to her daughter's demand for extra milk, or when she doesn't have time to read her more than two books. She says it again when she's trying to make the little girl sleep on a schedule, and to explain why she occasionally lets her cry a bit at night.

I hear other British and American mums say 'I'm a bad mother' too. The phrase has become a kind of verbal tic. Emily says 'I'm a bad mother' so often that – though it sounds negative – I realize that she must find the phrase soothing.

For Anglophone mothers, guilt is an emotional tax we pay for going to work, not buying organic vegetables, or plopping our kids in front of the television so we can surf the web or make dinner. If we feel guilty, then it's easier to do these things. We've 'paid' for our lapses.

Here too, the French are different. French mothers absolutely recognize the temptation to feel guilty. They feel as overstretched and inadequate as we Anglophones do. After all, they're working while bringing up small children. And like us, they often aren't living up to their own standards as either workers or parents.

The difference is that French mothers don't valorize this guilt. On the contrary, they consider it unhealthy and unpleasant, and they try to banish it. 'Guilt is a trap,' says my friend Sharon, the literary agent. When she and her Francophone girlfriends meet for drinks, they reassure each other that 'The perfect mother doesn't exist.'

The standards are certainly high for French mums. They're supposed to be sexy, successful, and have a home-cooked meal on the table each night. But they try not to add guilt to their burden. My friend Danièle, the French journalist, co-authored a book called *La mère parfaite, c'est vous* (*The Perfect Mother Is You*).

Danièle still remembers dropping her daughter off at crèche at five months old. 'I felt sick to leave her, but I would have felt sick to stay with her and not work,' she explains. She forced herself to face down this guilt, and then let it go. 'Let's just feel guilty and go on living,' she told herself. Anyway, she adds, reassuring both of us, 'The perfect mother doesn't exist.'

What really fortifies French women against guilt is their belief that it's unhealthy for mothers and children to spend all their time together. They believe there's a risk of smothering kids with attention and anxiety, or of developing the dreaded *relation fusionnelle*, where a mother's and a child's needs are too intertwined. French children – even babies and toddlers – get to cultivate their inner lives without a mother's constant interference.

'If your child is your only goal in life, it's not good for the child,' Danièle says. 'What happens to the child if he's the only hope for his mother? I think this is the opinion of all psychoanalysts.'

There's the risk of taking this separation too far. When French Justice Minister Rachida Dati went back to work five days after giving birth to her daughter, Zohra, there was a collective gasp from the French press. In a survey by French *Elle*, 42 per cent of respondents described Dati as 'too careerist'. (There was less controversy about the fact that Dati was a 43-year-old single mother, and that she wouldn't name the father.)

When we Anglophones talk about work–life balance, we're describing a kind of juggling, where we're trying to keep all parts of our lives in motion without screwing up any of them too badly.

The French also talk about *l'équilibre*. But they mean it differently. For them, it's about not letting any one part of your life – including parenting – overwhelm the rest. It's more like a balanced meal, where there's a good mix of proteins, carbohydrates, fruit, vegetables and sweet things. In that sense, the 'careerist' Rachida Dati had the same problem as stay-at-home mums: a life too heavily weighted towards one element.

Of course, for some French mothers *l'équilibre* is just an ideal. But at least it's a calming ideal. When I ask my Parisian friend Esther, who works full time as a lawyer, to assess herself as a mother, she says something that I find breathtaking in its simplicity and lack of neurotic tension. 'In general I don't doubt whether I'm good enough, because I really think I am.'

Inès de la Fressange isn't an ordinary French woman. In the 1980s she was Karl Lagerfeld's muse and main model at Chanel. Then de la Fressange was asked to be the new face of Marianne, the symbol of the French Republic, who appears on stamps and on busts in town halls. Past Mariannes have included Brigitte Bardot and Catherine Deneuve. She and Lagerfeld parted ways after she accepted. He allegedly said he didn't want to 'dress a monument'.

Now in her early fifties, de la Fressange is still a doe-eyed, languid brunette whose long legs don't seem to fit under café tables. She's had her own eponymous fashion label, and still occasionally struts the catwalk. In 2009, readers of *Madame Figaro* voted her the best embodiment of the Parisian woman.

De la Fressange is also a mother. Her two equally leggy and photogenic daughters – the teenaged Nine and tween-aged Violette – have already launched their own fashion and modelling careers. De la Fressange used to make light of her own charms by calling herself the 'swarthy asparagus'. She says she's an imperfect mother too. 'I forget about morning yoga, and I always put on lip gloss and mascara in the car mirror. What's important is to rid yourself of guilt over not being perfect.'

Obviously, de la Fressange isn't typical. But she incarnates a certain French ideal about striking a balance. In an interview with *Paris Match* she describes how, three years after her husband died, she met a man at a ski resort in the French Alps, where she was holidaying with her daughters.

She put off her suitor for a few months, explaining that she wasn't ready. But as she tells *Paris Match*: 'Finally, it was me who called him to say, "OK, I'm a mother and a working girl, but also a woman." For the girls, I thought it was good to have a mother in love.'

# 9

# Caca Boudin

WHEN BEAN IS ABOUT THREE, SHE STARTS USING AN expression I've never heard before. At first I think it's *caca buddha*, which sounds like it could be vaguely offensive to my Buddhist friends (as in English, *caca* is a French kid's term for poo). But after a while I realize she's saying *caca boudin* (pronounced boo-dah). *Boudin* means sausage. My daughter is going around shouting – if you'll pardon my French – 'poo sausage' all the time.

Like all good curse words, *caca boudin* is versatile. Bean shouts it gleefully when she's running through the house with her friends. She also uses it to mean 'whatever', 'leave me alone' and 'none of your business'. It's an all-purpose retort.

Me: 'What did you do at school today?'

Bean: '*Caca boudin.*' (snortle)

Me: 'Would you like some more broccoli?'

Bean: '*Caca boudin!*' (hysterical laughter)

Simon and I aren't sure what to make of *caca boudin*. Is it rude or cute? Should we be angry or amused? We don't understand the social context. To be safe, we tell her to stop saying it. She compromises by continuing to say it, but then adding, 'We don't say *caca boudin*. It's a bad word.'

Bean's budding French does have perks. When we go back to America for Christmas, my mother's friends keep asking her to pronounce the name of her hairdresser, Jean-Pierre, with her Parisian accent. (Jean-Pierre has given Bean a pixie haircut that they coo is oh-so-French too.) Bean is happy to sing, on demand, some of the dozens of French songs she's learned in school. I'm amazed the first time she opens a present and says, spontaneously, *oh là là!*

But it's becoming clear that being bilingual is more than just a party trick, or a neutral skill. As Bean's French improves, she's starting to bring home not just unfamiliar expressions, but also new ideas and rules. Her new language is making her into not just a French speaker but a French person. And I'm not sure that I'm comfortable with that. I'm not even sure what a 'French person' is.

The main way that France enters our house is through school. Bean has started *école maternelle*, France's free state nursery school. It's all day, four days a week, and not on Wednesdays. *Maternelle* isn't compulsory, and kids can go part-time. But pretty much every three-year-old in France goes to *maternelle* full-time, and has a similar experience there. It's France's way of turning toddlers into French people.

The *maternelle* has lofty goals. It is, in effect, a national project to turn the nation's solipsistic three-year-olds into civilized, empathetic people. A booklet for parents from the education ministry explains that in *maternelle* kids 'discover the richness and the constraints of the group that they're part of. They feel the pleasure of being welcomed and recognized, and they progressively participate in welcoming their fellow students.'

Charlotte, who's been a teacher at *maternelle* for thirty years (and still charmingly has the kids call her *maîtresse* – teacher or, literally, 'mistress'), tells me that in the first year the kids are very egotistical. 'They don't realize that the teacher is there for everyone,' she says. Conversely, the pupils only gradually grow to understand that when the teacher speaks to the group, what she's saying is also intended for each of them individually. Kids typically do activities of their choosing in groups of three or four.

To me, *maternelle* seems like art school for short people. During Bean's first year the walls of her classroom are quickly covered in the children's drawings and paintings. Being able to 'perceive, feel, imagine and create' are goals of *maternelle* too. The children learn to raise their hands *à la française*, with one finger pointed up in the air.

I was worried about enrolling Bean. The crèche was a big playroom. *Maternelle* is more like school. The classes are big. And I've been warned that parents get very little information about what goes on there. One mum from my playgroup says she stopped asking her daughter's teacher for feedback after the teacher eventually explained: 'If I don't say anything, that means she's fine.' Bean's first-year teacher is a glum woman whose only comment about Bean, the entire year, is that she's 'very calm'. (Bean adores this teacher, and loves her classmates.)

Despite all the artwork, there's a lot of emphasis on learning to follow instructions. One morning during Bean's first year there are twenty-five identical yellow stick figures with green eyes hanging up in the classroom. As someone who can't write anything without a deadline, I recognize the need for some constraints. But seeing all those nearly identical pictures is unsettling. (Bean's later work becomes more free-form.)

It takes me a while to realize that, in Bean's first-year classroom, there isn't even an alphabet on the wall, alongside all those paintings and drawings. At a meeting for parents, no one mentions reading. There's more fuss about feeding lettuce to the classroom's tank of *escargots* (tiny ones, not to be eaten).

In fact, as I'll discover, kids aren't taught to read in *maternelle*, which lasts until the year kids turn six. They just learn letters, sounds, and how to write their own names. I'm told that some kids pick up reading on their own, though I couldn't say which ones, since their parents don't mention it. Learning to read isn't part of the French curriculum until the school year that kids turn seven.

This relaxed attitude goes against my most basic American belief that earlier is better. But even the most upwardly mobile parents of Bean's schoolfriends aren't in any rush. 'I prefer that they don't spend time learning to read now,' Marion, who's herself a journalist, tells me. She and her husband say that at this stage it's much more important for children to learn social skills, how to organize their thoughts, and how to speak well.

And indeed, while reading isn't taught at *maternelle*, speaking definitely is. In fact, it turns out that the main goal of *maternelle* is for kids of all backgrounds to perfect their spoken French. That booklet for parents says this French should be 'rich, organized, and comprehensible to others' (that is, they need to speak it much better than I do). Charlotte, the teacher, tells me that the children of immigrants typically enter *maternelle* in September speaking bare-bones French, or none at all. By March, she says, they're usually competent if not fluent.

The French logic seems to be that if children can speak clearly, they can also think clearly. In addition to polishing their spoken grammar, the government's booklet says French kids learn to 'observe, ask questions, and make their interrogations increasingly rational. He learns to adopt a point of view other than his own, and this confrontation with logical thinking gives him a taste of reasoning. He becomes capable of counting, of classifying, ordering, and describing . . .' All those philosophers and intellectuals I see pontificating on evening television in France apparently began their analytical training in nursery school.

I'm grateful for the *maternelle*. I haven't forgotten that my friends in London are battling for places in public or private nurseries. But France is far from perfect. Teachers effectively have tenure, whether they're any good or not. There are chronic funding problems, and the occasional shortage of places. Bean's class has twenty-five kids, which feels like quite a lot but isn't even the maximum. (There's a teacher's assistant who helps with supplies, trips to the bathroom and small disputes.)

On the plus side, *maternelle* is free (lunch is on a sliding scale ranging from 13 centimes to five euros per day, based on parents' income). It's an eight-minute walk from our house. And the *maternelle* makes it very easy for mothers to work. It lasts from 8:20 to 4:20, four days a week. For another small fee there's a 'leisure centre' on the premises that can look after kids until the early evening, and all day on Wednesdays. The centre is also open on most school holidays and much of the summer, when they take the kids to parks, on picnics and on visits to museums. Bean recently spent the whole day on a farm.

*Maternelle* is clearly a big part of what's turning my little Anglo-American girl into a French person. It's even making me more French. Unlike at the crèche, the other parents immediately take an interest in Bean, and by association in me. They now seem to view our family as part of the cohort that they'll be travelling all through school with (whereas after the crèche the kids scattered to different schools). A few of the mothers from Bean's class have little babies and are on maternity leave. When I pick up Bean from school and take her to the park across the street, I sit with some of these mothers while our kids play. Gradually, we're even invited over to their homes for birthday parties, afternoon *goûters*, and dinners.

While the *maternelle* brings us all more into French life, it also makes us realize that French families observe social codes that we don't. After we finish dinner at the home of my friend Esther and her husband, who have a daughter Bean's age, Esther becomes agitated when her daughter won't come out of her room to say goodbye to us. She finally marches into the girl's room and drags her out.

'*Au revoir*,' the four-year-old finally says, meekly. Esther is soothed.

Of course I'd been making Bean say the 'magic words' please and thank you. But it turns out that in French there are four magic words: please, thank you, *bonjour* (hello) and *au revoir* (goodbye). Please and thank you are necessary, but not nearly sufficient. *Bonjour* and *au revoir* – and *bonjour* in particular – are crucial. I hadn't realized that learning to say *bonjour* is a central part of becoming French.

'Me, my obsession is that my children know to say *merci*, *bonjour*, *bonjour madame*,' Audrey Goutard, a French journalist with three kids, tells me. 'From the age of one, you can't imagine, I said it to them fifteen times a day.'

For some French parents, a simple *bonjour* isn't enough. 'They should say it with confidence, it's the first part of a relationship,' another mother tells me. Virginie, the skinny stay-at-home mum, demands that her kids heighten the politeness by saying '*Bonjour, monsieur*' and '*Bonjour, madame*.'

Other parents, like my friend Esther, insist on *bonjours* at the threat of punishment. 'If she doesn't say *bonjour*, she stays in her room, no dinner with guests,' Esther explains. 'So she says *bonjour*. It's not the most sincere *bonjour*, but it's the repetition [that matters], I'm hoping.'

Benoît, a professor and father of two, tells me there was a family crisis when he took his kids to stay with their grandparents. His three-year-old daughter would wake up grumpy, and didn't want to say *bonjour* to her grandfather until she'd had breakfast. She finally compromised by agreeing to say '*pas bonjour papi*' (not good morning, Grandpa) to him on the way to the table. 'He was happy with that. In a way, she was acknowledging him,' Benoît explains.

Adults are supposed to say *bonjour* to each other too, of course. I think tourists are often treated gruffly in Parisian cafés and shops partly because they don't begin interactions with *bonjour*, even if they switch to English afterwards. It's crucial to say *bonjour* upon getting into a taxi, when a waitress first approaches your table in a restaurant, or before asking a salesperson if the trousers come in your size. Saying *bonjour* acknowledges the other person's humanity. It signals that you view him as a person, not just as someone who's there to serve you. I'm amazed that people seem visibly put at ease after I say a nice solid *bonjour*. It signals that – although I have a strange accent – we're going to have a civilized encounter.

In Britain and the US, a four-year-old kid isn't obliged to greet me when he walks into my house. He gets to skulk in under the umbrella of his parents' greeting. And in an Anglophone context, that's supposed to be fine with me. I don't need the child's acknowledgement because I don't quite count him as a full person; he's in a separate kids' realm. I might hear all about how gifted he is, but he never actually speaks to me.

When I'm at a family luncheon back in the US, I'm struck that the cousins and step-cousins at the table, who range in age from five to fourteen, don't say anything at all to me, unless I try to pry a few words out of them. Some can only muster one-word responses to my questions. Even the teenagers aren't used to expressing themselves with confidence to a grown-up they don't know well.

Part of what the French obsession with *bonjour* reveals is that, in France, it isn't accepted that kids can have this shadowy presence. The child greets, therefore he is. Just as any adult who walks into my house has to acknowledge me, any child who walks in must acknowledge me too. 'Greeting is essentially recognizing someone as a person,' says Benoît, the professor. 'People feel injured if they're not greeted by children that way.'

These aren't just social conventions; they're a national project. In a meeting for parents at Bean's school, her teacher tells us that one of the school's goals is for students to remember the names of adults (Bean calls her teachers by their first names) and to practise saying *bonjour*, *au revoir* and *merci* to them. The booklet by the French government says that in *maternelle* kids are supposed to show their grasp of 'civility and politeness', including 'greeting the teacher at the beginning and the end of the day, responding to questions, thanking the person who helps him, and not cutting someone off when they're speaking'.

French children don't always succeed in saying *bonjour* unprompted. Often there's a little ritual in which the parent

190

urges the child to say it ('Come say *bonjour*!'). The adult who's being greeted usually waits a beat and then tells the parent, in a friendly way, not to worry about it. This seems to satisfy the obligation too.

Making kids say *bonjour* isn't just for the benefit of grown-ups. It's also to help kids learn that they're not the only ones with feelings and needs.

'It avoids selfishness,' says Esther, who dragged out her daughter – an adorable, doted-on only child – to say goodbye to me. 'Kids who ignore other people, and don't say *bonjour* or *au revoir*, they just stay in their bubble . . . When will they get the sense that they are there to give, not just to receive?'

Saying 'please' and 'thank you' puts children in an inferior, receiving role. An adult has either done something for them, or the child is asking the adult for something. But *bonjour* and *au revoir* put the child and the adult on more equal footing, at least for that moment. It cements the idea that kids are people in their own right.

I can't help thinking that letting an Anglophone kid slink in the door without greeting me could set off a chain reaction in which he then jumps on my couch, refuses to eat anything but plain pasta, and bites my foot while I'm having dinner. If he's exempt from that first rule of civility, he – and everyone else – will be quicker to assume that he's exempt from many other rules too, or that he's not capable of following these rules.

Saying *bonjour* signals to the child, and to everyone else, that he's capable of behaving well. It sets the tone for the whole interaction between adults and children.

Parents acknowledge that greeting someone is in some ways an adult act. 'I don't think it's easy to say hello,' says Denise, a medical ethicist with two girls aged seven and nine. But Denise says it fortifies kids to know that their greeting matters to the adult. She explains: 'I think the child who doesn't say *bonjour* cannot really feel confident.'

Neither can the child's parents. That's because saying *bonjour* is also a strong marker of upbringing. Kids who don't say these French magic words risk having the label *mal élevé* – badly brought up – slapped on them.

Denise says her younger daughter had a friend over who shouted quite a lot, and jokingly called Denise *chérie* – darling. 'I told my husband, I will not invite him back,' she tells me. 'I don't want my child to play with children who are badly brought up.'

Audrey Goutard, the journalist, has written a book called *Le Grand Livre de la Famille*, in which she tries to upend some French parenting conventions. But even Goutard doesn't dare question the importance of *bonjour*. 'Honestly, in France, a child who arrives somewhere and doesn't say *bonjour monsieur*, *bonjour madame*, is a child that one rejects,' she tells me. 'A six-year-old who doesn't look up from the TV when you come in, at a friend's house . . . I'm going to say that he is "badly brought up". I won't say that it's normal.

'We're a society with a lot of codes. And this code, if you don't follow it, you're excluded from society. It's as stupid as that. So you give [your kids] less of a chance to be integrated, to meet people. I say in my book that it's better that your kids know this code.'

Yikes. I'd vaguely noticed French kids saying *bonjour*. But I hadn't realized how much rests on it. It's the sort of signifier that having nice teeth is in America. When you say *bonjour*, it shows that someone has invested in your upbringing, and that you're going to play by some basic social rules. Bean's cohort of three- and four-year-olds have already had several years' worth of *bonjours* drilled into them. Bean hasn't had any. With only please and thank you in her arsenal, she's at just 50 per cent. She may already have earned the dreaded label 'badly brought up'.

I try to appeal to the tiny anthropologist in her. I explain that *bonjour* is a native custom we have to respect.

'We live in France, and for French people it's very important to say *bonjour*. So we have to say it too,' I tell her. I coach her in the lift before we arrive at birthday parties, or at visits to the homes of French friends.

'What are you going to say when we walk in?' I ask anxiously.

'*Caca boudin*,' she says.

Usually when we walk in, she says nothing at all. So I go through the ritual of, very publicly, telling her to say *bonjour*. At least I'm acknowledging the convention. Maybe I'm even instilling the habit.

One day while Bean and I are walking to her school, she spontaneously turns to me and says, 'Even if I'm shy, I have to say *bonjour*.' Maybe it's something she picked up in school.

Anyway, it's true. And it's good that she knows it. But I can't help worrying that she's internalizing the rules a bit too much. It's one thing to play at being French. It's quite another to really go native.

Although I'm ambivalent about Bean growing up French, I'm thrilled that she's growing up bilingual. Simon and I speak only English to her. And at school, she speaks only French. I'm sometimes astonished that I've given birth to a child who can effortlessly pronounce phrases like '*carottes rapées*' and '*confiture sur le beurre*'.

I had thought that young kids just 'pick up' languages. But it's more like a long process of trial and error. A few people tell me that Bean's French still has an American twang. And though Bean has never lived outside the Paris ring road, thanks to us she evidently radiates some kind of Anglophoneness. When I take her to her Wednesday-morning music class one day (the babysitter usually takes her) I discover that the teacher has been speaking to Bean in pidgin English, though she speaks French to all the other children. Later, a dance teacher tells the class of little girls, in French, to lie down flat on the floor '*comme une crêpe*'. Then she turns to Bean and says, '*comme un* pancake'.

At first, even I can tell that Bean is making lots of mistakes in French, and coming up with some bizarre constructions. She usually says the English 'for' instead of its French equivalent, '*pour*'. And she only knows the vocabulary that she's learned in the classroom, which doesn't really equip her to talk about cars, or dinner. One day she suddenly asks me, 'Avion is the same as airplane?' She's figuring it out.

I'm not sure which mistakes come from being bilingual, and which come from being three. One day in the Métro Bean leans into me and says, 'You smell like *vomela*.' This turns out to be a combination of 'vomit' and 'Pamela'.

A minute later Bean leans into me again.

'What do I smell like now?' I ask.

'Like college,' she says.

At home, some French expressions edge out the English ones. We start saying '*coucou*' instead of 'peekaboo', and '*guili-guili*' when we tickle her, instead of 'coochi coochi coo'. Bean doesn't play 'hide-and-seek', she plays '*cache-cache*'. We put our rubbish in the *poubelle*; her dummy is a *tétine*. No one in our household farts, they make *prouts* (rhymes with 'root').

By the spring of Bean's first year in *maternelle*, friends tell me that her Anglophone twang is gone. She sounds like a genuine *Parisienne*. She's become so confident in French that I overhear her joking around with friends, in French, in an exaggerated American accent (probably mine). She likes to mix up the two accents on purpose, and decides that the French word for 'sprinkles' must be 'shpreenkels'.

Me: 'How do you say *d'accord* in English?'

Bean: 'You know! [sounding like someone from Alabama] Dah-kord.'

My father finds the idea of having a 'French' grandchild charming. He tells Bean to call him *grand-père*. She doesn't even consider doing this. She knows he's not French. She just calls him Grandpa.

At night Bean and I look at picture books. She's excited and relieved to confirm that, as with 'airplane', certain words in French and English refer to the same thing. When we read the famous line in the Madeline books, 'Something is not right!' she translates it into colloquial French: 'Quelque chose ne va pas!'

Although Simon has an English accent, Bean speaks mostly American English. I'm not sure if that's my influence, or Elmo's. The other Anglophone kids we know in Paris all have their own accents. Bean's friend with a dad from New Zealand and a mother who's half-Irish sounds like a Londoner. A boy with a Parisian mother and a Californian dad sounds like a French chef from 1970s American television. The little boy around the corner with a Farsi-speaking father and an Australian mum just sounds like a creaky Muppet.

In English, Bean occasionally emphasizes the wrong syllables of words (like the second syllable of 'salad'). She sometimes puts English sentences into a French word order ('Me, I'm not going to have an injection, me') or translates literally from French to English ('Because it's like that!'). She tends to say 'after' when what she means is 'later'. (In French they're the same word, après).

Sometimes Bean just doesn't know how native English speakers talk. In a weird appropriation of all the Disney princess DVDs she's been watching, when she wants to know if something looks good on her she simply asks, 'Am I the fairest?' These are all small things. There's nothing that a summer in London won't fix.

Another French word that infiltrates our English vocabulary is *bêtise* (pronounced beh-teeze). It means the small acts of naughtiness that kids do. When Bean stands up at the table, grabs an unauthorized sweet or pitches a pea on the floor, we say that she's 'doing a *bêtise*'. *Bêtises* are minor annoyances. They're bad, but they're not that bad. The accumulation of many of them may warrant a punishment. But just one *bêtise* on its own probably doesn't.

We've appropriated the French word because there's no good English equivalent. In English, you wouldn't tell a child that he's committed a 'small act of naughtiness'. We tend to label the kid rather than the crime, by telling him that he's being naughty, misbehaving, or just 'being bad', whatever the severity of the act. There's a difference between hitting a table and hitting a person. Being able to label an offence as a misdemeanour – a mere *bêtise* – helps me, as a parent, to respond appropriately. I don't have to freak out and crack down every time Bean does something wrong or challenges my authority. Sometimes it's just a *bêtise*. Having this word calms me down.

I acquire much of my new French vocabulary not just from Bean, but from the many French kids' books we somehow end up owning, thanks to birthday parties, impulse purchases and neighbours' garage sales. I'm careful not to read to Bean in French if there's a native speaker within earshot. I can hear my foreign accent, and the way I stumble over the odd word.

Usually I'm trying so hard not to mispronounce anything too egregiously that I only grasp the storyline on the third reading.

I soon notice that French and English kids' books aren't just in different languages. Often, they have very different storylines and moral messages. In the English books there's usually a problem, a struggle to fix the problem, and then a cheerful resolution. The spoon wishes that she was a fork or a knife, but eventually realizes how great it is to be a spoon. The boy who wouldn't let the other kids play in his box is then excluded from the box himself, and realizes that all the kids should play in the box together. Lessons are learned, and life gets better.

It's not just the books. I notice how deliriously hopeful I sound when I sing to Bean about how 'If you're happy and you know it clap your hands' and when we're watching a DVD of the musical *Annie*, about how the sun will come out tomorrow. In the English-speaking world, every problem seems to have a solution, and prosperity is just around the corner.

The French books I read to Bean start out with a similar structure. There's a problem, and the characters struggle to overcome that problem. But they seldom succeed for very long. Often the book ends with the protagonist having the same problem again. There is rarely a moment of personal transformation, when everyone learns and grows.

One of Bean's favourite French books is about two pretty little girls who are cousins and best friends. Éliette (the red-head) is always bossing around Alice (the brunette). One day, Alice decides she can't take it any more, and stops playing with Éliette. There's a long, lonely stand-off. Finally Éliette comes to Alice's house, begging her pardon and promising to change. Alice accepts the apology. A page later, the girls are playing doctor and Éliette is trying to jab Alice with a syringe. Nothing has changed; and that's the end.

Not all French kids' books end this way, but a lot of them do. The message is that endings don't have to be tidy to be happy. In Bean's French stories, life is ambiguous and complicated. There aren't bad guys and good guys. Each of us has a bit of both. Éliette is bossy, but she's also lots of fun. Alice is the victim, but she also seems to ask for it, and she goes back for more.

We're to presume that Éliette and Alice keep up their little dysfunctional cycle, because, well, that's what a friendship between two girls is like. I wish I had known that when I was four, instead of finally figuring it out in my thirties. Writer Debra Ollivier points out that Anglophone girls pick the petals off daisies saying, 'He loves me, he loves me not.' Whereas little French girls allow for more subtle varieties of affection, saying: 'He loves me a little, a lot, passionately, madly, not at all.'

In the French kids books, a person can have contradictory qualities. In one of Bean's Perfect Princess books, Zoé opens a present and declares that she doesn't like it. But on the next page, Zoé is a 'perfect princess' who jumps up and says *merci* to the gift-giver.

If there were an English version of this book, Zoé would probably overcome her bad impulses and morph fully into the 'perfect princess'. The French book is more like real life: Zoé continues to struggle with both sides of her personality. The book tries to encourage princess-like habits (there's a little certificate at the end for good behaviour). But it takes for granted that kids also have a built-in impulse to do *bêtises*.

There is also a lot more nudity and love in French books for four-year-olds. We have a book about a boy who accidentally goes to school naked. We have another about the school heartthrob who pees in his pants, then admires the little girl who lends him her trousers, while fashioning her bandana into a skirt. These books – and the French parents I know – treat the crushes and romances of preschoolers as meaningful and genuine.

I get to know a few people who grew up in France with Anglophone parents. When I ask whether they feel French or British, they almost all say that it depends on the context. They feel British when they're in France, and French when they're in Britain.

Bean seems headed for something similar. I'm able to transmit some American traits, like whining and sleeping badly, with little effort. But others require a lot of work. I begin ditching certain American holidays, based mainly on the amount of cooking each one requires. Thanksgiving is out. Halloween is a keeper. American Independence Day, 4 July, is close enough to Bastille Day – 14 July – that I sort of feel like we're celebrating both. I leave the transmission of British holidays and bad habits to Simon.

Making Bean feel 'Anglo-American' is hard enough. On top of that, I'd also like her to feel Jewish. Though I put her on the no-pork list at school, this apparently isn't enough to cement her religious identity. She keeps trying to get a grip on what this strange, anti-Santa label means, and how she can get out of it.

'I don't want to be Jewish, I want to be British,' she announces in early December.

I'm reluctant to mention God. I fear that telling her there's an omnipotent being everywhere – including, presumably, in her room – would terrify her (she's already afraid of witches and wolves). Instead, in the spring, I prepare an elegant Passover dinner. Halfway through the first benediction, Bean begs to leave the table. Simon sits at the far end with a sullen 'I told you so' look. We slurp our matzah-ball soup, then turn on some Dutch football.

The following Hanukah is a big success. The fact that Bean is six months older probably helps. So do the candles and the presents. What really wins Bean over is that we sing and dance the *hora* in our living room, then collapse in a dizzy circle.

But after eight nights of this, and eight carefully selected gifts, she's still sceptical.

'Hanukah is over, we're not Jewish any more,' she tells me. She wants to know whether 'Father Christmas' – a.k.a. the '*Père Noël*' she's been hearing about in school – will be coming to our house. On Christmas Eve, Simon insists on setting out shoes with presents in front of our fireplace. He claims he's loosely following the Dutch cultural tradition, not the religious one. (The Dutch put out shoes on December fifth.) Bean is ecstatic when she wakes up and sees the shoes, even though the only thing in them is a cheap yo-yo and some plastic scissors.

'*Père Noël* doesn't usually visit the Jewish children, but he came to our house this year!' she chirps. After that, when I pick her up at school, our conversations usually go something like this:

Me: 'What did you do at school today?'

Bean: 'I ate pork.'

As long as we're foreign, it's not a bad idea to be native English speakers. English is of course the language *du jour* in France. Most Parisians under forty can now speak it at least passably. Bean's teacher asks me and a Canadian dad to come in one morning to read some English-language books out loud, to the kids in Bean's class. Several of Bean's friends take English lessons. Their parents coo about how lucky Bean is to be bilingual.

But there's a downside to having foreign parents. Simon always reminds me that, as a child in Holland, he cringed when his parents spoke Dutch in public. At the year-end concert at Bean's *maternelle*, parents are invited to join in for a few songs. Most of the other parents know the words. I mumble along, hoping that Bean doesn't notice.

It's clear that Simon and I will have to compromise between the Anglo-American identity we'd like to give Bean, and the French one she is quickly absorbing. I get used to her calling Cinderella 'Cendrillon' and Snow White 'Blanche Neige'. I laugh when she tells me that a boy in her class likes *'speederman'* – complete with a guttural 'r' – instead of Spiderman. But I draw the line when she claims that the seven dwarves sing 'Hey-ho, hey-ho,' instead of the Anglo-American 'Heigh-ho, heigh-ho.' Some things are sacred.

Luckily, it turns out that bits of Anglophone culture are irresistibly catchy. As I'm walking Bean to school one morning, through the glorious medieval streets of our neighbourhood, she suddenly starts singing, 'The sun'll come out, tomorrow.' We sing it together all the way to school. My hopeful little American girl is still in there.

I finally decide to ask some French adults about this mysterious word, *caca boudin*. They're tickled that I'm taking *caca boudin* so seriously. It turns out that it is a swear word, but one that's just for little kids. They pick it up from each other, around the time that they start learning to use the toilet.

Saying *caca boudin* is a little bit of a *bêtise*. But parents understand that that's the joy of it. It's a way for kids to thumb their noses at the world, and to transgress. The adults I speak to recognize that since children have so many rules and limits, they also need some freedom to disobey. *Caca boudin* gives kids power and autonomy. Bean's former caregiver Anne-Marie smiles when I ask her about *caca boudin*. 'It's part of the environment,' she explains. 'We said it when we were little too.'

That doesn't mean that children can say *caca boudin* whenever they want. The parenting guide *Votre Enfant* suggests telling kids they can only say bad words when they're in the bathroom. Some parents tell me they forbid such words at the dinner table. They don't ban *caca boudin* entirely, they trust their kids to wield it appropriately.

When Bean and I visit a French family in Brittany, she and their little girl, Léonie, stick out their tongues at the little girl's grandmother. The grandmother immediately sits them down for a talk about when it's appropriate to do such things.

'When you're alone in your room you can. When you're alone in the bathroom you can . . . You can go barefoot, stick out your tongue, point at someone, say *caca boudin*. You can do all that when you're by yourself. But when you're at school, *non*. When you're at the table, *non*. When you're with Mummy and Daddy, *non*. In the street, *non*. *C'est la vie*. You must understand the difference.'

Once Simon and I learn more about *caca boudin*, we decide to lift our moratorium on it. We tell Bean that she can say it, but not too much. We like the philosophy behind it, and even occasionally say it ourselves. A mild swear word just for kids: how quaint! How French!

In the end, I think the social complexities of *caca boudin* are too subtle for us to master. When the father of one of Bean's schoolfriends comes to fetch his daughter from our house one Sunday afternoon, after a play date, he hears Bean shouting *caca boudin* as she runs down the hall. The father, a banker, looks at me warily. I'm sure he mentions the incident to his wife. His daughter hasn't been back to our house since.

# 10

# Double Entendre

So I FINISHED MY BOOK. AND FOR ABOUT FIFTEEN GLORIOUS minutes before breakfast one morning, I'm within 100 grams of my target weight. I'm all ready to be pregnant.

And yet, I'm not.

Everyone around me is. There seems to be a last gasp of fertility among my friends who are, like me, in their late thirties. Getting pregnant with Bean was a bit like having a pizza delivered. You want one? Phone up and get one! It worked on the first try.

But this time, there's no pizza. As the months go by, I feel the age gap between Bean and her theoretical, possibly counterfactual sibling widening. I don't feel like I have many months to spare. I'd envisioned having three kids. If I don't have the second baby soon, the third will become physically impossible.

My doctor tells me that my cycle has become attenuated. She says the egg shouldn't be sitting on the shelf so long before it breaks through to reach a possible mate. She prescribes Clomid, which makes me release more eggs, upping the odds that one will stay fit enough. Meanwhile, more friends call me with their wonderful news: they're pregnant! I'm happy for them. Really, I am.

After about eight months, I get the name of an acupuncturist who specializes in fertility. She has long black hair and an office in a low-end Parisian business district. (Most cities have one Chinatown. Paris has five or six.) The acupuncturist studies my tongue, sticks some needles in my arms, and asks about the length of my cycle.

'That's too long,' she says, explaining that the egg is withering on the shelf. She writes me a prescription for a liquid potion that tastes like tree bark. I drink it dutifully. I don't get pregnant.

Simon says he'd be happy with just one kid. To be polite, I consider this possibility for about four seconds. Something primal is driving me. It doesn't feel Darwinian. It feels like a carbohydrate high. I want more pizza. I go back to my doctor and tell her I'm ready to up the ante. What else has she got?

She doesn't think we need to go all the way to in-vitro fertilization. (The national insurance pays for up to six rounds of IVF, for women under age forty-three.) Instead, she teaches me to inject myself in the thigh with a drug that will force me to ovulate earlier, so the egg won't have time to wither. For this to work, I have to take the shot on day fourteen of my cycle. And in a primitive twist, just after taking the shot, I must have sex.

It turns out that at the next fourteen-day point, Simon will be in Amsterdam for work. For me, there's no question of waiting another month. I book a babysitter for Bean and arrange to meet Simon in Brussels, about halfway between Amsterdam and Paris. We plan to have a leisurely dinner, and then retire to our hotel room. At the very least, it'll be a nice escape. He'll return to Amsterdam the next morning.

On day fourteen, there's a massive storm and a freak rail-service breakdown in western Holland. Just as I arrive at Brussels station around 6 pm, Simon calls to say that his train has been halted in Rotterdam. It's unclear which trains – if any – will leave from there. He might not get to Brussels tonight. He'll call me back. As if on cue, it starts to rain.

I've carried the injection in a portable cooler, with a cold pack that only lasts a few hours. What if I get caught in a hot train? I dash into a convenience store at the station, buy a bag of frozen peas and shove them inside the cooler.

Simon calls back to say there's a train leaving Rotterdam for Antwerp. Can I meet him in Antwerp? On the giant overhead screen I see that there's a train leaving Brussels for Antwerp in a few minutes. In a scene where *The Bourne Identity* meets *Sex and the City*, I grab my pea-wrapped syringe and bolt up to the platform.

I'm in the rain, about to board the train to Antwerp, when Simon calls again. 'Don't get on!' he shouts. He's on a train bound for Brussels.

I take a taxi to our hotel, which is cosy and warm, and decked out for Christmas with a giant tree. I should be grateful just to be there, but the first room the porter takes me to doesn't quite have the conception vibe I'm looking for. He leads me to another room on the top floor, with a slanted ceiling. It seems like a better place to procreate.

While I wait for Simon to arrive I take a bath, put on a robe, then calmly jab myself with the syringe. I realize I wouldn't make a bad junkie. I hope, however, that I'll make an even better mother of two.

A few weeks later, I'm in London for work. I buy a pregnancy test at a pharmacy. Then I order a bagel at a deli, for the sole purpose of using the deli's dingy basement bathroom to take the test (OK, I also ate the bagel). To my amazement, the test is positive. I call Simon while I'm pulling my suitcase to a meeting. He immediately starts choosing nicknames. Since the baby was conceived in Brussels, maybe we'll call him Sprout?

Simon comes with me to the ultrasound. I lie back on the table watching the screen. The baby looks wonderful: heartbeat, head, legs. Then I notice a dark spot off to the side.

'What's that?' I ask the doctor. She moves the wand over a bit. Suddenly another little body pops on to the screen, with its own heartbeat, head and legs.

'Twins,' she says.

This is one of the best moments of my life. I feel like I've been given an enormous gift: two pizzas. It also seems like a very efficient way for a woman in her late thirties to breed.

When I turn to look at Simon, I realize that the best moment of my life may be the worst moment of his. He appears to be in shock. For once, I don't want to know what he's thinking. I'm giddy from the idea of twins. He's blown over by the enormity of it.

'I'll never be able to go to a café again,' he says. Already he foresees the end of his free time.

'You could get one of those home espresso makers,' the doctor suggests.

My French friends and neighbours congratulate us on the news. They treat the reason I'm having twins as none of their business. The Anglophones I know are generally less discreet.

'Were you surprised?' a mother in my playgroup asks, when I announce the news. When I offer an unrevealing 'yes' she tries again: 'Well, was your doctor surprised?'

I'm too busy to be bothered. Simon and I have decided that what we really need isn't a better coffee maker, it's a larger apartment (our current one has just two small bedrooms). This seems even more urgent when we discover that the two babies are two little boys.

I trek out to see several dozen apartments, all of which are either too dark, too expensive, or have long, scary hallways leading to tiny kitchens (apparently in the nineteenth century it wasn't chic to smell food while the servants were cooking it). The estate agents are always boasting that the place I'm about to see is 'very calm'. This seems to be a prized quality in both apartments and children.

All the focus on real estate keeps me from worrying too much about the pregnancy. I think I've also absorbed the French idea that there's no need to track the formation of each fetal eyebrow (though there are quite a few eyebrows to worry about in there). I do briefly indulge in some twin-specific angst, like about the babies being born prematurely. But mostly the health system does the worrying for me. Because it's twins, I get extra doctor's visits and ultrasound scans. At each visit, the handsome radiologist points out 'Baby A' and 'Baby B' on the screen, then makes the same bad joke: you're not obliged to keep those names. I flash him my best micro-smile.

This time around, it's Simon who's anxious – about himself, not the babies. He treats each cheese plate as if it's his last. I revel in all the attention. Despite the free IVF, twins are still a novelty in Paris (I'm told that doctors often implant just one embryo). Within two months I'm visibly pregnant. By six months, it looks like I'm about to deliver. Even some maternity clothes are too tight. Soon it's clear even to young children that there's more than one baby in there.

I also read up on the nomenclature. In French, twins aren't called 'identical' or 'fraternal'. They're '*vrai*' or '*faux*' – real or fake. I get used to telling people that I'm waiting for fake twin boys.

I needn't have worried about my fake boys coming out early. At nine months pregnant, I have two full-sized babies inside me, each weighing nearly as much as Bean did. People point at me from café tables. And I can no longer climb stairs.

'If you want an apartment, go find one,' I tell Simon. Less than a week later, after seeing exactly one apartment, he does.

It's old, even for Paris. It has no hallways, and a triple-width pavement in front. It needs a lot of work. We buy it. The day before I give birth, I have a meeting with an architect to plan the renovations.

The private hospital where I delivered Bean was small and spotless, with an around-the-clock nursery, endless fresh towels, and steak and *foie gras* on the room-service menu. I barely had to change a nappy.

I've been warned that the public maternity hospital where I'm planning to deliver the twins will be a less rarified experience. The medicine is excellent at French public hospitals, but the service is no-frills. They give you a list of things to bring to the birth, which includes nappies. There's no customizing with birth plans, bathtubs and 'walking epidurals'. They don't give the baby a chic little hat. People keep saying 'conveyor belt' to describe the efficient but impersonal experience.

I opt for Hôpital Armand-Trousseau because it's a ten-minute taxi ride from our house, and it's equipped to handle complications with twins. (I later learn that it's attached to the children's hospital where Françoise Dolto did her weekly rounds.) I don't want to give birth in a bathtub anyway. And I figure that, when the moment comes, I'll just use my New York *chutzpah* to customize things. I point out to Simon that we're already enjoying economies of scale: they're going to deliver our two babies for the price of one.

When I go into labour, the epidural isn't optional. The

doctor puts me in a sterile operating room, so he can do a C-section instantly if necessary. I'm flat on my back, my legs locked into a retro 1950s harness, surrounded by strangers in shower caps and surgical masks. I ask several times for someone to put pillows under my back, so I can see what's happening. No one even responds. Eventually, in a small concession, someone shoves a folded sheet under me, which just makes me more uncomfortable.

As soon as active delivery starts, my French evaporates. I can't understand anything the doctor says, and I can only speak English. This must have happened before, because a midwife immediately begins interpreting between me and the doctor. Maybe she's summarizing, or maybe her English isn't great. But she mostly just says 'push' and 'don't push'.

When the first baby emerges, the midwife hands him to me. I'm captivated. Here is Baby A at last! We're just getting acquainted when the midwife taps me on the shoulder.

'Excuse me, but you must deliver the other baby,' she says, taking Baby A to an undisclosed location. I realize, right then, that having twins is going to be complicated.

Nine minutes later, Baby B emerges. I say a quick hello, and then they whisk him away too. In fact, soon almost everyone is gone – Simon, the babies, and most of the enormous medical team. I'm still on my back, paralysed from the waist down. My legs are still up in the harness, spread wide apart. On a stainless-steel table in front of me are two red placentas, each the size of a human head. Someone has decided to open the dividing curtains that were the walls of my room, so now anyone who walks past has a bull's-eye view of my five-minutes-post-twins crotch.

The only person still with me is the anaesthetic nurse, who also isn't thrilled about being left behind. She decides to mask her irritation by making small talk: where am I from? Do I like Paris?

'Where are my babies? When can I see them?' I ask. (My French has reappeared.) She doesn't know. And she's not allowed to leave me to find out.

Twenty minutes pass. No one comes for us. Perhaps because of the hormones, none of this bothers me. Though I'm grateful when the nurse finally uses surgical tape to put up a little modesty cloth between my knees. After that, she no longer wants to chat. 'I hate my job,' she says.

Eventually someone wheels me into a recovery room, where I reunite with Simon and the babies. We take pictures, and for the first and only time I attempt to nurse both boys at once.

An orderly wheels us to the room where the boys and I will be staying for the next few days. A boutique hotel it's not. It's more like a Travelodge. There's a skeletal staff to help out, and a nursery that's open from about 1 to 4 am. Because I have an older child, and am thus deemed unable to mess up too badly, the staff leaves me practically on my own. At mealtimes someone brings in plastic trays with a parody of hospital food: limp French fries, chicken nuggets and chocolate milk. It takes me a few days to realize that none of the other mothers is eating this: there's a communal refrigerator down the hall, where they store groceries.

Simon is at home looking after Bean, so most of the time

I'm alone with the boys, who howl for hours at a stretch. I usually wedge one between my legs, in some approximation of a hug, while I try to nurse the other. With the constant blur of noise and body parts, it feels like there are more than two of them. When I finally get them both to sleep, after hours of wailing and drinking, Simon shows up. 'It's so peaceful in here,' he says. I try not to think about the fact that my belly looks like a giant mound of flesh-coloured Jell-O.

Amid all this, we have to name the boys. (The city of Paris gives you three days. By day two, an angry-looking bureaucrat marches into your hospital room holding a clipboard.) Simon asks only that Nelson is somewhere in the mix, after his hero Nelson Mandela. Mostly he's worried about selecting the perfect nicknames. He wants to call one boy Gonzo and the other Chairman. I have a thing for contiguous vowels, and am considering calling them both Raoul.

We settle on Joel – whom we'll only ever call Joey – and Leo, who defies all attempts at nicknames. They're the most fraternal twins I've ever seen. Joey looks like me, except with platinum-blond hair. Leo is a swarthy little Mediterranean man. If they weren't exactly the same size and constantly together, you wouldn't guess that they were related. I'll later discover that someone who asks whether the boys are identical has no interest in babies.

After four long days, we're allowed to leave the hospital. Being at home with the boys is only marginally easier. In the early evenings, they wail for hours.

Both boys wake up all through the night. Simon and I pick a baby before we go to sleep, and are responsible for that one the whole night. We each angle to pick the 'better' baby, but who that is keeps changing. Anyway, we haven't yet moved into the larger apartment, so we're all sleeping in the same room. When one baby wakes up, everyone else does too. At about six months old, the boys start to sleep until six am.

It still feels like there are more than two of them. I never thought I'd dress twins alike, but I'm suddenly tempted to do so just to create a little bit of order, at least visually – like making kids at a tough school wear uniforms.

Amazingly, I manage to find time to be neurotic. I'm obsessed with the idea that we've given the boys the wrong names, and that I should go back to the town hall and call Leo Joel and Joel Leo. I spend my few leisure minutes ruminating on this.

Then comes the small matter of the circumcisions. Most French babies aren't circumcised. In the main, just Jews and Muslims do it. Because it's August in Paris, even the *mohels*, who do ritual circumcisions, are on holiday. We wait for one who's been recommended (a man who is reassuringly both a *mohel* and a paediatrician) to come back.

Unlike the birth, the circumcision isn't two for the price of one. There isn't even a package discount. Before the little ceremony, I confess to the *mohel* that I fear I've given the boys the wrong names, and that I may need to switch them. He doesn't offer me any spiritual advice. But being French, he explains that the bureaucracy to do this would be awful.

Somehow this information, plus the consecration of the circumcisions, erases my doubt. After the ceremony, I never worry about their names again.

Thankfully, my mother has arrived from Miami. She, Simon and I spend most of our time in the living room, holding the boys. One day a woman rings the doorbell. She explains that she's a psychologist from the PMI office in our neighbourhood. She says that she pays house calls to all mothers of twins, which I think is a tactful way of saying that she wants to make sure I'm not having a breakdown. A few days later, a midwife from the same PMI stops by, and stands with me as I'm changing Joey's nappy. His poo, she declares, is 'excellent'. I take that to be the official view of the French state.

We're able to put some of what we've learned about French parenting to use on the boys. We slowly nudge them on to the national meal plan, with four feeds a day. From the time they're a few months old, except for the *goûter*, they rarely snack.

Unfortunately, we don't get to try out the Pause on them. Having newborn twins who don't even have a room of their own – and an older child who's just a few feet away – makes it difficult to try out anything.

So once again, we suffer. After about a month of almost no sleep, Simon and I are zombies. We fall back on our Filipina nanny and her network of cousins and friends. We eventually have four different women to help us, on shifts covering practically twenty-four hours a day. We're bleeding cash, but at least we're sleeping a bit. I start to view mothers of multiples as a persecuted minority, like Tibetans.

Both boys have trouble breastfeeding. So I spend a lot of time upstairs in my bedroom, bonding with my electric breast pump. Bean eventually figures out that she can spend time alone with me if she sits with me while I pump. She learns to assemble the bottles and receptacles, as if she's putting together a rifle. She does a great impression of the 'wapa wapa' sound the pump makes.

Most of the time, I look like a stunned animal. I come downstairs to deliver my bottles of milk, or send Bean down with them and go back to sleep. There are so many babysitters around that I feel more like a supporting cast member than a lead actress. I'm convinced the boys don't know that, among all these women, I'm their mother. I must seem detached because at one point a friend grabs me by the shoulders, stares me in the eye and asks whether I'm OK. This isn't easy for her; she's quite a bit shorter than me.

'I'm OK, but I'm running out of money,' I say. I spend so much time singing 'Silent Night' to the boys – more as a command than a lullaby – that one of the babysitters asks if I've become a Catholic.

Meanwhile, our renovations are under way. Between pumping sessions, I dash over to inspect the new apartment. I meet with the head of the building association, an economist in his sixties, to discuss whether we can leave our double buggy in the vestibule downstairs. He won't commit.

'The previous owners were excellent neighbours,' he says.

'Excellent how?' I ask.

'They were very discreet,' he says.

The apartment itself is an enormous mess. I had approved the plans one night, while the boys were having a full-on fit of colic. It's suddenly clear that I had no idea how to read them. Two-hundred-year-old doors and walls, which I had thought were fine, have disappeared. They've been replaced with new, flimsier ones. It's only when the renovations are done and we move in that I realize I've turned our nineteenth-century Parisian apartment into what looks like a high-rise condominium in Miami, but with mice. I didn't understand quite how beautiful Paris is – the heavy doors, the intricate mouldings – until I destroyed a small part of it, at enormous expense.

Now I spend a lot of time ruminating on this. 'You know how Édith Piaf said, "*Je ne regrette rien*"?' I ask Simon. 'Well, for me it's "*Je regrette tout*".'

Occasionally our life changes from expensive and exhausting to merely surreal. When the boys are a bit older, a single girlfriend of mine stops by before bedtime one night. She watches as the boys – in footed pyjamas – silently pull themselves up and down on the furniture, in a kind of Dadaist dance. Later they'll march around silently while holding their toothbrushes aloft, like talismans. Simon watches them and pretends to narrate a documentary. 'For these boys, in their culture, toothbrushes are these curious status symbols,' he explains.

Mostly our new life is full of extreme emotions. Simon

mopes around in exhaustion and despair, taking little passive-aggressive snips at me. 'Maybe in eighteen years I'll get to have a cup of coffee,' he says. He describes the dread he feels when he approaches our house and hears the wailing coming from inside. Three kids under the age of three are a lot, even among our very fertile cohort.

Amid all the crying and complaining, there are hopeful moments. My whole mood lifts one afternoon when Leo is cheerful and calm for five whole minutes. The first night that he sleeps seven straight hours, Simon jumps around the house singing the Frank Zappa song 'Titties and Beer'.

Even so, I still feel much as I did at the moment of the boys' birth: that my attention is hopelessly divided. I ask my friend Hélène – who also has twins and a singleton – whether she's considering having more. 'I don't think so, I'm at the limit of my competence,' she says. I know exactly what she means. Only I fear that I've surpassed my competence. Even my mother, who spent years begging for grandchildren, tells me not to have any more kids.

As if to cement my status, Bean comes home from school one day and announces that I'm a 'maman crotte de nez'. I immediate type this into Google Translate. It turns out that she has called me a 'mummy bogey'. Given the circumstances, it's a very good description.

# 11

# I Adore This Baguette

FRIENDS TELL ME THAT PARENTS OF TWINS HAVE A HIGH divorce rate. I'm not sure this is statistically true, but I can certainly understand how the rumour got started. In the months after the twins are born, Simon and I bicker constantly. During one argument, he tells me that I'm 'rebarbative'. I have to look up this word. The dictionary says 'unattractive and objectionable: a rebarbative modern building'. I march back to Simon.

'Unattractive?' I ask. Even in our current state, that's a low blow.

'OK, you're just objectionable,' he says.

To remind myself to be civil, I tape up signs around the apartment that read 'Don't Snap at Simon'. There's one on the bathroom mirror. Simon and I are too tired to realize that we're fighting because we're tired. I no longer care what he's thinking about, though it's probably still Dutch football.

During rare moments of leisure, Simon likes to burrow in bed with a magazine. If I dare to interrupt him, he says:

"There's nothing you can say to me that's more interesting than this article I'm reading in the *New Yorker*.'

One day I have a revelation. 'I think we're actually quite compatible,' I tell him. 'You're irritable, and I'm irritating.'

Apparently we send out a scary vibe. A childless couple we know come to visit from Chicago and conclude, after four days, that they don't want kids after all. At the end of one weekend *en famille*, Bean decides that she doesn't want to have kids either. 'Children are too difficult,' she says.

On a positive note for our relationship, we get places in the crèche for both boys (even my mother is relieved to hear this). Twins are still uncommon enough in France that our application got priority status. The crèche committee took such pity on us that they assigned the boys to a tiny crèche two blocks from our new home, which I'd been told had no vacancies.

The crèche offers some hope for the future. But we still have to survive as a family and, perhaps more dauntingly, as a couple until we hand the boys over in a few months. We've decided to keep them at home until they're a year old.

It's not always obvious that Simon and I will make it that long. It seems no coincidence that as the labour-intensive parenting style has become de facto for the middle classes, research shows that marital satisfaction has fallen and that mothers find it more pleasant to do housework than to take care of their kids. Social scientists now pretty much take for granted that today's parents are less happy than non-parents. Studies show that parents have higher rates of depression, and that their unhappiness increases with each additional child (or in Simon's case, with merely seeing those additional children on an ultrasound).

Maybe we just need a date night? While I've been living in France, date nights have become the new penicillin for Anglophone couples with kids. Hate your spouse? Have a date night! Want to strangle your kids? Go out to dinner! The Obamas go on date nights. Even social scientists now study them. A paper on middle-class Canadians found that when couples got leisure time alone together, it 'helped them tremendously as a couple, rejuvenated them personally, and re-inspired their parenting'. But they rarely got this time. 'Many [participants] felt pressured by the wider culture to always place the needs of the children above the needs of the partner-ship,' the authors conclude. One husband said that while speaking to his wife, 'we would be interrupted on a minute-to-minute basis' by the children.

This is, of course, another consequence of concerted cultivation, which eats up leisure time and makes fomenting the child's development the family's overwhelming priority. I see this all around me when I visit America and the UK. A cousin of mine – who's a nurse with four kids – has family near by who'd be willing to babysit. But after a week of getting everybody to school, gymnastics, track meets and church, she and her husband – who works nights as a policeman – don't even consider going out. They're too tired. A schoolteacher from Manchester tells me that she's taking her toddler on her honeymoon, even though her mother has volunteered to look after him. 'I'd just feel too bad leaving him behind,' she explains.

Every Anglophone mother I speak to has a cautionary tale about a mother in her social circle who refuses to leave her child with anyone. These mums aren't urban myths; I frequently meet them. At a wedding I sit next to a stay-at-home mother from Colorado, who explains that she has a full-time babysitter but never leaves the sitter alone with her three kids. (Her husband has skipped the wedding to look after them.) An artist from Michigan tells me that she couldn't bring herself to use a babysitter for her son's whole first year. 'He seemed so tiny, he was my first kid. I'm really pretty neurotic. The idea of handing him over to someone . . .' Her voice trails off.

Other Anglophone parents I meet have adopted such specific diets and discipline techniques that it's hard for anyone else – even a grandparent – to take over and follow all the rules. A grandfather from Virginia says his daughter became livid when he pushed her baby's buggy the 'wrong' way over a bump. The baby's mum had read that there's a smaller chance of brain damage if babies go over bumps backwards.

Obviously, Simon and I aren't against babysitters. We're currently employing half the Philippines. But since the boys were born, I haven't spent more than a few hours away from home. Mostly I do what that mother from Colorado does: I use the babysitter as a kind of assistant who changes nappies and does the laundry. But I'm usually on the premises.

This system has the advantage of both depleting our savings

and destroying our relationship, simultaneously. I feel rebarbative much of the time. I realize I'm losing my mind a little bit when – about fifteen minutes before one of our babysitters is supposed to arrive – my phone beeps, indicating that I have a new text message. I panic, fearing that the babysitter is late. In fact, it's a message from a news service that I subscribe to, informing me that there's been a deadly earthquake in South America. For an instant, I'm relieved.

Of course, it's easier to get along with your spouse if your baby sleeps through the night by three months old, your kids play by themselves, and you're not constantly shuttling them from one activity to the next. What also seems to help is that French couples view romance differently, even when they have young kids. I get an inkling of this when my obstetrician writes me a prescription for ten sessions of *rééducation périnéale* – perineal re-education. She did this after Bean was born, and again after the birth of the boys.

Before my first re-education, I had only been vaguely aware that I had a perineum, or what exactly it is. It turns out to be the hammock-like pelvic-floor area, which often gets stretched out during pregnancy and birth. The stretching makes the birth canal a little less 'tight', and can cause mothers to pee a bit when they cough or sneeze. To prevent this, mothers in British antenatal classes are advised to do pelvic floor exercises on their own. Some of them probably do.

In France, getting a woman's pelvic floor back into shape is a priority. Friends tell me that their French obstetricians gauge whether a few sessions of perineal re-education are needed by asking, 'Is *le monsieur* happy?'

I think my *monsieur* would be happy to have any access to my perineum. The region hasn't exactly lain fallow in the year or so since the boys were born. But I wouldn't say there's any danger of overuse. For a while, as soon as Simon went anywhere near my breasts, it was like a fire alarm: they began spurting milk. Anyway, sleep is more of a priority.

I'm intrigued enough by perineal re-education to give it a try. My first re-educator is a slim Spanish woman named Mónica, with an office in the Marais. Our introductory session begins with a forty-five-minute interview, during which she asks me dozens of questions about my bathroom habits and my sex life.

Then I disrobe from the waist down, and lie down on a padded table covered with crinkly paper. Mónica slips on surgical gloves and leads me in what I can best describe as assisted crunches for the crotch, in sets of fifteen ('and up, and release'). It's a bit like Pilates for the below-the-belt region.

Afterwards, Mónica shows me a slender white wand that she'll introduce in the next phase. It resembles a device you might see for sale in an adults-only shop. The wand will add electro-stimulation to my mini-sit-ups. By the tenth session we'll be ready to try out a kind of video game, in which sensors on my groin measure whether I'm contracting the muscles enough to stay above a running orange line on the computer screen.

Perineal re-education is at once extremely intimate and strangely clinical. Throughout the exercises, Mónica and I address each other using the formal *vous*. But she asks me to close my eyes, so I can better isolate the muscles where her hand is. My doctor writes me a prescription for abdominal re-education too. She's noticed that, more than a year after the twins are born, I still have a kind of bulge around my waist that's part fat, part stretch, and part unknown substance. Frankly, I'm not sure what's in there. I decide that it's time to take action when I'm standing up on the Paris métro and a decrepit old woman offers me her seat. She thinks I'm pregnant.

Not all French women do re-education after they give birth. But many do. Why not? France's national insurance picks up most or all of the cost of re-education, including the price of the white wand. The state even helps pay for some tummy tucks, usually when the mother's belly hangs below her pubis, or when it's inhibiting her sex life.

Of course, all this re-education just gets mothers out of the starting gate. What do French women do once their bellies and their pelvic floors are back in fighting shape?

Some do focus only on their kids. But unlike in the US or Britain, the culture doesn't encourage or reward this. Sacrificing your marriage and your sex life for your kids is considered wildly unhealthy and out of balance.

The French know that having a baby changes things, especially at first. Couples typically assume that there's a very intense stretch after the birth, when it's all-hands-on-deck for the baby. After that, gradually, the mother and father are supposed to find their equilibrium as a couple again.

'There's this fundamental assumption [in France] that every human being has desire. It never disappears for very long. If it does it means you're depressed and you need to be treated,' explains Marie-Anne Suizzo, the University of Texas sociologist who studied French and American mothers.

The French mothers I meet talk about '*le couple*' in a wholly different way from the Anglophone parents I know. 'For me, the couple comes before the children,' says Virginie, the skinny stay-at-home mum who taught me to 'pay attention' to what I eat.

Virginie is principled, smart, and a devoted mother. But she has no intention of letting her romantic life slacken just because she has three kids.

'The couple is the most important. It's the only thing that you choose in your life. Your children you didn't choose. You chose your husband. So, you're going to make your life with him. So you have an interest in it going well. Especially when the children leave, you want to get along with him. For me, it's *prioritaire*.'

Not all French parents would agree with Virginie's ranking. But in general, the question for French parents isn't whether they'll resume having full romantic lives again, but when. 'No ideology can dictate the moment when the parents will feel truly ready to find each other again,' says the French psycho-sociologist Jean Epstein. 'When conditions permit, and when they feel ready, the parents will give the baby his rightful place, outside their couple.'

Anglophone experts do sometimes mention that parents should take time for themselves. In *Dr Spock's Baby and Child Care* (which my friend Dietlind hands over to me before leaving Paris) there's a two-paragraph section called 'Needless self-sacrifice and excessive preoccupation'. It says that today's young parents tend to 'give up all their freedom and all their former pleasures, not as a matter of practicality but as a matter of principle'. Even when these parents occasionally sneak off by themselves, 'They feel too guilty to get full enjoyment.' The book urges parents to carve out quality time together, but only after making 'all the necessary sacrifice of time and effort to your children'.

French experts don't treat having quality time together as an afterthought; they're adamant and unambiguous about it. That's perhaps because they're very sanguine and up-front about how having a baby can strain a marriage. 'It isn't for nothing that a good number of couples separate in the first few years, or the first few months following the arrival of a child. Everything changes,' one article says.

*Le couple* doesn't just get a cursory mention in the French parenting books I read; it's treated as a central topic. Some French parenting websites sometimes have as many articles on '*le couple*' as they do on pregnancy. 'The child must not invade the parents' whole universe . . . for family balance, the parents also need personal space,' writes Hélène de Leersnyder, the paediatrician. 'The child understands without a clash, and always very young, that his parents need time that's not about work, the house, shopping, children.'

Once French parents emerge from the initial cocooning period, they take this call to coupledom seriously. There is actually a time of day in France known as 'adult time' or 'parent time'. It's when the kids go to sleep. Anticipation of 'adult time' helps explain why – once the fairy tales are read and the songs are sung – French parents are strict about enforcing bedtime. They treat 'adult time' not as an occasional, hard-won privilege but as a basic human need. Judith, an art historian in Brittany with three young kids, explains that all three are asleep by 8 or 8:30, because 'I need a world for myself'.

French parents don't just think these separations are good for parents. They also genuinely believe that they're important for kids, who must understand that their parents have their own pleasures. 'Thus the child understands that he is not the centre of the world, and this is essential for his development,' the French parenting guide *Your Child* explains.

French parents don't just have their nights to themselves. After Bean starts school, we are confronted with a seemingly endless series of mid-term two-week holidays. During these times I can't even arrange a play date. Most of Bean's friends have been dispatched to stay with their grandparents in the countryside or the suburbs. Their parents use this time to work, travel, have sex and just be alone.

Virginie says she takes a ten-day holiday alone with her husband every year. It's non-negotiable. Her kids, aged four to fourteen, stay with Virginie's parents in a little village about two hours by train from Paris. Virginie says guilt doesn't enter into her holiday planning. 'What you build between the two of you when you're away for ten days has to be good for the kids too,' she says. She says that kids occasionally need space from their parents too. When they all reunite after the trip, it's very sweet.

The French parents I meet seem to grab adult time whenever they can. Caroline, the physiotherapist, tells me without a trace of guilt that her mother is picking up her three-year-old son from *maternelle* on Friday afternoon, and looking after him until Sunday. She says that on their weekend off, she and her husband plan to sleep late and go to the movies.

French parents even get pockets of 'couple time' when their kids are home. A 42-year-old with three kids aged three to six tells me that on weekend mornings, 'The kids don't have the right to enter our room until we open the door.' Until then, miraculously, they've learned to play by themselves. (Inspired by her story, Simon and I eventually try this. To our amazement, it mostly works. Though we have to re-teach it to the kids every few weeks.)

I have trouble explaining the concept of 'date night' to my French colleagues. For starters, there's no 'dating' in France. Here, when you start going out with someone, it's automatically supposed to be exclusive. To my French friends, a 'date' sounds too tentative, and too much like a job interview, to be romantic. It's the same once a couple lives together. 'Date night', with its implied sudden switch from sweatpants to stilettos, sounds contrived to my French friends. They take issue with the implication that 'real life' is unsexy and exhausting, and that they should schedule romance like it's a trip to the dentist.

When the American movie *Date Night* comes to France, it's renamed *Crazy Night*. The couple in the film are supposed to be typical suburbanites with kids. American and British reviewers have no trouble relating to them. A writer for the Associated Press describes the pair as 'tired, ordinary but reasonably content'. In an opening scene, they're awoken in the morning when one of their children pounces on their bed. French critics are horrified by such scenes. A reviewer for *Le Figaro* describes the kids in the film as 'unbearable'.

Despite having kids who don't pounce on them in the morning, French women would seem to have more to complain about than American women do. They lag behind Britons and Americans in key measures of gender equality, such as the percentage of women in the legislature and heading large companies. And they have a bigger gap than we do between what men and women earn.

French inequality is especially pronounced at home. French women spend 89 per cent more time than men doing household work and looking after children. In America, women spend 31 per cent more time than men on household activities, and 25 per cent more time on childcare.

Despite all this, my British and American girlfriends with kids seem a lot angrier at their husbands and partners than my French girlfriends are. 'I am fuming that he doesn't bother to be competent about a whole slew of stuff that I ask him to do,' my friend Anya writes to me in an e-mail about her husband. 'He's turned me into a shrewish nag and once I get mad, it's hard for me to cool back down.' American friends – or even acquaintances – regularly pull me aside at dinner parties to grumble about something their husbands have just done. Whole lunches are devoted to complaints about how, without them, their households would have no clean towels, living plants or matching socks.

Simon gets many points for effort. He gamely takes Bean across town one Saturday, to get some American-sized passport photos. She sets off looking completely normal, but somehow returns with photos that make her look like a five-year-old psychopath having a bad-hair day.

Since the boys were born, Simon's incompetence seems less charming. I no longer find it adorably mystifying when he breaks the second hands on all his watches, or reads our expensive English-language magazines in the shower. Some mornings, our whole marriage seems to hinge on the fact that he doesn't shake the orange juice before he pours it.

For some reason, we mostly fight about food. (I put up a 'Don't Snap at Simon' sign in the kitchen.) He leaves his beloved cheeses unwrapped in the refrigerator, where they quickly dry out. When the boys are a bit older, Simon gets a phone call when he's in the middle of brushing Leo's teeth. I take over, only to discover that Leo has an entire dried apricot in his mouth. When I complain, Simon says he feels disempowered by my 'elaborate rules'.

When I get together with my Anglophone girlfriends, it's

just a matter of time before we start venting about our men. At one dinner in Paris, three of the six women at the table discover – in a ricochet of me-too's – that their husbands all retreat to the bathroom for a long session, just when it's time to put the kids to bed. Their complaining is so intense, I have to remind myself that these are women in solid marriages; they're not on the verge of divorce.

When I get together with French women, this type of complaining doesn't happen. When asked, French women acknowledge that they sometimes have to prod their husbands to do more around the house. Most say they've had their sulky moments, when it felt like they were carrying the whole household, while their husbands lay on the couch.

But somehow, in France, this imbalance doesn't lead to what a writer in the bestselling American anthology *The Bitch in the House* calls 'the awful, silent process of tallying up and storing away and keeping tabs on what he helped out with and what he did not'. French women are no doubt tired from playing mother, wife and worker simultaneously. But they don't reflexively blame their husbands for this, or at least not with the venom that Americans women often do.

Possibly, French women are just more private. But even the French mothers I get to know well don't seem to be secretly boiling over with the belief that the life they have isn't the one they deserve. Their unhappiness doesn't manifest as rage against their partners.

Partly, this is because French women don't expect men to be their equals. They view them as a separate species, which by nature isn't good at booking babysitters, buying tablecloths, or remembering to schedule check-ups with the paediatrician. 'I think French women accept more the differences between the sexes,' says Debra Ollivier, author of *What French Women Know*. 'I don't think that they expect men to step up to the plate with the same kind of meticulous attention and sense of urgency.'

When the French women I know mention their partners' inadequacies, it's to laugh about how adorably inept the men are. 'They're just not capable, we're superior!' jokes Virginie, as her girlfriends chuckle. Another mother breaks into peals of laughter when she describes how her husband blow-dries her daughter's hair without brushing it first, so the little girl goes to school looking like she's just stuck her finger in an electric socket.

This outlook creates a virtuous cycle. French women don't harp on men about their shortcomings or mistakes. So the men aren't demoralized. They feel more generous towards their wives, whom they praise for their feats of micromanagement and their command of household details. This praise – instead of the tension and resentment that tends to build in Anglophone households – seems to make the inequality easier to bear. 'My husband says, "I can't do what you do,"' another Parisian mum, Camille, proudly tells me. None of this follows the Anglophone feminist script. But it seems to make things go more smoothly.

Fifty-fifty equality just isn't the gold standard for the Parisian women I know. Maybe this will change one day. But for now, the mothers I meet care more about finding a balance that works. Laurence, a management consultant with three kids, has a husband who works long hours during the week (she has switched to part-time). The couple used to fight all weekend about who does what. But lately Laurence has been urging her husband to go to his Aikido class on Saturday mornings, since he's more relaxed afterwards. She'd rather do a bit more childcare, in exchange for a spouse who's cheerful and calm.

French mothers also seem better at giving up some control, and lowering their standards, in exchange for more free time and less stress. 'You just have to say, I'm going to come home and there's going to be a week's worth of laundry in a pile,' Virginie tells me, when I mention that I'm taking Bean to visit my family for a week, and leaving Simon in Paris with the boys.

If you drop the forlorn hope of fifty-fifty equality, and relax your exacting feminist standards, it becomes easier to enjoy the fact that some urban French husbands do quite a lot of childcare, cooking and dishwashing. A 2006 French study found that just 15 per cent of fathers of infants participated equally in the babies' care, and 11 per cent took primary responsibility. But 44 per cent played very active, supporting roles. You see these dads, adorably scruffy, pushing buggies to the park on Saturday mornings, and bringing home bags of groceries afterwards.

This latter category of dads often focuses on housework and cooking in particular. French mothers tell me that their husbands handle specific domains, like homework or cleaning up after dinner. Perhaps having this clear division of labour is the secret. Or maybe French couples are just more fatalistic about marriage.

'One of the great feelings of a couple and of marriage is gratitude to the person who hasn't left,' says Laurence Ferrari, the anchorwoman of France's top nightly news programme. Ferrari, forty-four, is a pretty blonde who's six months pregnant with her second husband's baby. She's speaking to the raffish, professionally provocative French philosopher Pascal Bruckner. They are discussing 'Love and marriage: are they a good combination?' for a French magazine.

Ferrari and Bruckner are part of the French elite – a rarified circle of journalists, politicians, academics and businessmen who socialize with and marry each other. Their views represent an exaggerated, perhaps aspirational version of how ordinary French people think.

'Today, marriage no longer has a bourgeois connotation. To the contrary, for me, it's an act of bravado,' Ferrari says.

Marriage is a 'revolutionary adventure', Bruckner replies. 'Love is an indomitable feeling. The tragedy of love is the fact that it changes, and we're not the masters of this change.'

Ferrari concurs. 'It's because of that that I persist in saying, marriage for love is a magnificent risk.'

In a sign of how far we've come socially, Simon and I are invited away for the weekend – with kids – to the country home of our French friends Hélène and William. They, too, have twins and a singleton. Hélène, who's tall with a heart-shaped face and ethereal blue eyes, grew up in Reims, the capital of the Champagne region. Her family's holiday home is nearby in the Ardennes, close to the Belgian border.

Many of the First World War battles took place in the Ardennes. For four years, French and German soldiers dug trenches here, and fired artillery and machine guns at each other. The two sides lived in such close proximity that they knew each other's work shifts and habits, the way neighbours do. Sometimes they'd hold up handwritten signs for the other side to read.

In the small town where Hélène's family home is, it feels as if the shelling only recently stopped. People don't say 'First World War', they say 'fourteen to eighteen'. Many of the homes destroyed in the war were never rebuilt, leaving a lot of the landscape as open fields.

Hélène and William are ultra-dedicated parents all day long. But each night we're there, as soon as the kids are down, they bring out the cigarettes and the wine, turn on the radio, and have what is obviously adult time. They want to *profiter* – to take advantage of the company and the warm summer night.

On weekends, William gets up early with the kids. One morning he pops out of the house – while Simon babysits – to fetch some fresh *pains au chocolat* and a crusty baguette. Hélène eventually wanders downstairs in her pyjamas, her hair adorably mussed, and plops down at the breakfast table.

'*J'adore cette baguette!*' she says to William, as soon as she sees the bread he's bought.

It's a very simple, sweet, honest thing to say. And I can't imagine saying anything like it to Simon. I usually say that he's bought the wrong baguette, or I worry that he's left a mess that I'll have to clean up. He doesn't make me beam with delight, at least not first thing in the morning. That sheer girlish pleasure – *j'adore cette baguette* – sadly doesn't exist between us.

I tell Simon the baguette story as we're driving home from the Ardennes, past fields of yellow flowers and the occasional stone war memorial. 'We need more of that *j'adore cette baguette*,' he says. He's right; we absolutely do.

# 12

# You Just Have to Taste It

THE MAIN QUESTION PEOPLE ASK ABOUT TWINS, BESIDES HOW they were conceived, is how they're different from each other. Some parents have this all figured out: 'One's a giver and one's a taker,' the mother of two-year-old girls cooed, when I met her in a park in Miami. 'They get along perfectly!'

It's not quite that smooth with Leo and Joey. They seem like an old married couple – inseparable, but always bickering. (Perhaps they've learned that from Simon and me.) The differences between them become clearer when they start to talk. Leo, the swarthy one, says nothing but the odd noun for several months. Then suddenly at dinner one night, he turns to me and says, in a kind of robot voice, 'I am eating.'

It's no accident that Leo has mastered the present continuous. He lives in the present continuous. He's in constant, rapid motion. He doesn't walk anywhere, he runs. I can tell who's approaching by the speed of the footsteps.

Joey's preferred grammatical form is the possessive: *my* rabbit, *my* mummy. He moves slowly, like an old man, because he's trying to carry his key possessions with him at all times.

His favoured items vary, but there are always many of them (at one point he sleeps with a small kitchen whisk). He eventually puts everything into two briefcases, which he drags from room to room. Leo likes to swipe these, then run away. If I had to sum up the boys in a sentence, I'd say one's a taker and one's a hoarder.

Bean's preferred grammatical form is still the command. We can no longer blame her teachers; it's clear that giving orders suits her. She's constantly speaking up for a cause, usually her own. Simon refers to her as 'the union organizer', as in: 'The union organizer would like spaghetti for dinner.'

It was hard enough trying to instil French habits in Bean when she was an only child. Now that there are three kids in the house – and just two of us – creating some French *cadre* (framework) is even harder. But it's also a lot more urgent. If we don't control the kids, they're going to control us.

One realm in which we're succeeding is with food. Food is of course a source of national pride in France, and something that French people love to talk about. My French colleagues spend most of lunch discussing what they had for dinner. When Simon goes out for post-game beers with his French football team, he says they talk about food, not girls.

It becomes clear how French our kids' eating habits have become when we visit America. My mum is excited to introduce Bean to that American classic, macaroni and cheese from a box. But Bean won't eat more than a few bites. 'That's not cheese,' she says (I think I detect her first sneer).

We're on holiday when we visit America, so we end up

eating out a lot. On the plus side, American restaurants – like British ones – are a lot more kid-friendly than those in France. There are unheard-of conveniences like high chairs, crayons, and changing tables in the bathrooms. (You might occasionally find one of these things in Paris. But almost never all three at once.)

But I grow to dread the ubiquitous 'kids' menus' in American restaurants. It doesn't matter what type of restaurant we're in – seafood, Italian, Cuban. The kids' menus all have practically identical offerings: hamburgers, fried chicken fingers (now euphemistically called chicken 'tenders'), plain pizza, and perhaps spaghetti. There are almost never any vegetables, unless you count French fries or potato crisps. Occasionally, there's fruit. Kids aren't even asked how they want their hamburgers cooked. Perhaps for legal reasons, all the burgers come out a depressing shade of grey.

It isn't just restaurants that treat kids like they don't have fully developed taste buds. On one trip home I sign Bean up for a few days of tennis camp, which includes lunch. 'Lunch' for ten children turns out to be a bag of white bread and two packets of American cheese. Even Bean, who'd eat pasta or hamburgers for every meal if I let her, is taken aback. 'Tomorrow is pizza!' one of the coaches chirps.

The reigning view seems to be that kids have finicky, limited palates, and that adults who venture beyond grilled cheese do so at their peril. This belief is, of course, self-fulfilling. Many of the kids I meet in America and Britain do have finicky and limited palates. Frequently they spend a few years on a kind of mono-diet. A friend in Atlanta has one son who ate only white foods like rice and pasta. Her other son ate only meat. Another friend's baby nephew in Boston was supposed to start eating solid foods around Christmas. When the boy refused to eat anything but foil-wrapped chocolate Santas, his parents hoarded bags of them, afraid they'd be out of stock after the holidays.

Catering to picky kids is a lot of work. A mother I know in Long Island makes a different breakfast for each of her four kids, plus a fifth one for her husband. An American father who's visiting Paris with his family informs me in reverent tones that his seven-year-old is very particular about textures. He says the boy likes cheese and tortillas separately, but refuses to eat them when they're cooked together because the tortilla becomes – he whispers this while looking at his son – 'too crispy'.

Instead of resisting this pickiness, the parenting establishment seems to be capitulating to it. *What to Expect: The Toddler Years* says: 'Letting a young child go for months on nothing but cereal, milk and pasta, or bread and cheese (assuming a few well-chosen fruits and/or vegetables are thrown in for good balance) isn't indulgent or unacceptable, but perfectly respectable. In fact, there's something inherently unfair about insisting that children eat what's put in front of them when grown-ups enjoy a great deal of freedom of choice at the table.'

And then there's snack food. When I'm with Anglophone friends and their kids, little bags of pretzels and Cheerios seem to appear all the time, in between meals. Dominique, a French mother who lives in New York, says at first she was shocked to learn that her daughter's nursery feeds the kids every hour, all day long. She was surprised to see parents giving their kids snacks throughout the day at the playground too. 'If a toddler starts having a tantrum, they will give food to calm him down. They use food to distract them from whatever the crisis is,' she says.

The whole picture is different in France. In Paris, I mostly shop at the local supermarket. But just by going with the flow in Paris, my kids have never tasted high-fructose corn syrup or long-life bread. Instead of Fruit Shoots, they have fruit. They're so used to fresh food that processed food tastes strange to them.

As I've mentioned, French kids typically only eat at meal-times, and at the afternoon *goûter*. I've never seen a French child eating pretzels (or anything else) in the park at 10 am. There are kids' menus at some French restaurants – usually at corner bistros or pizza places. These menus don't always have *haute cuisine* either. There's often steak with *frites*. ('At home we never have *frites*, [my kids] know it's their only way of getting them,' my friend Christine says.)

But at most restaurants, kids are expected to order from the regular menu. When I ask for spaghetti with tomato sauce for Bean at a nice Italian restaurant, the French waitress very gently suggests that I order her something a bit more adventurous – say the pasta dish with aubergine.

It's not that French children are clamouring for more

vegetables. Of course they like certain foods more than others. And there are plenty of finicky French three-year-olds. But I've never met one who ate just one type of food. Their parents wouldn't let them exclude whole categories of textures, colours and nutrients, just because the children want to. The extreme pickiness that's come to seem normal in America and Britain looks, to French parents, like a dangerous eating disorder or, at best, a wildly bad habit.

The consequences of these differences are important. Just 3.1 per cent of French five- and six-year-olds are obese; in Britain, nearly 10 per cent of four- and five-year-olds are obese. As they get older, the gap between French and British children just keeps widening. In America and the UK, I see overweight children even in prosperous neighbourhoods. But in five years of hanging out at French playgrounds, I've seen exactly one child who might qualify as obese (and I suspect she was just visiting).

With food in particular, I can't help but ask the same question that I've been asking about so many other aspects of French parenting: how do French parents do it? How do they make their kids into little *gourmets*? And in the process, why don't French kids get fat? I see the results all around me, but how do French kids get to be this way?

I suspect that it starts with babies. When Bean is around six months old and I'm ready to feed her solid foods, I notice that French supermarkets don't sell the ground rice that my mother and all my Anglophone friends say should be a baby's first food. I have to trek to health food stores to buy an expensive, organic version imported from Germany, tucked away below the recycled nappies.

It turns out that French parents don't start their babies off on bland, colourless grains. From the first bite, they serve babies flavour-packed vegetables. The first foods that French babies typically eat are steamed and puréed green beans, spinach, carrots, peeled courgette, and the white part of leeks.

American babies eat vegetables too, of course, sometimes even from the start. But we Anglophones tend to regard vegetables as obligatory, vitamin-delivery devices, and mentally group them in the 'dull' category. A friend of mine gets so giddy when her kids eat avocado and broccoli that she shouts out the names of all the nutrients they're getting.

Although we're desperate for our kids to eat vegetables, we don't always expect them to. Bestselling cookbooks teach parents how to sneak vegetables into meatballs, fish fingers and macaroni and cheese, without kids even noticing. I once watched as friends of mine urgently spooned vegetables coated in yogurt into their kids' mouths after a meal, while the kids watched television, seemingly oblivious to what they were eating. 'Who knows how much longer we'll be able to do this,' the wife explained.

French parents treat their *légumes* with a whole different level of intention and commitment. They describe the taste of each vegetable, and talk about their child's first encounter with celery or leeks as the start of a lifelong relationship. 'I wanted her to know the taste of carrot by itself. Then I wanted her to know the taste of courgette,' my neighbour Samia swoons. Like other French parents I spoke to, Samia views vegetables – and fruit – as the building blocks of her daughter's incipient culinary *éducation*, and a way of initiating her into the richness of taste.

My English baby books recognize that certain foods are an acquired taste. They say that if a baby rejects a food, parents should wait a few days and then offer the same food again. My Anglophone friends and I all do this. But we assume that if it doesn't work after a few tries, our babies just don't like avocado, sweet potatoes or spinach.

In France, the same advice to keep re-proposing foods to babies is elevated to a mission. Parents take for granted that, while kids will prefer certain tastes to others, the flavour of each vegetable is inherently rich and interesting. Parents see it as their job to bring the child round to appreciating this. They believe that just as they must teach the child how to sleep, how to wait, and how to say *bonjour*, they must teach her how to eat.

No one suggests that introducing all these foods will be easy. The French government's free handbook on feeding kids says all babies are different. 'Some are happy to discover new foods. Others are less excited, and diversification takes a little bit longer.' But the handbook urges parents to be dogged about introducing a child to new foods, and not to give up even after he's rejected a food three or more times.

French parents advance slowly. 'Ask your child to taste just one bite, then move on to the next course,' the handbook suggests. The author adds that parents should never offer a different food to replace the rejected one. And they should react neutrally if the child won't eat something. 'If you don't react too much to his refusal, your child will truly abandon this behaviour,' the authors predict. 'Don't panic. You can keep giving him milk to be sure he's getting enough food.'

This long-term view of cultivating a child's palate is echoed in Laurence Pernoud's legendary parenting book *J'élève mon enfant* (*I Raise My Child*). Her section on feeding solids to babies is called 'How little by little a child learns to eat everything'.

'He refuses to eat artichokes?' Pernoud writes. 'Here again, you have to wait. When, a few days later, you try again, try putting a little bit of artichoke into a lot of purée' (of potatoes, say).

The government food guide says parents should offer the same ingredients cooked many different ways. 'Try steaming, baking, in parchment, grilled, plain, with sauce or seasoned,' the handbook's authors say. 'Your child will discover different colours, different textures and different aromas.'

The handbook also suggests a talking cure, *à la* Dolto. 'It's important to reassure him, and to talk to him about this new food,' it says. The conversation about food should go beyond 'I like it' or 'I don't like it'. They suggest showing kids a vegetable and asking, 'Do you think this is crunchy, and that it'll make a sound when you bite it? What does this flavour remind you of? What do you feel in your mouth?' They suggest flavour games like offering different types of apples and having the child decide which is the sweetest and the most acidic. In another game, the parent blindfolds the child and has him eat and identify foods he already knows.

All the French baby books I read urge parents to remain calm and cheerful at mealtimes, and above all to stay the course, even if their child doesn't take a single bite. 'Don't force him, but don't give up on proposing it to him,' the government handbook explains. 'Little by little, he'll get more familiar with it, he'll taste it . . . and without a doubt, he'll end up appreciating it.'

To get more insight into why French children eat so well, I attend the Commission Menus in Paris. It's here that those sophisticated menus posted at Bean's crèche every Monday get vetted. The commission's goal is to thrash out what the crèches of Paris will be serving for lunch for the next two months.

I'm probably the first foreigner ever to attend this meeting. It's held in a windowless conference room inside a government building on the banks of the Seine. Heading the meeting is Sandra Merle, the chief nutritionist of Parisian crèches. Merle's deputies are also there, along with a half-dozen chefs who work in various crèches.

The commission is a microcosm of French ideas about kids and food. Lesson number one is that there's no such thing as 'kids' food'. When a dietician reads out the proposed menus, including all four courses for each lunch, there is no mention of French fries, chicken nuggets, pizza or even ketchup. The proposed menu for one Friday is a salad of shredded red cabbage and *fromage blanc*. Then there's a white fish called 'colin' (hake) in dill sauce, with organic potatoes *à l'anglaise*. The cheese course is a *coulommiers* cheese (a soft cheese similar to Brie), and dessert is a baked organic apple. Each dish is cut up or puréed according to the age of the kids.

The commission's second lesson is the importance of variety. Members take a leek soup off the menu when someone points out that the children will have eaten leeks the previous week. Merle deletes a tomato dish she had planned for late December – another repeat – and replaces it with a boiled-beetroot salad.

Merle stresses visual and textural variety too. She says that if foods are all the same colour one day, she inevitably gets complaints from crèche directors. She reminds the crèche chefs that if the older kids (meaning two- and three-year-olds) have a puréed vegetable as a side dish, they should have a whole fruit for dessert, since they might find two puréed dishes too babyish.

Some of the chefs boast about their recent successes. 'I served mousse of sardines, mixed with a little cream,' says a chef with curly black hair. 'The kids loved it. They spread it on bread.'

There is much praise of soup. 'They love soup, it doesn't matter which beans or which vegetables,' another chef says. 'The soup with leeks and coconut milk, they really like it,' a third chef adds.

When someone mentions *fagots de haricots verts*, everyone laughs. It's a traditional Christmas dish that all the crèches were supposed to prepare last year. The dish requires blanching green beans, wrapping clusters of the beans in thin slices of smoked pork, piercing the combination with a toothpick and then grilling it. Apparently, this was too much even for the aesthetics-obsessed crèche chefs (though they don't baulk at being told to cut a kiwi into the shape of a flower).

Not surprisingly, another driving principle of the Commission Menus is that if at first the kids don't like something, they should try it and try it again. Merle reminds the chefs to introduce new foods gradually, and to prepare them in different ways. She suggests introducing berries first as a purée, since kids will already be familiar with that texture. After that, the chefs can serve them cut into pieces.

One chef asks what to do about grapefruit. Merle suggests serving it sprinkled with sugar to start with, then gradually serving it without. The same goes for spinach. 'Our kids don't eat spinach at all. It all goes in the bin,' one chef grumbles. Merle tells her to mix it with rice to make it more appetizing, and says she'll send out a 'technical sheet' to remind everyone how to do this. 'You re-propose spinach in different ways throughout the year, eventually they will like it,' she promises. She says that once one kid starts eating spinach, the others will follow. 'It's the principle of nutritional education.'

Vegetables are a big concern for the group. One cook says her kids won't eat green beans unless they're lathered in crème fraîche or *béchamel* sauce. 'You need to strike a balance;

sometimes with sauce, sometimes without,' Merle suggests. Then there's a long discussion of rhubarb.

After about two hours under the fluorescent lights, I'm fading a bit. I'd like to go home and have dinner. But the commission is just getting to the menu for the upcoming Christmas meal.

'The *foie gras*, no?' one chef suggests as an appetizer. Another counters with duck mousse. At first I assume that they're both joking, but no one laughs. The group then debates whether to serve the children salmon or tuna for the main course (their first choice is monkfish, but Merle says it's too expensive).

And what about the cheese course? Merle vetoes goat's cheese with herbs, because the kids had goat's cheese at their autumn picnic. The group finally settles on a menu that includes fish, broccoli mousse and two kinds of cow's milk cheese. Dessert is an apple-cinnamon cake, a yogurt cake with carrots, and a traditional Christmas *galette* with pears and chocolate. ('You can't veer too much from tradition. Parents will want a *galette*,' someone says.) For the afternoon *goûter* that day, Merle worries that a mousse made of 'industrial chocolate' won't be sufficiently festive. They settle on a more elaborate *chocolat liégeois* – a chocolate mousse sundae in a glass, topped with whipped cream.

Not once does anyone suggest that a flavour might be too intense or complicated for a child's palate. None of the foods is outrageously strong – there are a lot of herbs but no mustards, pickles or olives. But there are mushrooms, celery and many other kinds of vegetables in abundance. The point isn't that every kid will like everything. It's that he'll give each food a chance.

Not long after I sit in on the Commission Menus, a friend loans me a book called *The Man Who Ate Everything* by the American food writer Jeffrey Steingarten. Steingarten writes that when he was named food critic for *Vogue*, he decided that his personal food preferences made him unfairly biased. 'I feared that I could be no more objective than an art critic who detests the colour yellow,' he writes. He embarks on a project to see if he can make himself like the foods he detests.

Steingarten's hated foods include kimchi (the fermented cabbage that's a national dish of Korea), swordfish, anchovies, dill, clams, lard, and desserts in Indian restaurants – which he says have 'the taste and texture of face creams'. He reads up on the science of taste, and concludes that the main problem with new foods is simply that they're new. So just having them around should chip away at the eater's innate resistance.

Steingarten bravely decides to eat one of his hated foods each day. He also tries to eat very good versions of each food: chopped anchovies in garlic sauce in northern Italy; a perfectly done capellini in white-clam sauce at a restaurant on Long Island. He spends an entire afternoon cooking lard from scratch, and eats kimchi ten times, at ten different Korean restaurants.

After six months, Steingarten still hates Indian desserts. ('Not every Indian dessert has the texture and taste of face cream. Far from it. Some have the texture and taste of tennis balls.') But he comes to like, and even crave, nearly all of his other formerly detested foods. By the tenth portion of kimchi, it 'has become my national pickle, too,' he writes. He concludes that 'No smells or tastes are innately repulsive, and what's learned can be forgot.'

Steingarten's experiment sums up the French approach to feeding kids: if you keep trying things, you eventually come round to liking most of them. Steingarten discovered this by reading up on the science of taste. But French parents seem to know this intuitively, and do it automatically. In France, the idea of reintroducing a broad range of vegetables and other foods isn't just one idea among many. It's the guiding culinary principle for kids. The ordinary French parents I meet are evangelical about the idea that there is a rich world of flavours out there, which their children must be educated to appreciate.

This isn't just some theoretical ideal that can only play out in the controlled environment of the crèche. It actually happens in the kitchens and dining rooms of ordinary French families. I see it first-hand when I visit the home of Fanny, the publisher, who lives in a high-ceilinged apartment in eastern Paris with her husband Vincent, four-year-old Lucie and three-month-old Antoine.

Fanny has pretty, rounded features and a thoughtful gaze. She usually arrives home by 6 pm and serves Lucie dinner at 6:30, while Antoine sits in a bouncy chair drinking his bottle. On week nights, Fanny and Vincent eat together once the kids are asleep.

Fanny says she rarely makes anything as complex as the braised endives and chard that Lucie used to eat at the crèche. Still, she views each night's dinner as part of Lucie's culinary education. She doesn't worry too much about how much Lucie eats. But she insists that Lucie has at least a bite of every item on her plate.

'She has to taste everything,' Fanny says, echoing a rule I hear from almost every French mother I speak to about food.

One extension of the tasting principle is that, in France, everyone eats the same dinner. There are no choices or substitutions. 'I never ask, "What do you want?" It's "I'm serving this,"' Fanny tells me. 'If she doesn't finish a dish, it's OK. But we all eat the same thing.'

British or American parents might see this as exercising power over their helpless offspring. Fanny thinks it empowers Lucie. 'She feels bigger when we all eat, not the same portions, but the same thing,' Fanny says. Fanny says Anglophone visitors are amazed when they see Lucie at a meal. 'They say, "How come your daughter already knows the difference between Camembert, Gruyère and Chèvre?"'

Fanny says she also tries to make the meal fun. Lucie is of course a seasoned chef, because she makes cakes most weekends. Fanny says she has Lucie play some role in making dinner too, by preparing some of the food or setting the table. 'We help her, but we make it playful. And it's every day,' Fanny says.

When it's time to eat, Fanny doesn't austerely wave her finger at Lucie and order her to taste things. They talk about the food. Often they discuss the flavour of each cheese. And having participated in preparing the meal, Lucie is invested in how it turns out. There's complicity. If a certain dish is a flop, 'We all have a laugh about it,' Fanny says.

Part of keeping the mood light is keeping the meal brief. Fanny says that once Lucie has tasted everything, she's allowed to leave the table. The book *Votre Enfant* says a meal with young kids shouldn't last more than thirty minutes. French kids learn to linger over longer meals as they get older. And as they start going to bed later, they eat more weeknight dinners with their parents. Eating together teaches the kids table manners, social skills, and how to make conversation.

Planning the dinner menu is a lesson in balance. I'm struck by how French mothers like Fanny seem to have the day's culinary rhythm mapped out in their heads. They assume that their kids will have their one big protein-heavy meal at lunchtime. For dinner they mostly serve carbohydrates like pasta, along with vegetables.

Fanny may have just raced home from the office, but as they do at the crèche she calmly serves dinner in courses. She gives Lucie a cold vegetable starter, such as shredded carrots in vinaigrette. Then there's a main course, usually pasta or rice with vegetables. Occasionally she'll cook a bit of fish or meat, but usually she expects Lucie to have most of her protein at lunch. 'I try to avoid proteins [at night] because I think I've been educated like that. They say once per day is enough. I try to focus on vegetables.'

Some parents tell me that, in winter, they often serve soup

for dinner, along with a baguette or maybe a bit of pasta. It's a filling meal, which also relies heavily on grains and vegetables. A lot of parents purée these soups. And that's dinner. Kids might drink some juice at breakfast, or at the afternoon *goûter*. But at lunch and dinner they drink water, usually at room temperature or slightly chilled.

Weekends are for family meals. Almost all the French families I know have a large lunch *en famille* on both Saturday and Sunday. The kids are almost always involved in cooking and setting up these meals. On weekends 'We bake, we cook, I have cookbooks for children, they have their own recipes,' says Denise, the medical ethicist and mother of two girls.

After all these preparations, they sit down to eat. Sociologists Claude Fischler and Estelle Masson, authors of the book *Manger*, say that a French person who eats a sandwich at his desk for lunch doesn't even count this as 'having eaten'. For the French, 'Eating means sitting at the table with others, taking one's time and not doing other things at the same time.' Whereas for Americans, 'Health is seen as the main reason for eating.'

At Bean's fifth birthday party, I announce that it's time for the cake. Suddenly all the kids – who've been raucously playing – file into our dining room and sit down at the table. They're all *sage* at once. Bean sits at the head of the table and hands out plates, spoons and napkins. Except for lighting the candles and carrying out the cake, I don't have much of a role. By five years old, sitting calmly at the table for any kind of eating is an automatic reflex for French kids. There's no question of eating on the couch, in front of the television, or while looking at the computer.

Of course, one of the benefits of having some *cadre* in your home is that you can go outside the *cadre* without worrying that it will collapse. Denise tells me that once a week she lets her two girls – who are seven and nine – have dinner in front of the television.

On weekends and during those ubiquitous school holidays, French parents are more relaxed about what time their kids eat and go to bed. They trust the *cadre* to be there when they need it again. Magazines run articles about easing kids back on to an earlier schedule, once school starts again. When we're on holiday with my friend Hélène and her husband William, I panic a bit when it's 1:30 and William still hasn't got home with some of the ingredients for our lunch.

But Hélène figures that the kids can adapt. They are people, after all, who like us are capable of coping with a bit of frustration. She breaks open a bag of potato crisps, and the six kids all gather at the kitchen table to eat them. Then they pile outside to play again, until lunch is ready. It's no big deal. We all cope. A little while later we all have a long, lovely meal at the table that we've set up under a tree.

If over-parenting were an airline, Park Slope, Brooklyn, would be its hub. Every parenting trend and new product seems to originate or refuel there. Park Slope is home to 'New York's first baby-wearing and breastfeeding boutique', and to a

$15,000-per-year nursery where teachers 'actively discourage and stop superhero play'. If you live in Park Slope, 'Baby Bodyguards' will kid-proof your duplex for $600. (The company's founder explains that 'Once I gave birth and my son became part of the external world, my fear and anxiety kicked in.')

Despite Park Slope's reputation for zealous parenting, I'm unprepared for what I witness in a playground there on a sunny Sunday morning. At first, the father and son I spot just seem to be doing a particularly energetic version of narrated play. The boy looks about six. The father – in expensive jeans and stylish weekend stubble – has followed him to the top of the jungle gym. In a bilingual twist, he's giving the boy a running commentary in both English and what sounds like American-accented German.

The son seems used to his father heading down the slide behind him. When they move to the swings, the father continues his bilingual soliloquy, while pushing. This is all still within the bounds of what I've seen elsewhere. But then the mother arrives. She's a rail-thin brunette in her own pair of expensive jeans, carrying a bag of produce from the farmers' market next door.

'Here's your parsley snack! Do you want your parsley snack?' she says to the boy, handing him a green sprig.

Parsley? A snack? I think I understand the intention: these parents don't want their son to be fat. They want him to have a varied palate. They see themselves as original thinkers who can provide him with unusual experiences, German and parsley surely being just a small sample. And I grant them that parsley doesn't run the risk of ruining their son's – or frankly anyone's – appetite.

But there's a reason why parsley has never caught on as a snack. It's a seasoning. It doesn't taste good all by itself. I get the feeling that these parents are trying to remove their son from the collective wisdom of our species, and the basic chemistry of what tastes good. I can only imagine the effort this requires. What happens when he discovers cookies?

When I mention the 'parsley snack' incident to American parents, they're not surprised. They concede that parsley isn't a snack. But they admire the effort. At that impressionable age, why not try? In the hothouse environment of Park Slope, some parents have gone beyond the American Question: how do we speed up the stages of development? They're now asking how they can override basic sensory experiences.

I realize I'm guilty of this too when I take Bean to her first Halloween party, when she's about two. The French haven't embraced this holiday yet, the way the British have. (I go to one adult Halloween party in Paris, where all the women are dressed as sexy witches, and most of the men are Draculas.) Each year a group of Anglophone mothers in Paris takes over the top floor of a Starbucks near the Bastille and sets up little trick-or-treat stations around the room.

As soon as Bean grasps the concept – all these people are *giving her sweets* – she begins to eat them. She doesn't just eat a few sweets; she tries to eat all the sweets in her bag. She sits in a corner of the room stuffing pink, yellow and green gooey masses into her mouth. I have to intervene to slow her down.

It occurs to me then that I've taken the wrong approach to sweets. Before this Halloween, Bean had rarely eaten refined sugar. To my knowledge, she hadn't had a single gummy bear. Like the parsley parents, I'd tried to pretend that sweets didn't exist.

I've watched other Anglophone parents agonize about giving their kids any sugar at all. One afternoon a British mother I know tells me her little girl can't have a cookie although all the other kids are having them, explaining, 'She doesn't need to know about that.' Another mum I know – a psychologist – looked to be in agony over whether to let her eighteen-month-old have an iced lolly, even though it was at the end of a hot summer day and all our kids were playing outside. (She finally conceded.) I once saw an American couple with three advanced degrees between them convene a nervous meeting over whether their four-year-old can have a lollipop.

But refined sugar does exist. And French parents know it. They don't try to eliminate all sweets from their children's diets. Rather, they fit sweets inside the *cadre*. For a French kid, sweets have their place, and are a regular enough part of their lives that they don't gorge like freed prisoners the moment they get their hands on any. Mostly, children seem to eat them at birthday parties, special times at school, and as a special treat. At these occasions, they're usually free to eat all they want. When I try to limit the boys' intake of candy and chocolate cake at the crèche's Christmas party, one of their caregivers intervenes. She tells me I should just let them enjoy the party and be free. I think of my skinny friend Virginie, who pays strict attention to what she eats on weekdays, then eats whatever she wants on weekends. Kids, too, need moments when the regular rules don't apply.

But parents decide when these moments are. When I drop Bean off at a birthday party for Abigail, a little girl in our building, she's the first guest to arrive (we haven't yet figured out that you're not supposed to be punctual for kids' birthdays). Abigail's mum has just set out plates of cookies and sweets on a table. Abigail asks her mum if she can have some of the sweets. Her mum says *non*, and explains that it isn't yet time to eat them. Abigail looks longingly at the candy, then runs off with Bean to play in another room.

Chocolate has a more regular place in the lives of French kids. French parents talk about chocolate as if it's just another food group, albeit one to eat in moderation. When Fanny describes what Lucie eats in a typical day, the menu includes cookies or a piece of cake. 'And obviously she'll want chocolate in there somewhere,' Fanny says.

Hélène gives her kids hot chocolate when it's cold outside. She serves it for breakfast, along with a hunk of baguette, or makes it their afternoon *goûter*, along with some cookies. My kids love reading books about T'choupi, a French children's book character modelled on a penguin. When he's sick, his mum lets him stay home and drink hot chocolate. I take my kids to see a performance of *Goldilocks and the Three Bears*, at a theatre near our house. The bears don't eat oatmeal, they eat *bouillie au chocolat* (hot chocolate thickened with flour).

'It's a compensation for going to school, and I guess it gives them some energy,' explains Denise, the medical ethicist. She shuns McDonald's, and makes her daughters' dinner from scratch each night. But she gives each girl a bar of chocolate for breakfast, along with some bread and a bit of fruit.

French kids don't get a huge amount of chocolate – it's a small bar, or a drink's worth, or a strip on a *pain au chocolat*. They eat it happily, but don't expect a second helping. But chocolate is a nutritional fixture for them, rather than a forbidden treat. Bean once comes home from the summer camp at her school with a chocolate sandwich: a baguette with a bar of chocolate inside. I'm so surprised I take a picture of it. (I later learn that the chocolate sandwich – usually made with dark chocolate – is a classic French *goûter*.)

With sweets, too, the *cadre* is key. French parents aren't afraid of sugary foods. Everything, even cake and chocolate, has its place. In general, French parents will serve cake or cookies at lunch, or at the *goûter*. But they don't give kids chocolate or rich desserts with dinner. 'What you eat in the evening just stays with you for years,' Fanny explains.

For dessert with dinner, Fanny typically serves fresh fruit or a fruit compote – those ubiquitous little tubs of apple sauce with other puréed fruits mixed in (these come with or without added sugar). There's a 'compotes' section in French supermarkets. Fanny says she also buys all different types of plain yogurt, and then gets jams for Lucie to mix in.

As in most realms, French parents aim at mealtimes to give kids both firm boundaries and freedom within those boundaries. 'It's things like sitting at the table and tasting everything,' Fanny explains. 'I'm not forcing her to finish, just to taste everything and sit with us.'

I'm not sure exactly when I started serving my kids meals in courses. But I now do it at every meal. It's a stroke of French genius. This starts with breakfast. When the kids sit down, I put plates of cut-up fruit on the table. They nibble on this while I'm getting their toast or cereal ready. They can have juice at breakfast, but they know that for lunch and dinner we drink water. Even the union organizer doesn't complain about that. We talk about how clean water makes us feel.

At lunch and dinner I serve vegetables first, when the kids are hungriest. We don't move on to the main course until they at least make a dent in the starter. Usually they finish it. Except when I introduce an entirely new dish, I rarely have to resort to the tasting rule. If Leo won't eat a food the first time I serve it, he'll usually agree to at least smell it, and he'll take a nibble soon after that.

Bean sometimes exploits the letter of the rule by eating a single piece of courgette, and then insisting that she has fulfilled her obligation. She recently declared that she will taste everything 'except salad', by which she means the actual green lettuce leaves. But for the most part, she quite likes the starters we serve. These include sliced avocado, tomato in vinaigrette, or steamed broccoli with a little soy sauce. We all have a good chuckle when I serve *carottes râpées* – shredded carrots in vinaigrette – and try to pronounce it.

My kids come to the table hungry because, except for the *goûter*, they don't snack. It helps that other kids around them aren't snacking either. But even so, getting to this point required a steely will. I simply don't cave in to demands for a filling piece of bread or a whole banana between meals. And as the kids have got older, they've mostly stopped asking. If they do, I just say, 'No, you're having dinner in thirty minutes.' Unless they're very tired, they're usually fine with that. I feel a swell of accomplishment when I'm in the supermarket with Leo and he points to a box of cookies and says '*goûter*'.

I try not to be too fanatical about this (or as Simon describes it, 'more French than the French'). When I'm cooking I occasionally give the kids a little preview of dinner – a piece of tomato or a few chickpeas. When I'm introducing a new ingredient, like pine nuts, I'll offer them a few bites while I'm cooking, to get them in the mood. Obviously they drink water whenever they want.

Sometimes keeping my kids in the food *cadre* feels like a lot of work. Especially when Simon is away, I'm often tempted to skip the starter, plop a bowl of pasta in front of them and call it dinner. When I occasionally do this, they're quite happy to gobble it down. There's certainly no clamouring for salad and vegetables.

But usually the kids don't have a choice. Like a French mum, I've accepted that it's my duty to teach them to like a variety of tastes, and to eat meals that are *équilibrés*. (Though my fanaticism about this is entirely American.) Also like a French mum, I try to keep the balance of the whole day's menu in my head. We mostly stick to the French formula of large protein-heavy lunches and lighter carbohydrate-driven dinners, though always with vegetables. The kids do eat a lot of pasta, though I try to vary the shape and the sauce. Whenever I have time, I make a big pot of soup for dinner (though I can't bring myself to purée it), and serve it with rice or bread.

It's no surprise that the kids find the food more appetizing when the ingredients are fresh, and it looks good. I consider the balance of colours on their plate, and occasionally slip in some slices of tomato or avocado if dinner looks monotone. We have a collection of colourful melamine plates. But for dinner I use white plates, which makes the colours of the food 'pop', and signals to the kids that we're having a grown-up meal.

I try to let them help themselves as much as possible. Beginning when the boys were quite young, I passed around a bowl of grated Parmesan on pasta nights and let them sprinkle it on all by themselves. They get to put a spoonful of sugar in their hot chocolates and occasionally in their yogurts.

Bean frequently asks for a slice of Camembert, or a hunk of whatever cheese we've got, at the end of the meal. Except for special occasions, we don't do cake or ice cream at night. I still can't bring myself to serve them chocolate sandwiches.

It's taken a while to make all this second nature. It helps that the boys in particular really like to eat. One of their teachers at the crèche calls them *gourmands*, which is a polite way of saying that they eat a lot. She says their favourite word is *'encore'* – more. They've developed the annoying habit, possibly learned at the crèche, of holding up their plates at the end of the meal, to show that they've finished. Whatever sauce or liquid is left spills on to the table (I think at the crèche they've already mopped up the liquid with slices of baguette).

Sweets are no longer non grata in our house. Now that we offer them in moderation, Bean doesn't treat each sweet as if it's her last. When it's really cold out, I make the kids hot chocolate in the morning. I serve it with yesterday's baguette, softened slightly in the microwave, and slices of apple in a little serving bowl, which the kids dip in their drinks. It feels like a very French breakfast.

## Chocolat chaud à la Hélène
(makes about 6 cups)

*1 litre half-fat milk*
*1–2 tsp cocoa powder*
*sugar to taste*

In a saucepan, mix one heaped teaspoon unsweetened cocoa powder with a small splash of cold or room-temperature milk. Mash the milk and powder together until they form a thick paste. Add the rest of the milk and mix. (The chocolate should spread evenly into the milk.) Cook on medium heat until the milk begins to boil. Allow the hot chocolate to cool, skim off any skin that has formed, then pour it into mugs with spoons inside. Let kids add their own sugar at the table.

## Quick breakfast version

In a large mug, make a paste with 1 teaspoon cocoa powder and a small splash of milk. Fill the mug with milk and mix. Heat the mug in the microwave for two minutes, or until very hot. Mix in a teaspoon of sugar. Pour a bit of this hot cocoa concentrate into several mugs. Add cold or room-temperature milk to each mug. Serve with a crusty baguette, or any toasted bread.

# 13

# It's Me Who Decides

LEO, THE SWARTHY TWIN, DOES EVERYTHING QUICKLY. I DON'T mean that he's gifted. I mean that he moves at twice the speed of ordinary humans. By age two, he's developed a runner's physique from dashing from room to room. He even speaks quickly. As Bean's birthday approaches, he begins singing 'Happybirthdaytoya!' in a high-pitched squeak; the whole song is over in a few seconds.

It's very hard to wrestle with this little tornado. Already, he can practically outrun me. When I go to the park with him, I'm in constant motion too. He seems to regard the gates around play areas as an invitation to leave.

One of the most impressive parts of French parenting – and perhaps the toughest one to master – is authority. Many French parents I meet have an easy, calm manner with their children that I can only envy. Their kids actually listen to them. French children aren't constantly dashing off, talking back or engaging in prolonged negotiations. But how exactly do French parents pull this off? And how can I acquire this magical authority too?

One Sunday morning, my neighbour Frédérique witnesses me trying to cope with Leo when we take our kids to the park. Frédérique is a travel agent from Burgundy. She's in her mid-forties, with a raspy smoker's voice and a no-nonsense manner. After years of paperwork she adopted Tina, a beautiful red-headed three-year-old, from a Russian orphanage. At the time of our outing, she's been a mother for all of three months.

But already Frédérique is teaching me about *éducation*. Just by virtue of being French, she has a whole different vision of what's *possible* and *pas possible*. This becomes clear in the sandbox at the park. Frédérique and I are sitting on the perimeter of the sandbox, trying to talk. But Leo keeps dashing outside the fence surrounding the sandbox. Each time he does this, I get up to chase him, scold him and drag him back while he screams. It's irritating and exhausting.

At first, Frédérique watches this little ritual in silence. Then, without any condescension, she says that if I'm running after Leo all the time, we won't be able to indulge in the small pleasure of sitting and chatting for a few minutes.

'That's true,' I say. 'But what can I do?'

Frédérique says I should be more stern with Leo, so he knows that it's not OK to leave the sandbox. 'Otherwise it doesn't work,' she says. In my mind, spending the afternoon chasing Leo is inevitable. In her mind, it's *pas possible*.

Frédérique's strategy doesn't seem to hold out much promise for me. I point out that I've been telling Leo to stop leaving the sandbox for the last twenty minutes. Frédérique smiles.

She says I need to make my 'no' stronger, and to really believe in it.

The next time Leo tries to run outside the gate, I say 'no' more sharply than usual. He leaves anyway. I follow and drag him back.

'You see?' I say to Frédérique. 'It's not possible.'

Frédérique smiles again, and says I need to make my 'no' more convincing. What I lack, she says, is the belief that he's really going to listen. She tells me not to shout, but rather to speak with more conviction.

I'm scared that I'll terrify him.

'Don't worry,' Frédérique says, calmly urging me on.

Leo doesn't listen the next time either. But I can feel that my 'no's' are coming from a more convincing place. They're not louder, but they're more self-assured. I feel like I'm impersonating a different sort of parent.

By the fourth try, when I'm finally brimming with conviction, Leo approaches the gate but – miraculously – doesn't open it. He looks back and eyes me warily. I widen my eyes and try to emit disapproval.

After about ten minutes, Leo stops trying to leave altogether. He seems to forget about the gate, and just plays in the sandbox with Tina, Joey and Bean. Soon Frédérique and I are chatting, with our legs stretched out in front of us.

I'm shocked that Leo suddenly views me as an authority figure.

'See that,' Frédérique says, not gloating. 'It was your tone of voice.'

She points out that Leo doesn't appear to be traumatized. For the moment – and possibly for the first time ever – he actually seems like a French child. With all three kids suddenly *sage* at once, I can feel my shoulders falling a bit. It's an experience I've never really had in the park before. Maybe this is what it's like to be a French mother?

I feel relaxed, but also foolish. If it's that easy, why haven't I been doing this for the last four and a half years? Saying no isn't exactly a cutting-edge parenting technique. What's new is Frédérique's coaching me to drop my ambivalence and to be certain about my own authority. What she tells me springs from her own upbringing and deepest beliefs. It comes out sounding like common sense.

Frédérique has the same certainty that what's most pleasant for us parents – being able to have a relaxing chat at the park, while the kids play – is also best for the children. This seems to be true. As we're chatting, it becomes clear that Leo is a lot less stressed than he was half an hour earlier. Instead of a constant cycle of escape and reimprisonment, he's playing happily with the other kids.

I'm ready to bottle my new technique – the fully felt 'no' – and sell it off the back of a wagon. But Frédérique warns me that there's no magic elixir for making kids respect your authority. It's always a work in progress. 'There are no fixed rules,' she says. 'You have to keep changing what you do.'

That's unfortunate. So what else explains why French parents like Frédérique have so much authority with their kids? How exactly do they summon this authority, day after day, dinner after dinner? And how can I get some more of it?

A French colleague of mine says that if I'm interested in authority, I must speak to her cousin Dominique. She says that Dominique, a French singer who's raising three kids in New York, is an unofficial expert in the differences between French and American parents.

Dominique, forty-three, looks like the heroine of a *nouvelle vague* film. She has dark hair, delicate features and an intense, gazelle-like gaze. If I were thinner, better looking and could sing, I'd say that she and I were living mirror-image lives: she's a Parisian who's raising her children in New York. I'm an ex-New Yorker who's raising kids in Paris. Living in France has made me calmer and less neurotic, whereas despite Dominique's sultry good looks she has adopted the bubbly self-analysis that comes from living in Manhattan. She speaks enthusiastic French-accented English, peppered with 'like' and 'oh my God'.

Dominique arrived in New York as a 22-year-old student. She planned to study English for six months, then go home. But New York quickly became home. 'I felt really good and stimulated and had great energy, something I hadn't felt in a long, long time in Paris,' she says. She married an American musician.

Beginning when she first got pregnant, Dominique was also enchanted with American parenting. 'There's a great sense of community that, in a way, you don't have as much in France

. . . If you like yoga and you're pregnant, boom! You get into this group of pregnant women doing yoga.'

She also started to notice the way kids are treated. At a big dinner with her husband's family, she was astonished to see that when a three-year-old girl arrived, all twenty adults at the table stopped talking and focused on the little girl.

'I thought, oh, this is incredible, this culture. It's like the kid is a god, it's really amazing. I'm like, no wonder Americans are so confident and so happy, and the French are so depressed. Here we are – just look at the attention.'

But over time Dominique started to view this type of attention differently. She noticed that the same three-year-old girl who'd stopped conversation at that family dinner was developing an oversized sense of entitlement.

'I was like, "That's it, this kid really annoys me." She's thinking that because she's here, everyone has to stop their life and pay attention."'

Dominique, whose own kids are eleven, eight and two, says her doubts grew when she overheard kids at her children's nursery responding to teachers' instructions with: 'You are not the boss of me.' ('You would never see that in France, never,' Dominique says.) When she and her husband were invited for dinner at the homes of American friends with young kids, she often ended up doing most of the cooking, because the hosts were busy trying to make their kids stay in bed.

'Instead of just being firm, and saying, "No more of that, I'm not giving you more attention, this is bedtime, and this is parents' time. Now it's my time as an adult with my friends. Go to bed, that's it" – well, they don't do that. I don't know why they don't do that, but they don't do that. They can't do it. They keep just serving the kids. And I see that and I'm just blown away.'

Dominique still adores New York, and much prefers American schools to French ones. But in matters of parenting, she has increasingly reverted to French habits, with their clear rules and boundaries.

'The French way sometimes is too harsh. They could be a little more gentle and friendly with kids, I think,' she says. 'But I think the American way takes it to the extreme, of raising kids as if they are ruling the world.'

I find it hard to argue with my would-be doppelgänger. I can picture those dinner parties she's describing. American parents – myself included – are often deeply ambivalent about being in charge. In theory, we believe that 'kids need limits'. This is a truism of American parenting. However, in practice we're often unsure where these limits should be, or we're uncomfortable policing them.

'I feel more guilty for getting angry than I feel angry,' is how a college friend of Simon's justifies his three-year-old daughter's bad behaviour. A girlfriend of mine says her three-year-old son bit her, but she 'felt bad' yelling at him, because she knew that it would make him cry. So she let it go.

Anglophone parents worry that being too strict will break their kids' creative spirits. A visiting American mother was shocked when she saw a playpen in our apartment in Paris. Apparently, back home, even playpens are now seen as too confining. (We didn't know. In Paris they're *de rigueur*.)

A mother from Long Island tells me about her badly behaved nephew, whose parents were – in her view – alarmingly permissive. But she says the nephew has since grown up to become head of oncology at a major American medical centre, vindicating the fact that he was an unbearable child. 'I think kids who are very intelligent and not much disciplined are insufferable when they're kids. But I think they are less stifled creatively when they're older,' she says.

It's very hard to know where the correct limits lie. By forcing Leo to stay in a playpen, or in the sandbox, am I preventing him from one day curing cancer? Where does his free expression end and pointless bad behaviour begin? When I let my kids stop and study every manhole cover we pass on the pavement, are they following their bliss, or turning into brats?

A lot of Anglophone parents I know find themselves in an awkward in-between zone, where they're trying to be both dictator and muse to their children. The result is that they end up constantly negotiating with their kids. I get my first taste of this when Bean is about three. Our new house rule is that she's allowed to watch forty-five minutes of television per day. One day, she asks to watch a bit more.

'No. You've already had your TV time for today,' I say.

'But when I was a baby I didn't watch any TV,' she says.

Like us, most Anglophone parents I know have at least some limits. But with so many different parenting philosophies in play, there are some parents who oppose authority altogether. I meet one of them on a visit to America.

Liz is a graphic designer in her mid-thirties, with a five-year-old daughter named Ruby. She easily ticks off her main parenting influences: the paediatrician William Sears, the author Alfie Kohn and the behaviourist B. F. Skinner.

When Ruby acts up, Liz and her husband try to convince the girl that her behaviour is morally wrong. 'We want to extinguish unacceptable behaviours without resorting to power plays,' Liz tells me. 'I try not to exploit the fact that I'm larger and stronger than her by physically restraining her. Similarly, I try not to resort to the fact that I have all the money by saying, "You can have this thing or not."'

I'm touched by the exacting effort that Liz has put into constructing her approach to parenting. She hasn't merely adopted someone else's rules; she has carefully digested the work of several thinkers and come up with a thoughtful hybrid. The new way of parenting that she's created is, she says, a complete break from the way that she herself grew up.

Liz says that this eclectic style, and her desire not to be judged for it, have isolated her from many of her neighbours and peers. She says her own parents are bewildered and overtly disapproving of how she's bringing up Ruby, and that she can no longer discuss it with them. Visits home are tense, especially when Ruby acts up.

But Liz and her husband remain determined not to flaunt their authority. Lately Ruby has been hitting them both. Each time, they sit her down and discuss why hitting is wrong. This well-intentioned reasoning isn't helping. 'She still hits us,' Liz says.

*　*　*

France feels like a different planet. Even the most bohemian parents boast about how strict they are, and seem unequivocal about being at the top of the family hierarchy. In a country that reveres revolution and climbing the barricades, there are apparently no anarchists at the family dinner table.

'It's paradoxical,' admits Judith, the art historian and mother of three in Brittany. Judith says she's 'anti-authority' in her political views, but that when it comes to parenting she's the boss, full stop. 'It's parents, then children,' she says of the family pecking order. In France, she explains, 'Sharing power with a child doesn't exist.'

In the French media and among the older generation, there's talk of that encroaching 'child-king' syndrome. But when I talk to parents in Paris, what I hear all the time is 'C'est moi qui décide' – it's me who decides. There's another slightly more militant variation, 'C'est moi qui commande' – it's me who gives the orders. Parents say these phrases to remind both their kids and themselves who's the boss.

To Anglophones, this hierarchy can look like tyranny. Robynne is an American who lives just outside Paris with her French husband and their two kids, Adrien and Léa. Over a family dinner at her apartment one night, she tells me about taking Adrien to the paediatrician when he was a toddler. Adrien cried and refused to step on the scales, so Robynne knelt down to convince him.

The doctor interrupted. 'He said, "Don't explain to him why. Just say, "That's why. That's what you're doing, you're going on the scales, that's it, there's no discussion.'" Robynne was shocked. She says she eventually changed paediatricians because she found this one too severe.

Robynne's husband Marc has been listening to this story. 'No, no, that's not what he said!' he interjects. Marc, a professional golfer who grew up in Paris, is one of those French parents who seems to wear his authority quite effortlessly. I notice the way his kids listen carefully when he speaks to them, and respond immediately.

Marc says the doctor wasn't being wantonly bossy. On the contrary, he was helping with Adrien's *éducation*. Tellingly, Marc's recollection of the conversation goes like this:

'He said that you have to be sure of yourself, you have to take your kid and put him on the scales ... If you give him too many choices, he doesn't feel reassured. You have to show him a way ... You have to show him that's the way it is and it's not a bad way or a good way, it's just the way.

'It's a simple gesture but it's the start of everything. You have certain things that don't need explanation. You need to weigh the kid so you take the kid and put the kid on the scales. Period. Period!'

He says the fact that Adrien found the experience unpleasant was part of the lesson. 'Sometimes there are things in life you don't really like, and you have to do them,' Marc says. 'You don't always do what you love or what you want to.'

When I ask Marc how he got his authority, it's clear that it's not as effortless as it looks. He's put enormous effort into establishing this dynamic with his kids. Having authority is something that he thinks very hard about, and considers a priority. All this effort springs from his belief that having a parent who's confident is reassuring to kids.

'For me it's better to have a leader, someone who shows the way,' he says. 'A kid has to feel like the mum is in control, or the dad.'

'Just like when you're on a horse,' Adrien, now aged nine, chips in.

'Good comparison,' Robynne says.

Marc adds, 'We have a saying in French: it's easier to loosen the screw than to tighten the screw. Meaning that you have to be very tough. If you're too tough, you loosen. But if you are too lenient . . . afterwards, to tighten, forget about it.'

Marc is describing the *cadre* that I've heard so much about. French parents seem to spend the early years of a child's life constructing this *cadre*. They do it in part by establishing their own right to say, sometimes, 'Just get on the scales.'

We American and British parents assume that we'll have to chase our kids around the park all afternoon, or spend half a dinner party putting them to bed. It's irritating, but it's come to seem normal.

For French parents, living with a child king seems wildly out of balance, and bad for the whole family. They think it would drain much of the pleasure from daily life, for both the parents and the kids. They know that building this *cadre* requires enormous effort, but they believe that the alternative is unacceptable. It's obvious to French parents that the *cadre* is the only thing standing between them and two-hour 'good nights'.

For Anglophones, 'It's accepted that when you have kids, your time is not your own,' Marc tells me. In his view, 'The kids need to understand that they're not the centre of attention. They need to understand that the world doesn't revolve around them.'

So how do parents build this *cadre*? The process of constructing it does occasionally seem harsh. But it isn't just about saying no, and establishing that 'it's me who decides'. Another way that French parents and educators build the *cadre* is simply by talking a lot about the *cadre*. That is, they spend a lot of time telling their kids what's permissible and what's not.

All this talk seems to will the *cadre* into existence. It starts to take on an almost physical presence, much like a good mime can convince you there's actually a wall. This ongoing conversation about the *cadre* is often very polite. Parents say 'please' a lot, even to babies.

Parents often invoke the language of rights. Rather than saying 'Don't hit Jules,' they typically say, 'You don't have the right to hit Jules.' This is more than a semantic difference. It feels different to say it this way. The French phrasing suggests that there's a fixed and coherent system of rights, which both children and adults can refer to. It also makes clear that the child *does* have the right to do other things.

Kids pick up this phrase, and police each other. A playground chant for little kids is the rhyming, *Oh là là, on a pas le droit de faire ça!* (Oh la la, we don't have the right to do that!)

Another phrase that adults use a lot with children is 'I don't agree,' as in, 'I don't agree with you throwing your peas on the floor.' Parents say this in a serious tone, while looking directly at the child. 'I don't agree' is also more than just 'no'. It establishes the adult as another mind, which the child must consider. And it credits the child with having his own view about the peas, even if this view is being overruled. It makes throwing the peas seem like something the child has rationally decided to do, so he can decide to do otherwise too.

This may help explain why mealtimes are so calm in France. Instead of waiting for a big crisis and resorting to dramatic punishments, parents and carers focus on making lots of small, polite, preventative adjustments, based on well-established rules.

I see this at the crèche, when I sit in with the eighteen-month-olds for another fabulous, four-course lunch. Six little kids, wearing matching pink terrycloth bibs, are sitting around a rectangular table as Anne-Marie oversees the meal. The atmosphere is extremely calm. Anne-Marie describes the foods in each course, and tells the children what's coming next. I notice that she also closely watches everything they do, and – without raising her voice – comments on small infractions.

'*Doucement* – gently – we don't do that with a spoon,' she says to a boy who has started banging his spoon on the table. 'No, no, no, we don't touch the cheese, it's for later,' she tells another. When she speaks to a child, she always makes eye-contact with him.

French parents and carers don't always resort to this level of micromanagement. I've noticed that they tend to do it more at mealtimes, when there are more small gestures and rules, and more risk of chaos if things go wrong. Anne-Marie does this combination of conversation and gentle-but-firm corrections throughout the thirty-minute meal. By the end, the kids' faces are smeared with food. But there is just a crumb or two on the floor.

Like Marc and Anne-Marie, the French parents and caregivers I meet have authority without seeming like dictators. They don't aspire to raise obedient robots. On the contrary, they listen and talk to their kids all the time. In fact, the adults I meet who have the most authority all speak to children not as a master to a subject, but as one equal to another. 'You must always explain the reason for something that's forbidden,' Anne-Marie tells me.

When I ask French parents what they most want for their children, they say things like 'to feel comfortable in their own skin' and 'to find their path in the world'. They want their kids to develop their own tastes and opinions. In fact, French parents worry if their kids are too docile. They want them to have *caractère*.

But they believe that children can only achieve these goals if they respect boundaries and have self-control. So alongside *caractère*, there has to be *cadre*.

It's hard to be around so many well-behaved kids, and around parents with such high expectations. Day after day, I am mortified that the boys start shouting loudly or whining, practically every time we walk through the courtyard between our lift and the main entrance to our building. It's like an announcement to the dozens of people whose apartments open on to the courtyard: the Anglos have arrived!

Bean and I are invited to a schoolmate's home for *goûter* one afternoon, during the Christmas holidays. Once we're all sitting around the table (I'm served tea), Bean decides that it's a good moment to do some *bêtises*. She takes a swig of her hot chocolate, then spits it back into her mug.

I'm embarrassed. I'd kick her under the table if I could be sure which set of legs was hers. I do tell her to stop, but I don't want to ruin the moment by making too much of a fuss. Meanwhile, our hostess's three daughters are sitting *sagely* around the table, nibbling on their cookies. They're apparently not even tempted to imitate Bean.

I see how French parents construct *cadres*. What I don't understand is how they calmly keep their kids in the *cadre*. I can't help but think of an adage I once heard: if you want to keep a man in a ditch, you have to get in the ditch with him. It's a bit like that at our house. If I send Bean to her room, I have to stay in the room with her, otherwise she'll come out again.

Empowered by that episode in the park with Leo, I'm trying to be strict all the time. But this doesn't always work. I'm not sure when to tighten the screw, and when to loosen it.

For some guidance, I make a lunch date with Madeleine, a French nanny who worked for Robynne and Marc. She lives in a small city in Brittany, in western France, but is currently working the overnight shift with a new baby in Paris. (The child is 'searching for his nights', Madeleine says.)

Madeleine, sixty-three, is herself the mother of three boys. She has short, greying brown hair and a warm smile, and radiates that total certainty I see in Frédérique and other French parents I meet. Like them, she has a calm conviction that her methods really do work.

'The more spoiled a child is, the more unhappy he is,' she tells me, almost as soon as we sit down.

So how does she keep her charges in line?

'*Les gros yeux*' – the big eyes – she says. Madeleine demonstrates these for me at the table. As she does so, she suddenly morphs from a grandmotherly lady in a matching pink scarf and sweater, into a scary-looking owl. Even just for show, she has a lot of conviction.

I want to learn the big eyes too. When our salads arrive, we practise. At first, I have trouble doing the owl without cracking up. But as with Frédérique in the park, when I finally hit the point of real conviction, I can feel the difference. Then, I don't feel like laughing.

Madeleine says that she's not trying to frighten children into submission. She's asserting her authority. But she says the big eyes work best when she has a strong connection with the child, and when there's mutual respect. Madeleine says the most satisfying part of her job is developing 'complicity' with a child, as if they're seeing the world the same way, and she can almost tell what the child is about to do. Getting to this point requires carefully observing him, talking with him, and trusting him with certain freedoms. And it means understanding that he's a person too.

Indeed, to build a relationship with a child in which the big eyes work, she says strictness must come with flexibility, including giving kids autonomy and choices. 'I think you need to leave [kids] a bit of liberty, let their personalities show,' she says.

Madeleine doesn't see any contradiction between having this strong reciprocal relationship and also being very firm. Her authority seems to come from inside the relationship with children, not from above it. She's able to balance complicity and authority. 'You must listen to the child, but it's up to you to fix the limits,' she says.

The big eyes are famous in France. Bean mentioned getting them at the crèche. Many French adults still remember being on the receiving end of the big eyes and other, similar expressions.

'She had this look,' Clotilde Dusoulier, the Parisian food writer, says of her mother. With both her parents, 'There was this tone of voice they used when all of a sudden they felt you had stepped over a line. They had a facial expression that was stern and annoyed and not happy. They would say, "No, you don't say that." You would feel chastised and a bit humiliated. It would pass.'

What's interesting to me is that Clotilde remembers *les gros yeux* – and the *cadre* the look enforced – very fondly. 'She's always been very clear on what was OK and what wasn't,' she says of her mother. 'She managed to be both affectionate and have authority without ever raising her voice.'

* * *

Speaking of voice-raising, I seem to do it quite a lot. Shouting does sometimes succeed in getting the kids to brush their teeth, or wash their hands before dinner. But it takes a lot out of me, and creates an awful ambience. The louder I yell, the worse I feel about it afterwards.

French parents do speak sharply to their kids. But they prefer surgical strikes to constant carpet-bombing. Shouting is saved for important moments, when they really want to make a point. When I shout at my kids in the park or at home when we have French friends over, my friends suddenly look alarmed, as if they think that there's been a serious offence.

Anglophone parents like me often view imposing authority in terms of discipline and punishment. French parents don't talk much about these things. Instead, they talk about the *éducation* of kids. As the name suggests, this is about gradually teaching children what's acceptable and what's not.

This difference makes the whole tone in France a lot more gentle. When Leo refuses to use his cutlery at dinner, I try to imagine that I'm teaching him to use a fork much like I'd teach him a letter of the alphabet. This makes it easier for me to be patient and calm. I no longer feel disrespected and angry when he doesn't immediately comply. And with some of the stress off the situation, he's more amiable about trying. I don't yell, and dinner is more pleasant for everyone.

It takes me a while to realize that French and Anglophone parents also use the word 'strict' quite differently. When British or American parents describe someone as 'strict', they typically mean that the person has an all-encompassing authority. The image of a stern, joyless schoolteacher comes to mind. I don't know many American parents who use this word to describe themselves.

When French parents describe themselves as 'strict' they mean something different. They mean that they're very strict about a few things, and pretty relaxed about everything else. That's the *cadre* model: a firm framework surrounding a lot of freedom.

'We should leave the child as free as possible, without imposing useless rules on him,' Françoise Dolto says in *Les Étapes majeures de l'enfance* (*The Major Stages of Childhood*). 'We should leave him only the *cadre* of rules that are essential for his security. And he'll understand from experience, when he tries to transgress, that they are essential, and that we don't do anything just to bother him.' In other words, being strict about a few key things makes parents seem more reasonable and companionable, and thus makes it more likely that children will obey.

True to Dolto's spirit, Parisian parents tell me that they don't usually get worked up about minor *bêtises* – those small acts of naughtiness. They assume that these are just part of being a kid. 'I think if every misbehaviour is treated on the same level, how will they know what's important?' my friend Esther tells me.

But these same parents say that they immediately jump on certain types of infractions. Their zero-tolerance areas vary. But almost all the parents I know say that their main non-negotiable realm is 'respect for others'. They're referring to all those *bonjours*, *au revoirs*, and *mercis*, and also about speaking respectfully to parents or other adults.

Physical aggression is another common no-go area. American kids often seem to get away with hitting their parents, even though they know they're not supposed to. The French adults I know simply don't tolerate this. Bean hits me once in front of our neighbour Pascal, a bohemian fiftyish bachelor. Pascal is normally an easy-going guy. But he immediately launches into a stern lecture about how 'one does not do that'. I'm awed by his sudden conviction. I can see that Bean is awed too.

At bedtime you can really see the French balance between being very strict about a few things and very relaxed about most others. A few parents tell me that at bedtime, kids must stay in their rooms. But within their rooms, the kids can do what they want.

I introduce this concept to Bean, and she really likes it. She doesn't focus on the fact that she's confined to her room. Instead she keeps saying, proudly, 'I can do whatever I want.' She usually plays or reads for a while, then puts herself to bed.

When the boys are about two, and they're sleeping in beds rather than cots, I introduce this same principle. Since they're sharing a room, things tend to get a bit more boisterous. I hear a lot of crashing Lego. Unless it sounds dangerous, however, I avoid going back in after I've said good night. Sometimes, if it's getting late and they're still going strong, I come in and tell them that it's bedtime, and that I'm turning off the lights.

They don't seem to view this as a violation of the do-what-you-want principle. By that point they're usually exhausted, and they climb into bed.

To pry myself further out of my black-and-white way of looking at authority, I visit Daniel Marcelli. Marcelli is head of child psychiatry at a large hospital in Poitiers and the author of more than a dozen books, including a recent one called *Il est permis d'obéir* (*It Is Permissible to Obey*). The book is meant for parents. But typically, it's also a meditation on the nature of authority. Marcelli develops his arguments in long expositions, quoting Hannah Arendt, and delighting in paradoxes.

His favourite paradox is that in order for parents to have authority, they should say yes most of the time. 'If you always forbid, you're authoritarian,' Marcelli tells me, over coffee and chocolates. He says the main point of parental authority is to authorize children to do things, not to block them.

Marcelli gives the example of a child who wants an orange, or a glass of water, or to touch a computer. He says the current French 'liberal education' dictates that the child should ask before touching or taking these things. Marcelli approves of this asking, but he says the parents' response should almost always be 'yes'.

Parents 'should only forbid him every once in a while . . . because [something is] fragile or dangerous. But fundamentally, [the parent's job] is to teach the child to ask before taking.'

Marcelli says that embedded in this dynamic is a longer-term goal, with its own paradox: if all is done right, the child will eventually reach a point where he can choose to disobey too.

'The sign of a successful education is to teach a child to obey until he can freely authorize himself to disobey from time to time. Because how can one learn to disobey certain orders if one has not learned to obey?'

'Submission demeans,' Marcelli explains, 'whereas obedience allows a child to grow up.' (He also says that children should watch a bit of television, so they have a shared culture with other kids.)

To follow Marcelli's whole argument about authority, it would help to have been raised in France, where philosophy is taught in high school. What I do understand is that part of the delight of building such a firm *cadre* for kids is that they can sometimes leave the *cadre*, and it will remain intact.

Marcelli is also echoing another point I've heard a lot in France: without limits, kids will be consumed by their own desires. ('By nature, a human being knows no limits,' Marcelli tells me.) French parents stress the *cadre* because they know that, without boundaries, children will be overpowered by their own impulses. The cadre helps to contain all this inner turmoil, and calm it down.

That could explain why my children are practically the only ones having tantrums in the park in Paris. A tantrum happens when a child is overwhelmed by his own desires, and doesn't know how to stop himself. The other kids are used to hearing *non*, and having to accept it. Mine aren't. My 'no' feels contingent and weak to them. It doesn't stop the chain of wanting.

Marcelli says that kids with a *cadre* can absolutely be creative and 'awakened' – a state that French parents also describe as 'blossoming'. The French ideal is to promote the child's blossoming within the *cadre*. He says a small minority of French parents think that blossoming is the only important thing, and don't build any *cadre* for them. It's pretty clear how Marcelli feels about this latter group. Their children, he says, 'don't do well at all, and despair in every sense'.

I'm quite taken with this new view. From now on I'm determined to be authoritative but not authoritarian. When I'm putting Bean to bed one evening, I actually mention to her that I know she needs to do *bêtises* sometimes. She looks relieved. It's a moment of complicity.

'Can you tell that to Daddy?' she asks.

Bean, who after all spends her days in a French school, has a better grasp of discipline than I do. One morning I'm in the lobby of our apartment building, and I'm late. I need the boys to get into the pram, so I can rush Bean to school and then take the boys to crèche. Simon is away.

But the boys refuse to get into their double pram. They want to walk, which will take even longer. What's more, we're in the courtyard of our building, so the neighbours can hear and even watch this whole exchange. I summon whatever pre-coffee authority I can muster, and insist that they get in. This has no effect.

Bean has been watching too. She believes that I should be able to galvanize two little boys.

'Just say "One, two, three,"' she says, with considerable irritation. Apparently, this is what her teachers say when they want an uncooperative child to comply.

Saying 'One, two, three' isn't rocket science. It certainly happens in Britain and America too. But the logic behind it is very French. 'This gives him some time, and it's respectful to the child,' Daniel Marcelli says. He says the child should be allowed to play an active role in obeying, which requires giving him time to respond.

In *It Is Permissible to Obey*, Marcelli gives the example of a child who seizes a sharp knife. 'His mother looks at him and says, her face "cold", her tone firm and neutral, her eyebrows lightly furrowed: "Put that down!"' In this example, the child looks at his mother but doesn't move. Fifteen seconds later, his mother adds, in a firmer tone, 'You put it down right away,' and then ten seconds later, 'Do you understand?'

In Marcelli's telling, the little boy then puts the knife on the table. 'The mother's face relaxes, her voice becomes sweeter, and she says to him, "That's good." Then she explains to him that it's dangerous and that you can cut yourself with a knife.'

Marcelli notes that although the child was obedient in the end, he was also an active participant. There was reciprocal respect. 'The child has obeyed, his mother thanks him but not excessively, her child recognizes her authority . . . For this to happen, there must be words, time, patience, and reciprocal recognition. If his mother had rushed over to him and snatched the knife from his hands, he wouldn't have understood much of anything.'

It's hard to strike this balance between being the boss but also listening to a child and respecting him. One afternoon, as I'm getting Joey dressed to leave the crèche, he suddenly collapses in tears. I'm all charged up in my new 'It's me who decides' mode. I have the fervour of a convert. I decide that this is like the incident with Adrien on the doctor's scales: I'm going to force him to get dressed.

But Fatima, his favourite carer at the crèche, hears the ruckus and comes into the changing room, concerned. She takes the opposite tack from me. Joey may throw fits all the time at home, but at the crèche it's quite unusual. Fatima leans into Joey, and starts stroking his forehead.

'What is it?' she keeps asking him gently. She views this tantrum not as some abstract, inevitable expression of the terrible twos, but as communication from a very small, rational being.

After a minute or two, Joey calms down enough to explain – through words and gestures – that he wants his hat from his locker. That's what this whole scene has been about (I think he'd tried to grab it earlier). Fatima takes Joey down from the changing table, then watches as he goes to the locker, opens it and takes out the hat. After that, he's *sage* and ready to go.

Fatima isn't a pushover. She has a lot of authority with the kids. She didn't think that just because she patiently listened to Joey, she was giving in to him. What she did was to calm him down, then give him a chance to express what he wanted.

Unfortunately, there are endless scenarios, and no one rule about what to do in every case. The French have a whole bunch of contradictory principles, and few hard-and-fast rules. Sometimes you listen carefully to your kid. And sometimes you just put him on the scales. It's about setting limits, but also about observing your child and building complicity, and then adapting to what the situation requires.

For some parents, all this probably becomes automatic. But for now, I wonder if this balance will ever come naturally to me. It feels like the difference between trying to learn salsa dancing as a thirty-year-old, and growing up dancing salsa as a child with your dad. I'm still counting steps, and stepping on toes.

In some Anglophone homes I've visited, it's not uncommon for a child to be sent to his room during practically every meal. Whereas in France, there are lots of small reminders about how to behave, but being *puni* is a big deal.

Often, parents send the punished child to his room, or to a corner. Sometimes, they spank him. I've only seen French kids spanked in public a few times, though friends of mine in Paris say they see it more frequently. At a staging of *Goldilocks and the Three Bears*, the actress playing mummy bear asks the audience what should happen to the baby bear, who's been acting up.

'*La fessée!*' – a spanking – the crowd of little kids shouts in unison. In a national poll, 19 per cent of French parents said they spank their kids 'from time to time'; 46 per cent said they spank 'rarely' and 2 per cent said they spank 'often'.' Another 33 per cent said they never spank their kids.

In the past, '*la fessée*' probably played a bigger role in French child-rearing and in enforcing adults' authority. But the tide is turning. All the French parenting experts I read about oppose it. Instead of spanking, they recommend that parents become adept at saying no. Like Marcelli, they say that 'no' should be used sparingly. But once uttered, it must be definitive.

This idea isn't new. In fact, it comes all the way from Rousseau. 'Give willingly, refuse unwillingly,' he writes in *Émile*. 'But let your refusal be irrevocable. Let no entreaties move you; let your "no", once uttered, be a wall of brass, against which the child may exhaust his strength some five or six times, but in the end he will try no more to overthrow it. Thus you will make him patient, equable, calm and resigned, even when he does not get all he wants.'

In addition to the rapid-movement gene, Leo has also been born with the subversive gene.

'I want water,' he announces at dinner one night.

'What's the magic word?' I ask sweetly.

'Water!' he says, smirking. (Strangely, Leo – who looks the most like Simon – speaks with a slight British accent. Joey and Dean both sound American).

Building a *cadre* for your kids is a lot of work. In the early years, it requires quite a lot of repetition and attention. But once it's in place, it makes life much easier and calmer (or so it seems). In moments of desperation I start telling my kids, in

French, 'C'*est moi qui décide*' – it's me who decides. Just uttering this sentence is strangely fortifying. My back stiffens a bit when I say it.

The French way also requires a paradigm shift. I'm so used to believing that everything revolves around the kids. Being more 'French' means moving the centre of gravity away from them, and letting my own needs spread out a bit too.

Feeling like I have some control also makes having three little kids a lot more manageable. When Simon is away one spring weekend, I let the kids drag carpets and blankets out on to our balcony and create a kind of Moroccan lounge. I bring them hot chocolate, and they sit around sipping it.

When I tell Simon about this later, he immediately asks, 'Wasn't it stressful?' It probably would have been a few weeks earlier. I'd have felt overpowered by them, or too worried to enjoy it. There would have been shouting, which – since our balcony overlooks the courtyard – our neighbours would have heard.

But now that I'm the decider, at least a little bit, having three kids on the balcony with hot chocolate actually feels manageable. I even sit down and have a cup of coffee with them.

One morning I'm taking Leo to crèche by himself (Simon and I have divided the morning duties). As we're riding down in the lift, I feel a sense of dread. I decide to tell Leo firmly that there will be no shouting in the courtyard. I present this new rule as if it's always existed, and explain it firmly, while looking into his eyes. I ask him whether he understands, and then pause to give him a chance to reply. After a thoughtful moment, he says yes.

When we open the glass door and walk out into the court-yard, it's strangely silent. There's no shouting or whining. There's just a very speedy little boy, tugging me along.

# 14

# Let Him Live His Life

ONE DAY, A NOTICE GOES UP AT BEAN'S SCHOOL. IT SAYS that parents of students aged four to eleven can register their kids for a summer trip to the Hautes-Vosges, a rural region about five hours by car from Paris. The trip, *sans* parents, will last for eight days.

I can't imagine sending Bean, who's five, on an eight-day school holiday. She's never spent more than a night alone at my mother's house. My own first overnight class trip, to SeaWorld, was when I was in secondary school.

This trip is yet another reminder that while I can now use the subjunctive in French, and even get my kids to listen to me, I'll never actually be French. Being French means looking at a notice like this and saying, as the mother of another five-year-old next to me does, 'What a shame. We already have plans then.' None of the French parents finds the idea of dis-patching their four- and five-year-olds for a week of group showers and dormitory life to be at all alarming.

I soon discover that this school trip is just the beginning. I didn't go to sleep-away camp until I was ten or eleven. But in

298

France, there are hundreds of different sleep-away *colonies de vacances* – holiday camps – for kids as young as four. The younger kids typically go away for seven or eight days to the countryside, where they ride ponies, feed goats, learn songs and 'discover nature'. For older kids, there are *colonies* that specialize in things like theatre, kayaking or astronomy.

It's clear that giving kids a degree of independence, and stressing a kind of inner resilience and self-reliance, is a big part of French parenting. The French call this *autonomie* – autonomy. They generally aim to give children as much autonomy as they can handle. This includes physical autonomy, like the class trips. It also includes emotional separation, like letting them build their own self-esteem that doesn't depend on praise from parents and other adults.

I admire a lot about French parenting. I've tried to absorb the French way of eating, of wielding authority, and of teaching my kids to entertain themselves. I've started speaking at length to babies, and letting my kids just 'discover' things for themselves, instead of pushing them to acquire skills. In moments of crisis and confusion, I often find myself asking: what would a French mother do?

But I have a harder time accepting some parts of the French emphasis on autonomy, like the school trips. Of course I don't want my kids to be too dependent on me. But what's the rush? Must the push for autonomy start so young? And aren't the French overdoing it a bit? In some cases, the drive to make kids self-reliant seems to clash with my most basic instincts to protect my kids, and to make them feel good.

American parents tend to dole out independence quite differently. It's only after I marry Simon, a European, that I realize I spent much of my childhood acquiring survival skills. You wouldn't know it from looking at me, but I can shoot a bow and arrow, right a capsized canoe, safely build a fire on someone's stomach, and – while treading water – convert a pair of blue jeans into an inflated life-jacket.

As a European, Simon didn't have this survivalist upbringing. He never learned how to pitch a tent or steer a kayak. He'd be hard-pressed to know which end of a sleeping bag to crawl into. In the wild he'd survive about fifteen minutes – and that's only if he had a book.

The irony is, while I have all these *faux* pioneering skills, I learned them in tightly scheduled summer camps, after my parents had signed legal disclaimers in case I drowned. And that was before there were webcams in classrooms and vegan, nut-free birthday cakes.

Despite their scouting badges and killer backhands, middle-class American (and British) kids are famously quite protected. 'The current trend in parenting is to shield children from emotional or physical discomfort,' the psychologist Wendy Mogel writes in *The Blessing of a Skinned Knee*. Instead of giving kids freedom, the well-heeled parents that Mogel counsels 'try to armour [their kids] with a thick layer of skills by giving them lots of lessons and pressuring them to compete and excel'.

It's not simply that Anglophones don't emphasize autonomy. It's that we're not sure it's a good thing. We tend to assume that parents should be physically present as much as possible, to protect kids from harm and to smooth out emotional turbulence for them. Simon and I have 'joked' since Bean was born that we'll just move with her to wherever she attends university. Then I see an article saying that some American colleges now hold 'parting ceremonies' for parents of incoming freshmen, to signal that the parents must leave.

French parents don't seem to have this fantasy of control. They want to protect their kids, but they aren't obsessed with far-flung eventualities. When they're travelling they don't, as I do, email their spouse once a day to remind him to bolt the front door and to make sure that all the toilet lids are closed (in case a child falls in).

In France, the social pressure goes in the opposite direction. If a parent hovers too much or seems to micromanage his child's experiences, someone else is apt to say some version of 'Just let him live his own life'. My friend Sharon, the literary agent with two kids, explains: 'Here there's an argument about pushing a child to the max. Everyone will say, "You have to let children live their lives."'

The French emphasis on autonomy comes all the way from Françoise Dolto. 'The most important thing is that a child will be, in full security, autonomous as early as possible,' Dolto says in *The Major Stages of Childhood*. 'The trap of the relationship between parents and children is not recognizing the true needs of the child, of which freedom is one... The child has the need to feel "loved in what he is becoming", sure of himself in a space, more freely day by day left to his own exploration, to his personal experience, and in his relations with those of his own age.'

Dolto is talking, in part, about leaving a child alone, safely, to figure things out for himself. She also means respecting him as a separate being who can cope with challenges. In Dolto's view, by the time a child is six, he should be able to handle everything in the house – and in society – that concerns him.

The French way can be tough for even the most integrated Anglophone expatriates to accept. My friend Andi, who's lived in France for more than twenty years, says that when her older son was six, she found out that he had an upcoming class trip.

'Everyone tells you how great it is, because in April there'll be a *classe verte*' – literally, a green class. 'And you say to yourself, "Hmm, what's that? Oh, a field trip. And it's a week? It lasts a week?"' At her son's school, the trips are optional until first grade. After that, the whole class of twenty-five kids is expected to go on a week-long trip with the teacher each spring.

Andi says that by American standards, she isn't a particularly clingy mother. However, she couldn't get comfortable with the idea of the 'green class' – near some salt marshes on the western coast of France. Her son had never even gone on a sleepover. Andi still corralled him into the shower each night. She couldn't imagine him going to bed without her tucking him in. She liked his teacher, but she didn't know the other adults who'd be supervising the trip. One was the teacher's nephew. Another was a supervisor from the playground. The third, Andi recalls, was just 'this other person [the teacher] knows'.

When Andi told her three sisters in America about the trip, she says, 'they completely freaked out. They said, "You don't have to do that!" One's a lawyer, and she's like, "Did you sign anything?"' Andi says they were mainly worried about paedophiles.

At a meeting to exchange information about the trip, another Anglophone mum from the class asked the teacher how she would cope with a scenario in which an electrical wire accidentally fell in the water, and a child then walked into the water. Andi says the French parents snickered. She was glad she hadn't asked the question, but it did reflect her own 'hidden neuroses'.

Andi's own main concern – which she didn't dare raise at the meeting – was what would happen if her son became sad or upset during the trip. When this happens at home, 'I try to help him identify his emotions. If he started crying and he didn't know why, I would say, "Are you scared, frustrated, are you angry?" That was my thing. I was like, "OK, we're going to go through this together."'

The French emphasis on autonomy extends beyond school trips. My heart regularly jumps when I'm walking around my neighbourhood, because French parents will often let small kids race ahead of them on the pavement. They trust that the kids will stop at the corner and wait for them. Watching this is particularly terrifying when the kids are on scooters.

When I run into my friend Hélène on the street, and we stop to chat, she lets her three girls wander off a bit, towards the edge of the pavement. She trusts that they won't suddenly dash into the street. Bean probably wouldn't do that either. But just in case, I make her stand next to me and hold my hand while Hélène and I talk.

I live in a world of worst-case scenarios. Simon reminds me that I once wouldn't let Bean sit in the stands to watch him play football, in case she got hit by the ball. The French are less panicked. By accident, I often run into the caregivers from the boys' crèche leading a group of toddlers down the street, to buy the day's baguettes. It's not an official outing, it's just taking a few kids for a walk. Bean went on a school trip to the zoo, which I only learn about by accident weeks later when I happen to take her to the same zoo. I am never asked to sign waivers. French parents don't seem to worry that anything untoward might happen on these trips.

There are also many small moments in France when I'd expect to help my kids along, but they're supposed to go it alone. When Bean has a recital for her dance class, I'm not even allowed backstage. I make sure she has a pair of white leggings, which is the only instruction that's been communicated to parents. I never speak to the dance teacher. Her relationship is with Bean, not with me. When we get to the theatre, I hand her over to an assistant who shuttles her backstage.

For weeks, Bean has been telling me, 'I don't want to be a marionette.' I wasn't sure what that meant. It becomes clear as soon as the curtains open. Bean comes onstage in full costume and make-up, with a dozen other little girls, doing jolty arm and leg movements to a song called 'Marionetta'. The girls are way out of synch with each other. They look like marionettes on the loose, who've had too much cognac.

But it's also clear that Bean, without my knowledge, has memorized an entire ten-minute dance routine. When she comes out from backstage after the show, I gush about what a wonderful job she did. But she looks disappointed.

'I forgot to not be a marionette,' she says.

French kids aren't just more independent in their extra-curricular activities. They also have more autonomy in their dealings with each other. French parents seem slower to intervene in playground disputes, or to mediate arguments between siblings. They expect kids to work these situations out for themselves. French playgrounds are famously free-for-alls, with teachers mostly watching from the sidelines.

When I pick up Bean from preschool one afternoon, she's just come from the playground and has a red gash on her cheek. It's not deep, but it's bleeding a bit. She won't tell me what happened (but she isn't in pain). Her teacher claims not to know what happened either. I'm practically in tears by the time I question the director of the school, but she, too, doesn't know anything about it. They seem surprised that I'm making such a fuss.

My mother happens to be visiting, and she can't believe this. She says that a similar injury in America would prompt official enquiries, calls home and lengthy explanations.

For French parents, such events are upsetting, but they

aren't Shakespearian tragedies. 'In France we like it when kids brawl a bit,' the journalist and author Audrey Goutard tell me. 'It's the part of us that's a bit French and a bit Mediterranean. We like that our children know how to defend their territory, and quarrel a bit with other children . . .We're not bothered by a certain violence between children.'

Bean's reluctance to say how she got the gash probably reflects another aspect of the autonomy ethos. 'Telling' on another child – the French use the verb *'rapporter'* – is viewed very badly. People tell me this is partly because of all the lethal informing on neighbours that went on during the Second World War. At the annual meeting of my apartment's building association, many of whose members were alive during the war, I ask if anyone knows who's been tipping over our buggy in the lobby.

'We don't *rapporter*,' an older woman says. Everyone laughs.

Britons don't like 'grasses' either. However, in France, even among kids, having the inner resolve to suffer some scrapes and keep your lips sealed is considered a life skill. Even within families, people are entitled to their secrets.

'I can have secrets with my son that he can't tell his mother,' Marc, the French golfer, tells me. I see a French movie in which a well-known economist picks up his teenage daughter from a Paris police station, after she's been brought in for shoplifting and possessing marijuana. On the drive home, she defends herself by saying that at least she didn't rat on the friend who was with her.

This don't-tell culture creates solidarity between kids. They learn to rely on each other and on themselves, rather than rushing to parents or school authorities for back-up. The trade-off is that there isn't quite the same reverence for truth at any cost. Marc and his American wife Robynne tell me about a recent case in which their son Adrien, who's now ten, saw another student setting off firecrackers at school. There was a big enquiry. Robynne urged Adrien to tell the school authorities what he'd seen. Marc advised him to consider the other boy's popularity, and whether he could beat Adrien up.

'You have to calculate the risks,' Marc says. 'If the advantage is not to do anything, he should do nothing. I want my son to analyse things.'

I see this emphasis on making kids learn their own lessons when I'm renovating our apartment. Like all the English-speaking parents I know, I'm eager for everything to be rigorously child-proof. I choose rubber flooring for the kids' bathroom, lest they slip on wet tiles. I also insist that every appliance has a kid-proof lock, and that the oven door is the type that doesn't get hot.

My contractor Régis, an earthy, roguish fellow from Burgundy, thinks I'm nuts. He says the way to 'child-proof' an oven is to let the kid touch it once, and realize that it's hot. Régis refuses to install rubber floors in the bathroom, saying that they would look terrible. I concede, but only when he also mentions the apartment's resale value. I don't budge on the oven.

On the day that I read an English story to Bean's class at *maternelle*, the teacher gives a brief English lesson beforehand.

She points to a pen and ask the kids to say the pen's colour in English. In response, a four-year-old boy says something about his shoes.

'That has nothing to do with the question,' the teacher tells him.

I'm taken aback by this response. I would have expected the teacher to find something positive to say, no matter how far the answer is off the subject. I come from the American tradition of, as the sociologist Annette Lareau describes it, 'treating each child's thought as a special contribution'. By praising kids for even the most irrelevant comments, we try to give them confidence and make them feel good about themselves.

In France, that kind of parenting is very conspicuous. I see this when I take the kids to the trampolines in the Tuileries gardens, just next to the Louvre. Each child gets his own trampoline inside a gated area, and parents watch from the surrounding benches. But one mum has brought a chair inside the gates and parked it directly in front of her son's trampoline. She shouts 'Whoah!' each time he jumps. I know, even before I approach to eavesdrop further, that she must be an Anglophone like me.

I know this because, although I manage to restrain myself at the trampolines, I feel compelled to say 'Whee!' each time one of my kids goes down a slide. This is shorthand for 'I see you doing this! I approve! You're wonderful!' Likewise, I praise even their worst drawings and artwork. I feel that I must: their self-esteem is in my hands.

French parents also want their child to feel good about himself and '*bien dans sa peau*' – comfortable in his own skin. But they have a different strategy for bringing this about. It's in some ways the opposite of the American strategy. They don't believe that praise is always good.

The French believe that kids feel confident when they're able to do things for themselves, and do those things well. After children have learned to talk, adults don't praise them just for saying something. They praise them for saying interesting things, and for speaking well. Raymonde Carroll, a French sociologist, says French parents train their children to verbally 'defend themselves well'. She quotes an informant who says: 'In France, if the child has something to say, others listen to him. But the child can't take too much time and still retain his audience; if he delays, the family finishes his sentences for him. This gets him in the habit of formulating his ideas better before he speaks. Children learn to speak quickly, and to be interesting.'

Even when French kids do say interesting things – or just give the correct answer – French adults are decidedly understated in response. They don't act like every job well done is an occasion for a 'good job'. When I take Bean to the free health clinic for a check-up, the paediatrician asks her to do a wooden puzzle. Bean fits all the pieces together. The doctor looks at the finished puzzle and then does something I'm not constitutionally capable of: practically nothing. She mutters the faintest '*bon*' – more of a 'let's move on' than a 'good' – then proceeds with the check-up.

Not only don't teachers and authority figures in France routinely praise children to their faces. To my great disappointment, they also don't routinely praise children to their parents. I had hoped this was a quirk of Bean's rather sullen first-year teacher. The following year, she has two different teachers. One is a dynamic, extremely warm young woman named Marina, with whom Bean has an excellent rapport. But when I ask Marina how things are going, she says simply that Bean is '*très compétente*'. (I type this into Google Translate, to make sure I haven't missed some nuance of *compétent* that might suggest brilliance. It just means 'very competent'.)

It's good that my expectations are low when Simon and I have a mid-term meeting with Agnès, Bean's other teacher. She, too, is lovely and attentive. And yet she also seems reluctant to label Bean, or make any general statements about her. She simply says, 'Everything is fine.' Then she shows us the one worksheet – out of dozens – that Bean had trouble finishing. I leave the meeting having no idea of how Bean ranks against her peers.

After the meeting, I'm miffed that Agnès didn't mention anything that Bean has done well. Simon points out that, in France, that's not her job. Her role is to discover problems. If the child is struggling, the parents need to know. If the child is coping, there's nothing more to say.

This focus on the negative, rather than on trying to boost kids' (and parents') morale with positive reinforcement, is a well-known (and often criticized) feature of French schools.

It's almost impossible to get a perfect score on the French *baccalauréat*, the final exam at the end of senior school. A score of 14:20 is considered excellent, and 16:20 is practically perfect.

Through friends I meet Benoît, who's a father of two and a professor at one of France's elite universities. Benoît says his senior-school-aged son is an excellent student. However, the most positive comment a teacher ever wrote on one of his papers was '*des qualités*' – some good qualities. Benoît says French teachers don't grade their students on a curve, but rather against an ideal, which practically no one meets. Even for an outstanding paper, 'the French way would be to say "correct, not too bad, but this and this and this and this are wrong".'

By senior school, Benoît says there's little value placed on letting students express their feelings and opinions. 'If you say, "I love this poem because it makes me think of certain experiences I had," that's completely wrong . . . What you're taught in high school is to learn to reason. You're not supposed to be creative. You're supposed to be articulate.'

When Benoît took a temporary posting at Princeton, he was surprised when students accused him of being a harsh grader. 'I learned that you had to say some positive things about even the worst essays,' he recalls. In one incident, 'I had to justify giving a student a D.' Conversely, I hear that an American who taught at a French high school got complaints from parents when she gave grades of 18:20 and 20:20. The parents assumed that the class was too easy, and that the grades were 'fake'.

311

\* \* \*

In general, the French parents I know are a lot more support-ive than French teachers. They do praise their kids and give them positive reinforcement. Even so, they don't smother them with praise, the way we Anglophones do.

I'm starting to suspect that the French may be right in giving less praise. Perhaps they realize that those little zaps of pleasure kids get each time a grown-up says 'good job' could – if they arrive too often – simply make kids addicted to positive feedback. After a while, they'll need someone else's approval to feel good about themselves. And if kids are assured of praise whatever they do, then they won't need to try very hard. They'll be praised anyway.

Since I'm American, what really convinces me is the research. Praise seems to be yet another realm in which French parents are doing – through tradition and intuition – what the latest scientific studies suggest.

In their 2009 book *NurtureShock*, Po Bronson and Ashley Merryman write that the old conventional wisdom that 'praise, self-esteem and performance rise and fall together' has been toppled by new research showing that excessive praise 'distorts children's motivations; they begin doing things merely to hear the praise, losing sight of the intrinsic enjoyment.'

Bronson and Merryman discover research showing that when heavily praised students get to college, they 'become risk-averse and lack perceived autonomy'. These students 'commonly drop out of classes rather than suffer a mediocre grade, and they have a hard time picking a major. They're afraid to commit to something because they're afraid of not succeeding.'

This new research also refutes the conventional Anglophone wisdom that when kids fail at something, parents should cushion the blow with positive feedback. A better tack is to gently delve into what went wrong, giving kids the confidence and the tools to improve. French schools have their problems, but this is exactly what Bean's French teachers were doing.

The French seem to proceed through parenting using a kind of scientific method, to test what works and what doesn't. In general, they seem unmoved by ideas about what *should* work on their kids, and clear-sighted about what actually does work. They conclude that some praise is good for a child, but that if you praise him too much, you're not letting him live his life.

Over the winter holidays I take Bean back to America. At a family gathering, she starts putting on a one-child show, which mostly involves acting like a teacher and giving the grown-ups orders. It's cute but, frankly, not brilliant. Yet gradually, every adult in the room stops to watch, and to remark on how adorable Bean is (she wisely drops in some French phrases, knowing that these always impress).

By the time the show is over, Bean is beaming as she soaks up all the praise. I think it's the highlight of her visit. I'm beaming too. I interpret the praise for her as praise for me, which I've been starving for in France. All through dinner afterwards, everyone talks – within earshot of both of us – about how terrific her performance was.

It's great on holiday. But I'm not sure I'd want Bean to get that kind of unconditional praise all the time. It feels good, but it seems to come bundled with troubling side effects, including letting a child constantly interrupt. It might also throw off Bean's internal calibration of what's truly entertaining, and what's not.

I've accepted that, if we stay in France, my kids probably won't ever learn to shoot a bow and arrow. (God forbid they're ever attacked by eighteenth-century American Indians.) I've even toned down my praise a bit. But adjusting to the overarching French view on autonomy is a lot harder. Of course I know that my children have an emotional life that's separate from mine, and that I can't constantly protect them from rejection and disappointment. Nevertheless, the idea that they have 'their lives' and I have mine doesn't reflect my emotional map.

Still, I have to admit that my kids seem happiest when I trust them to do things for themselves. I don't hand them knives and tell them to go carve a watermelon. They mostly know when things are way beyond their abilities. But I do let them stretch a bit, even if it's just to carry a breakable plate to the dinner table. After these small achievements, they're calmer and happier. Dolto is most certainly right that autonomy is one of a child's most basic needs.

She also may be right about age six being the threshold.

314

One night, I'm sick with the flu and keeping Simon awake with my coughing. So in the middle of the night I retreat to the couch. When the kids march into the living room at about 7:30 am, I can hardly move. I don't start my usual routine of putting out breakfast.

So Bean does. I lie on the couch, still wearing my eyeshades. In the background I hear her opening drawers, laying the table, and getting out the milk and cereal. She's five and a half years old. And she's taken my job. She's even subcontracted some of it to Joey, who's organizing the cutlery.

After a few minutes, Bean comes over to me on the couch. 'Breakfast is ready, but you have to do the coffee,' she says. She's calm, and very pleased. I'm struck by how happy – or more specifically how *sage* – being autonomous makes her feel. I haven't praised or encouraged her. She's just done something new for herself, with me as a witness, and is feeling very good about it.

Dolto's idea that I should trust my children, and that trusting and respecting them will make them trust and respect me, is very appealing. In fact, it's a relief. The clutch of mutual dependency and worry that often seems to bind Anglophone parents to their kids feels inevitable at times, but it never feels good. It doesn't seem like the basis for the best parenting.

Letting children 'live their lives' isn't about releasing them into the wild or abandoning them (though French school trips do feel a bit like that to me). It's about acknowledging that children aren't repositories for their parents' ambitions, or projects for their parents to perfect. They are separate and capable, with their own tastes, pleasures and experiences of the world.

My friend Andi ended up letting her older son go on that trip to the salt marshes. She says he loved it. It seems he didn't need to be tucked in every night; it was Andi who needed to do the tucking. When it was time for Andi's younger son to start taking the same class trips, she just let him go.

Maybe I'll get used to these trips too one day, though I haven't let Bean go on one yet. I want my kids to be self-reliant, resilient and happy. I just don't want to let go of their hands.

# Epilogue

# The Future in French

M Y MOTHER HAS FINALLY ACCEPTED THAT WE LIVE ACROSS an ocean from her. She's even studying French, though it's not going as well as she'd like. An American friend of hers, who lived in Panama but spoke little Spanish, suggests a technique: say a Spanish sentence in the present tense, then shout the name of the intended tense. 'I go to the store . . . *pasado!*' means that she went to the store. 'I go to the store . . . *futuro!*' means that she'll go later.

I've forbidden my mother from doing this when she comes to visit. To my astonishment, I now have a reputation to protect. I have three kids in the local school, and courteous relationships with neighbourhood fishmongers, tailors and café proprietors.

I still haven't swooned for Paris. I get tired of the elaborate exchange of *bonjours*, and of using the distancing *vous* with everyone but colleagues and intimates. Living in France feels a bit too formal, and doesn't bring out my freewheeling side. I realize how much I've changed when, on the Métro one morning, I instinctively back away from the man sitting next to the only empty seat, because I have the impression that he's deranged. On reflection, I realize my only evidence for this is that he's wearing shorts.

Nevertheless, I've come to feel at home in Paris. As the French say, I've 'found my place'. It helps that I've made some wonderful friends. It turns out that behind their icy facades, Parisian women need to mirror and bond too. They're even hiding a bit of cellulite. These friendships have turned me into a bona fide Francophone. I'm often surprised, mid-conversation, to hear coherent French sentences coming out of my own mouth.

It's also exciting to watch my kids become bilingual. One morning, as I'm getting dressed, Leo points to my brassiere.

'What's that?' he asks.

'A bra,' I say.

He immediately points to his arm. It takes me a second to understand that he means that the French word *bras* (with a silent 's') means 'arm'. He must have learned this word at his crèche. I quiz him and discover, to my surprise, that he knows all the main body parts in French.

What has really connected me to France is discovering the wisdom of French parenting. Thanks to living in Paris, I've learned that children are capable of feats of self-reliance and mindful behaviour that, as an Anglophone parent, I might never have imagined. I can't go back to not knowing this – even if we end up living elsewhere.

Of course, some French principles are easier to implement when you're actually on French soil. When the other children aren't having midday snacks at the playground, it's simpler not to give yours a snack either. It's also easier to enforce boundaries for your kids' behaviour when everyone around you is enforcing more or less the same ones (or as I often say to Bean, 'Do they let you do this in school?').

But much about 'French' parenting doesn't depend on where you live, or require access to certain types of cheese. It mostly requires a parent to shift how he conceives of his relationship to his children, and what he expects from them. That's as accessible in Canterbury or Cleveland as it is in Cannes.

Friends often ask whether I'm raising my kids to be more French or American. When I'm with them in public, I usually think they're somewhere in between: badly behaved compared to the French kids I know, and pretty good compared to the Americans.

They don't always say *bonjour* and *au revoir*, but they know that they're supposed to. Like a real French mother, I'm always reminding them of it. I've come to see this as part of an on-going process called their *éducation*, in which they increasingly learn to respect other people, and to wait. This *éducation* seems, gradually, to be sinking in.

I'm still striving for that French ideal: genuinely listening to my kids, but not feeling that I must always bend to their wills. And I still declare, 'It's me who decides,' in moments of crisis, to remind everyone that I'm in charge. I see it as my job to stop my kids from being consumed by their own desires. But I also try to say yes as often as I can.

Simon and I have stopped discussing whether we'll stay in France. If we do, I'm not sure what's in store as our children get older. By the time French kids become teenagers, their parents seem to give them quite a lot of freedom, and to be matter-of-fact about them having private lives, and even sex lives. Perhaps that gives the teenagers less reason to rebel.

They seem to have an easier time accepting that *maman* and *papa* have private lives too. After all, *maman* and *papa* have always acted as if they do. They haven't based life entirely around their children. Their offspring do plan to move out of their parents' homes eventually. But if a Frenchman in his twenties still lives with his parents, it isn't quite the humiliating tragedy that it is in America. They can let each other live their lives.

The summer before Bean starts primary school I realize that the French way of parenting has really got under my skin. Practically all of her French friends are spending weeks of their summer holidays with their grandparents. I decide that we should send her to stay in Miami with my mother. My mum will be visiting us in Paris anyway, so she and Bean can fly back together.

Simon is against it. What if Bean gets madly homesick and we're an ocean away? I've found a day camp in Miami with daily swimming lessons. Because of the timing, she'll have to start the camp mid-session. Won't it be difficult for her to make friends? He suggests we wait a year, until she's older.

But Bean thinks the trip is a spectacular idea. She says she'll be fine alone with her grandmother, and that she's excited about the camp. Simon finally acquiesces, perhaps calculating that with Bean away, he'll get to spend more time in cafés. I'll fly to Miami to bring her home.

I give my mother a few instructions: no pork, lots of sunblock. Bean and I spend a week fine-tuning the contents of her carry-on bag for the plane. We have a moment of melancholy, when I promise to call every day.

And I do. But as soon as she arrives in Miami, Bean is so absorbed in her adventure that she won't stay on the phone for more than a minute or two. I have to rely on reports from my mum's friends: 'She ate sushi with us tonight, taught us some French, told us about some pressing issues concerning her friends from school, and went off to bed with a smile on her face,' one of them emails me.

After just a few days, Bean's English – which was once mid-Atlantic-mysterious with a British twist – now sounds almost fully American. She says 'car' with a full, flat 'ahr'. However, she's definitely milking her status as an expatriate. My mum says they listened to her language tapes in the car, and that Bean declared, 'That man doesn't know French.'

Bean does try to figure out what's happened in Paris since she has been away. 'Is Daddy fat? Is Mummy old?' she asks us, after about a week. My mum says Bean keeps telling people when I'll arrive in Miami, how long I'll stay, and where we'll go after that. Just as Françoise Dolto predicted, she needs both independence and a rational understanding of the world.

When I tell friends about Bean's trip, their reactions split straight down national lines. The North Americans say that Bean is 'brave' and ask how she's coping with the separation. No Anglophone parents I know are sending kids her age off for ten-day stints with their grandparents, especially not across an ocean. But my French friends assume that detaching a bit is good for everyone. They take for granted that Bean is having fun on her own, and that I'm enjoying a well-deserved break.

As the kids become more independent, Simon and I are getting along better. He's still irritable, and I'm still irritating. But he's decided that it's OK to be cheerful sometimes, and to admit that he enjoys my company. Every once in a while, he even laughs at my jokes.

I've made concessions too. I micromanage him less, even when I come out in the morning and he's serving the kids unshaken orange juice. I've figured out that, like them, he craves autonomy. If that means a glass full of pulp for me, so be it. I no longer ask what he's thinking about. I've learned to cultivate – and appreciate – having some mystery in our marriage.

Last summer, we went back to the seaside town where I first noticed all those French children eating happily in restaurants. This time, instead of having one child, we have three. And instead of trying to manage in a hotel, we wisely rent a house with a kitchen.

One afternoon, we take the kids out for lunch at a restaurant near the port. It's one of those idyllic French summer days, when the whitewashed buildings glow in the midday sun. All five of us are able to enjoy it. We order our food calmly, and in courses. Everyone stays in their seats and enjoys their food – including some fish and vegetables. Nothing lands on the floor, and there's no shouting. It isn't as relaxing as dining out alone with Simon. But it really does feel like we're on holiday. We even have coffee at the end of the meal.

# Glossary of French Parenting Terms

*Attend* (ah-tahn) – Wait, stop. A command that a French parent says to a child. 'Wait' implies that the child doesn't require immediate gratification, and that he can entertain himself for a few seconds or minutes.

*Au revoir* – Goodbye. What a French child must say when he leaves the company of a familiar adult. It's one of the four French 'magic words' for kids. See *bonjour*.

*Autonomie* – Autonomy. The blend of independence and self-reliance that French parents encourage in their children from an early age.

*Bêtise* (beh-teeze) – A small act of naughtiness. Labelling an offence a mere *bêtise* helps parents respond to it with moderation.

*Bonjour* – Hello. What a child must say when he encounters a familiar adult.

*Caca boudin* (caca booh-dah) – Literally, 'caca sausage'. A curse word used almost exclusively by French preschoolers.

*Cadre* (kah-druh) – Frame or framework. A visual image that describes the French parenting ideal: setting firm limits for children, but giving them tremendous freedom within those limits.

*Caprice* (kah-preese) – A child's impulsive whim, fancy or demand, often accompanied by whining or tears. French parents believe it is damaging to accede to *caprices*.

*Classe verte* – Green class. An annual class trip in which children as young as six or seven spend a week or so in a natural setting. The teacher chaperones, along with a few other adults.

*Colonie de vacances* – Holiday camp. One of hundreds of group holidays for kids as young as four, without their parents, usually in the countryside.

*Complicité* – Complicity. The mutual understanding that French parents and caregivers try to develop with children, beginning from birth. *Complicité* implies that even small babies are rational beings, with whom adults can have reciprocal, respectful relationships.

*Crèche* (kresh) – A full-time French nursery, subsidized and regulated by the government. Middle-class French parents generally prefer crèches to nannies or childminding in private homes.

*Doucement* (doo-ceh-mahn) – Gently, carefully. A word that French parents and caregivers say frequently to small children. *Doucement* implies that children are capable of controlled, mindful behaviour.

*Doudou* (doo-doo) – The obligatory comfort object for young children. It's usually a floppy stuffed animal.

*École maternelle* – France's free state preschool. It begins in September of the year a child turns three.

*Éducation* (eh-doo-cah-see-ohn) – Upbringing; the way that French parents raise their kids.

*Enfant roi* (an-fahn rwa) – child king; an excessively demanding child who is constantly the centre of his parents' attention, and who can't cope with frustration.

*Équilibre* (Eh-key-lee-bre) – Balance. Not letting any one part of life – including being a parent – overwhelm the other parts.

*Éveillé/e* (eh-vay-yay) – Awakened, alert, stimulated. This is one of the ideals for French children. The other is for them to be *sage*.

*Gourmand/e* (goohre-mahn/d) – Someone who eats too quickly, too much of one thing, or too much of everything.

*Goûter* (gooh-tay) – The afternoon snack for kids, eaten at about 4 pm. The *goûter* is the only snack of the day. It can also be a verb: did you already *goûter*?

*Les gros yeux* (leh grohz yuh) – The big eyes. The look of admonishment that French adults give children. It signals that they should stop doing a *bêtise*.

*Maman-taxi* – Taxi mother. A woman who spends much of her

free time shuttling her children to extracurricular activities. This is not *équilibré*.

*N'importe quoi* (nem-port-a kwa) – Whatever; anything you like. A child who does *n'importe quoi* acts without limits or regard for others.

*Non* – No. Absolutely not.

*profiter* (proh-feeh-teh) – to enjoy the moment and take advantage of it.

*Punir* (pooh-near) – To punish. To be *puni* – punished – is serious and important.

*Rapporter* – To tell on someone; to grass. French children and adults believe that it's very bad to do this.

*Sage* (sah-je) – Wise and calm. This describes a child who is in control of himself or absorbed in an activity. Instead of saying 'be good', French parents say 'be *sage*'.

# Bibliography

Antier, Edwige, 'Plus on lève la main sur un enfant, plus il devient agressif', *Le Parisien*, 15 November 2009.

Auffret-Pericone, Marie, 'Comment réussir à se faire obéir?', *Enfant*, October 2009.

Badinter, Élisabeth, *L'Amour en Plus: Histoire de l'amour maternel*, Paris: Flammarion, 1980.

Badinter, Élisabeth, *Le Conflit: la femme et la mère*, Paris: Flammarion Lettres, 2010.

Belsky, Jay, 'Effects of Child Care on Child Development: Give Parents Real Choice', March 2009.

Bennhold, Katrin, 'Where having it all doesn't mean having equality', *New York Times*, 11 October 2010.

Bloom, Paul, 'Moral Life of Babies', *New York Times Magazine*, 3 May 2010.

Bornstein, Marc H., Catherine S. Tamis-LeMonda, Marie-Germaine Pecheux and Charles W. Rahn, 'Mother and infant activity and interaction in France and in the United States: a comparative study', *International Journal of Behavioral Development* (1991), 21–43.

Bronson, Po and Ashley Merryman, *NurtureShock: New Thinking About Children*, New York: Twelve, 2009.

Calhoun, Ada, 'The battle over "cry it out" sleep training', 17 March 2010, Salon.com.

Carroll, Raymonde, *Cultural Misunderstandings: The French-American Experience*, Chicago: University of Chicago Press, 1990.

Cimpian, Andrei, Holly-Marie C. Arce, Ellen M. Markman and Carol S. Dweck, 'Subtle linguistic cues affect children's motivation', *Association for Psychological Science*, 18:4, 2007.

Cohen, Abby J., 'A brief history of federal financing for child care in the United States', *The Future of Children: Financing Child Care*, 6 (1996).

Cohen, Michel, *The New Basics*, New York: Collins, 2004.

Delahaye, Marie-Claude, *Livre de Bord de la Future Maman*, Marabout, 2007.

De Leersnyder, Hélène, *L'enfant et son sommeil*, Paris: Robert Laffont, 1998.

Dolto, Françoise and Danielle Marie Lévy, *Parler juste aux enfants*, Paris: Gallimard, 2002.

Dolto, Françoise, *Les Étapes majeures de l'enfance*, Paris: Gallimard, 1994.

Dolto, Françoise, *Lettres de jeunesse: Correspondance 1913–1938*, Paris: Gallimard, 2003.

Dyck, Vera and Kerry Daly, 'Rising to the challenge: fathers' role in the negotiation of couple time', *Leisure Studies*, 25:2 (2006), 201–17.

Eisenberg, Arlene, Heidi E. Murkoff and Sandee Hathaway, *What to Expect: The Toddler Years*, London: Simon and Schuster, 1996.

Epstein, Jean, '*Parents, faites-vous confiance!*' Interview on aufeminin.com.

Ford, Gina, *The New Contented Little Baby Book*, London: Vermilion, 2006.

Franrenet, Sandra, 'Quelles punitions pour nos fripons?', madame.lefigaro.fr, 28 February 2011

Galinsky, Ellen, Kerstin Aumann and James T. Bond, *Times Are*

*Changing: Gender and Generation at Work and at Home*, Families and Work Institute, 2009.

Gerkens, Danièle, 'Comment rendre son enfant heureux?' Interview with Aldo Naori, *Elle* magazine, 26 February 2010.

Girard, Isabelle, *'Pascal Bruckner et Laurence Ferrari: Le Mariage? Un acte de bravoure'*, *Le Figaro – Madame*, 11 September 2010.

Guiliano, Mireille, *French Women Don't Get Fat*, New York: Alfred A. Knopf, 2005.

Hausmann, Ricardo, Laura D. Tyson and Saadia Zahidi, 'The Global Gender Gap Report 2010', World Economic Forum.

Hulbert, Ann, *Raising America: Experts, Parents, and a Century of Advice About Children*, New York: Vintage Books, 2004.

Kahneman, Daniel and Alan B. Krueger, 'Developments in the measurement of subjective well-being', *Journal of Economic Perspectives*, 20:1 (2006), 3–24.

Kamerman, Sheila, US Senate Testimony, 27 March 2001.

Kamerman, Sheila, 'A global history of early childhood education and care', background paper, Unesco, 2006.

Krueger, Alan B., Daniel Kahneman, Claude Fischler, David Schkade, Norbert Schwarz and Arthur A. Stone, 'Time use and subjective well-being in France and the US', *Social Indicators Research* 93 (2009), 7–18.

Krueger, Alan B., ed., *Measuring the Subjective Well-Being of Nations: National Accounts of Time Use and Well-Being*, Chicago: University of Chicago Press, 2009.

Lareau, Annette, *Unequal Childhoods: Class, Race and Family Life*, Berkeley: University of California Press, 2003.

Lareau, Annette, 'Questions and answers about unequal childhoods', http://sociology.sas.upenn.edu/a_lareau2

Marbeau, J. B. F., *The Crèche or a Way to Reduce Poverty by Increasing the Population* (trans. Vanessa Nicolai), Montreal: 1994 (first published 1845).

Marcelli, Daniel, *Il est permis d'obéir*, Paris: Albin Michel, 2009.

Melmed, Matthew, Statement submitted to the Committee on Education and Labor, US House of Representatives, Hearing on Investing in Early Education: Improving Children's Success, 23 January 2008.

Mindell, J. A. et al., 'Behavioral treatment of bedtime problems and night wakings in young children: AASM Standards of Practice', *Sleep*, 29 (2006), 1263–76.

Mischel, Walter, in G. Lindzey and W. M. Runyan (eds), *A History of Psychology in Autobiography*, Washington, DC: American Psychological Association, 2007.

Mogel, Wendy, *The Blessing of a Skinned Knee*, New York: Scribner, 2001.

Murkoff, Heidi, Arlene Eisenberg and Sandee Hathaway, *What to Expect When You're Expecting*, New York: Pocket Books, 2002.

Ollivier, Debra, *What French Women Know About Love, Sex, and Other Matters of Heart and Mind*, New York: G. P. Putnam's Sons, 2009.

Parker, Kim, 'The harried life of the working mother', Pew Research Center, 1 October 2009.

Pernoud, Laurence, *J'élève mon enfant*, Paris: Éditions Horay, 2007.

Pinella, Teresa and Leann L. Birch, 'Help me make it through the night: behavioral entrainment of breastfed infants' sleep patterns', *Paediatrics*, 1993: 91(2), 436–43.

Prochner, Larry, 'The American creche: "Let's do what the French do, but do it our way"', *Contemporary Issues in Early Childhood*, 4:3 (2003).

Richardin, Sophie, 'Surfez sur les vagues du désir!', *Neuf Mois*, February 2009.

Rossant, Lyonel and Jacqueline Rossant-Lumbroso, *Votre Enfant: Guide à l'usage des parents*, Paris: Robert Laffont, 2006.

# BIBLIOGRAPHY

Rousseau, Jean-Jacques, *Émile or On Education*, trans. Allan Bloom, New York: Basic Books, 1979.

Rousseau, Jean-Jacques, *Émile, or On Education*, trans. NuVision Publications LLC, 2007.

Sawica, Leslie, coordinator, *Le guide des nouvelles mamans*, free booklet prepared with support from the French health ministry.

Senior, Jennifer, 'All Joy and No Fun', *New York Magazine*, 12 July 2010.

Sethi, Anita, Walter Mischel, J. Lawrence Aber, Yuichi Shoda and Monica Larrea Rodriguez, 'The role of strategic attention deployment in development of self-regulation: predicting preschoolers' delay of gratification from mother–toddler interactions', *Developmental Psychology*, 36:6 (Nov 2000), 767–77.

Skenazy, Lenore, *Free-Range Kids*, San Francisco: Jossey-Bass, 2009.

Steingarten, Jeffrey, *The Man Who Ate Everything*, New York: Vintage Books, 1997.

Suizzo, Marie-Anne, 'French and American mothers' childrearing beliefs: stimulating, responding, and long-term goals', *Journal of Cross-Cultural Psychology*, 35:5 (September 2004), 606–26.

Suizzo, Marie-Anne, 'French parents' cultural models and childrearing beliefs', *International Journal of Behavioral Development*, 26:4 (2002), 297–307.

Suizzo, Marie-Anne, 'Mother–child relationships in France: balancing autonomy and affiliation in everyday interactions', *Ethos*, 32:3 (2004), 292–323.

Suizzo, Marie-Anne and Marc H. Bornstein, 'French and European American child-mother play: culture and gender considerations', *International Journal of Behavioral Development*, 30:6 (2006), 498–508.

Thirion, Marie and Marie-Josèphe Challamel, *Le sommeil, le rêve et l'enfant: de la naissance à l'adolescence*, Paris: Albin Michel, 2002.

Turkle, Sherry, *Psychoanalytic Politics: Jacques Lacan and Freud's French Revolution*, New York: The Guilford Press, 1992.

Turkle, Sherry, 'Tough Love', Introduction to *When Parents Separate* by Françoise Dolto, Boston: David R. Godine, 1995.

Twenge, Jean M., W. Keith Campbell and Craig A. Foster, 'Parenthood and marital satisfaction: a meta-analytic review', *Journal of Marriage and Family*, 65: 3 (August 2003), 574–83.

Warner, Judith, *Perfect Madness: Motherhood in the Age of Anxiety*, New York: Riverhead Books, 2005.

Zellman, Gail L. and Anne Johansen, 'Examining the Implementation and Outcomes of the Military Child Care Act of 1989', research brief, 1998, Rand Corporation.

Zigler, Edward, Katherine Marsland and Heather Lord, *The Tragedy of Child Care in America*, New Haven and London: Yale University Press, 2009.

Citations without an author:

*ABCs of Parenting in Paris*, fifth edition, France: MESSAGE Mother Support Group, 2006.

CIA, *The World Factbook*. https://www.cia.gov/library/publications/the-world-factbook/

Direction de la recherche, des études, de l'évaluation et des statistiques (DREES), April 2006, *Le temps des parents après une naissance*.

INSEE, Time-Use Surveys, 1986 and 1999.

Lemangeur-ocha.com, 'France, Europe, the United States: what eating means to us: Interview with Claude Fischler and Estelle Masson', posted online 16 January 2008.

Mairie de Paris, 'Mission d'information et d'évaluation sur l'engagement de la collectivité parisienne auprès des familles en matière d'accueil des jeunes enfants de moins de trois ans', 15 June 2009.

# BIBLIOGRAPHY

Military.com, 'Military Child Care', www.military.com/benefits/ resources/family-support/child-care.

National Institutes of Health, 'Child Care Linked To Assertive, Noncompliant, and Aggressive Behaviors; Vast Majority of Children Within Normal Range', 16 July 2003.

OECD, '*Éducation et accueil des Jeunes Enfants*', May 2003.

Pew Global Attitudes Project, 'Men's Lives Often Seen as Better: Gender Equality Universally Embraced, but Inequalities Acknowledged', 1 July 2010.

Unicef, 'Child poverty in perspective: an overview of childhood well-being in rich countries', Innocenti Report Card 7, 2007, UNICEF Innocenti Research Center, Florence.

US Bureau of Labor Statistics, American Time Use Survey Summary, 2009 results.

# Notes

## Prologue: French Children Don't Throw Food

**French parents are very concerned about their kids.** In a 2002 survey by the International Social Survey Program, 90 per cent of French adults agreed or strongly agreed with the statement 'Watching children grow up is life's greatest joy.' In the US it was 85.5 per cent; in the UK it was 81.1 per cent.

**more attention to the upbringing of children than can possibly be good for them.** Joseph Epstein, 'The Kindergarchy: Every Child a Dauphin', *The Weekly Standard*, 9 June 2008. Epstein may also have coined the word 'kindergarchy'.

**their own kids would benefit from more stimulation too.** Judith Warner describes this in *Perfect Madness: Motherhood in the Age of Anxiety*, New York: Riverhead Books, 2005.

**when I discover a research study.** Alan B. Krueger, Daniel Kahneman, Claude Fischler, David Schkade, Norbert Schwarz and Arthur A. Stone, 'Time Use and Subjective Well-Being in France and the US', *Social Indicators Research* 93 (2009), 7–18.

**only the Irish have a higher birth rate.** According to 2009 figures from the OECD, France's birth rate is 1.99 per woman. Belgium's is 1.83; Italy's is 1.41; Spain's is 1.4 and Germany's is 1.36.

# 1: Are You Waiting for a Child?

**a book by Edmund White.** Edmund White, *The Flâneur: A Stroll Through the Paradoxes of Paris*, London: Bloomsbury, 2001.

# 2: Paris Is Burping

**the under-five mortality rate is 50 per cent lower in France.** Save the Children, *The Complete Mothers' Index*, 2010.

**America's was thirty-seventh.** *The World Health Report 2000 – Health systems: improving performance*, World Health Organization, 2000.

**to prepare them for looking after an infant.** 'It's good for women to suffer the pain of a natural birth, says medical chief', by Denis Campbell, *Observer*, 12 July 2009.

**about 87 per cent of women have epidurals.** Maman.fr, '*Les Tops des Maternités*'.

# 3: Doing Her Nights

**A meta-study of dozens of peer-reviewed sleep papers.** Jodi Mindell et al., 'Behavioral treatment of bedtime problems and night wakings in young children: an American Academy of Sleep medicine review', *Sleep*, 29 (2006), 1263–76.

**The authors of the meta-study point to a paper.** Teresa Pinella and Leann L. Birch, 'Help me make it through the night: behavioral entrainment of breast-fed infants' sleep patterns', *Pediatrics*, 1993: 91 (2), 436–43.

# 4: Wait!

**Most could only wait about thirty seconds.** Mischel's experiments were recounted by Jonas Lehrer in the *New Yorker*, 18 May 2009.

**Hold on, I'm talking to papa.** Walter Mischel cautions that even if young French children are good at waiting, that doesn't mean they'll become successful adults. Many other things affect them too. And while Americans typically don't expect small children to wait well, they trust that the same children will somehow acquire this skill later in life. 'I believe an undisciplined child isn't doomed to become an undisciplined adult,' Mischel says. 'Just because a kid is throwing around food at age seven or eight, at a restaurant . . . doesn't mean that the same child isn't going to become a superb business person or scientist or teacher or whatever fifteen years later.'

**ended up eating it.** Mischel found that kids can easily learn to distract themselves. In a subsequent marshmallow test, experimenters told the children that instead of thinking about the marshmallow, they should think about something happy like 'swinging on a swing with Mummy pushing' or pretend it was just a *picture* of a marshmallow. With this instruction, overall waiting times increased dramatically. Waiting times improved even though kids knew that they were trying to trick themselves. The moment the experimenter walked back into the room, children who had been busy self-distracting for fifteen minutes gobbled up the marshmallow.

**now includes snacks.** Jennifer Steinhauer, 'Snack Time Never Ends', *New York Times*, 20 January 2010.

**But the French mums said it was very important.** Marie-Anne Suizzo, 'French and American mothers' childrearing beliefs: stimulating, responding, and long-term goals', *Journal of Cross-Cultural Psychology*, 35:5 (September 2004), 606–26.

**an enormous US government study of the effects of childcare.** *NICHD Study of Early Child Care and Youth Development*.

**Anglophone kids doing quite a lot of *n'importe quoi.*** A 2006 study of white, middle-class Canadian couples found that when the kids were around – which was very often – it was impossible for parents to have quality time together. One participant said that while speaking to his wife, 'we would be interrupted on a minute-to-minute basis'. The authors conclude that, 'For any experience of being a couple together, they simply had to get away from the children.' Vera Dyck and Kerry Daly, 'Rising to the challenge: fathers' role in the negotiation of couple time', *Leisure Studies*, 25:2 (2006), 201–17.

**A French psychologist writes.** The psychologist is Christine Brunet, quoted in *Journal des Femmes*, 11 February 2005.

**an obligatory rite of passage.** Anne-Catherine Pernot-Masson, quoted in *Votre Enfant*.

## 5: Tiny Little Humans

**a mother writes in the *Telegraph.*** Judith Woods, 'I'm a pushy parent, and proud', *Daily Telegraph*, 6 January 2010.

**as far away as Normandy or Burgundy.** Elisabeth Badinter, *L'amour en plus: histoire de l'amour maternel*, Paris: Flammarion, 1980.

**to replace the mother in the family shop.** Ibid.

**writes a French social historian.** Ibid.

**because doing so would give the children pleasure.** Marie-Anne Suizzo, 'French and American mothers' childrearing beliefs: stimulating, responding, and long-term goals', *Journal of Cross-Cultural Psychology*, 35:5 (September 2004), 606–26.

**I don't know where she got her answers.** 'Dolto: une vie pour l'enfance', Télérama hors série, 2008.

**she would ask her young patients.** Recollection of the psychoanalyst Alain Vanier, reported in Dolto: une vie pour l'enfance, Télérama hors série, 2008.

**some of them are small. But they communicate.** The psychologist is Muriel Djéribi-Valentin, interviewed by Jacqueline Sellem in 'Françoise Dolto: quand l'enfant est un sujet à part entière', translated by Kieran O'Meara for l'Humanité in English.

**give the baby a tour of the house.** Marie-Anne Suizzo found that 86 per cent of Parisian mothers she interviewed 'specifically stated that they talk to their infants to communicate with them'. Marie-Anne Suizzo, 'Mother–child relationships in France: balancing autonomy and affiliation in everyday interactions', Ethos, 32:3 (2004), 292–323.

**writes Yale psychologist Paul Bloom.** Paul Bloom, 'Moral Life of Babies', New York Times Magazine, 3 May 2010.

**that eight-month-olds understand probabilities.** Alison Gopnik writes that these new studies 'demonstrate that babies and very young children know, observe, explore, imagine and learn more than we would ever have thought possible'. Gopnik is a psychologist at the University of California at Berkeley and author of The Philosophical Baby.

# 6: Daycare?

**perfect conviction that the children understand.** A 2009 report by the Paris mayor's office said that caregivers shouldn't speak badly about a child's parents, origins, or appearance, even if the child is an infant, and even if the remark is made to someone else. 'The implicit message in this type of reflection is always perceived intuitively by the children. The younger they are, the more they understand what is contained behind the words,' the report says.

**but must be trained in-house.** OECD, 'Starting Strong II: Early Childhood Education and Care', 2006.

**the way kids develop and behave later in life.** NICHD Study of Early Child Care and Youth Development.

**One of the study's researchers.** Jay Belsky, 'Effects of child care on child development: give parents real choice', March 2009.

# 7: Bébé au Lait

**do some breastfeeding.** OECD, 'France Country Highlights, Doing Better for Children', 2009.

**90 per cent of mothers in London.** WHO Global Data Bank on Infant and Young Child Feeding, 2007–2008. In America, 74 per cent of mothers do at least some breastfeeding, and a third are still nursing exclusively at four months.

**a columnist writes in the *Daily Mail*.** 'Why do babies turn so many brilliant women into slummy mummies?' by Helen Kirwan-Taylor, *Mail Online*, 2 September 2009.

**there's no reason to feel badly about that.** When French and American mothers ranked the importance of 'always put[ting] the baby's needs before one's own', American mothers gave it 2.89 out of 5; French mothers gave it 1.26 out of 5. The 2004 study, by Marie-Anne Suizzo, is called 'French and American mothers' childrearing beliefs: stimulating, responding, and long-term goals'. It was published in the *Journal of Cross-Cultural Psychology*.

**a fashion spread in a French mothers' magazine.** 'Géraldine Pailhas, des visages, des figures', by Violaine Belle-Croix, *Milk Magazine*, 13 September 2010.

**is also required to keep her looking and feeling seductive.** 'French women know that an inner life is a sexy thing. It needs to be nurtured, developed, pampered . . .' Debra Ollivier writes in *What French Women Know*.


# 8: The Perfect Mother Doesn't Exist

**the most satisfying kind of marriage is one in which both husband and wife have jobs.** Given the baby boom and the shortage of places in crèches, the French state pays some mothers about 500 euros a month to look after their own children until the youngest is three. Mothers are also entitled to work part-time for the first three years.

**they're broadcasting them.** Judith Warner writes in *Perfect Madness* that after her first child was born, 'I talked and sang and made up stories and did funny voices and narrated car rides and read at mealtimes until, when my daughter turned four and a half, I realized that I had turned into a human television set, so filled with twenty-four-hour children's programming that I felt as though I had no thoughts left of my own.'

**to make childcare less pleasant for mothers.** Alan B. Krueger, Daniel Kahneman, Claude Fischler, David Schkade, Norbert Schwarz and Arthur A. Stone, 'Time use and subjective well-being in France and the US', *Social Indicators Research*, 93 (2009), 7–18.

**Annette Lareau observed among white and African-American middle-class parents.** Annette Lareau, *Unequal Childhoods: Class, Race and Family Life*, Berkeley: University of California Press, 2003.

**she's also supposed to attend *the practices*.** Annette Lareau writes that most of the middle-class families she observed were frenetically busy, with parents working full-time, then shopping, cooking, overseeing baths and homework, and driving kids back and forth to activities. 'Things are so hectic that the house sometimes seems to become a holding pattern between activities,' she writes.

**more time on childcare than parents did in 1965.** Robert Pear, 'Married and Single Parents Spending More Time with Children, Study Finds', *New York Times*, 17 October 2006.

## 9: Caca Boudin

**passionately, madly, not at all.** Debra Ollivier, *What French Women Know About Love, Sex, and Other Matters of Heart and Mind*, New York: G. P. Putnam's Sons, 2009.

## 11: I Adore This Baguette

**marital satisfaction has fallen.** Jean M. Twenge, W. Keith Campbell and Craig A. Foster, 'Parenthood and marital satisfaction: a meta-analytic review', *Journal of Marriage and Family*, 65: 3 (August 2003), 574–83.

**mothers find it more pleasant to do housework than to take care of their kids.** In a well-known 2004 study, working mothers in Texas said childcare was one of their most unpleasant daily activities. They preferred housework. Daniel Kahneman, et al., 'A survey method for characterizing daily life experience: the day reconstruction method', *Science*, 3 December 2004.

**their unhappiness increases with each additional child.** Ibid., Jean M. Twenge.

**A paper on middle-class Canadians.** Dyck, Vera and Kerry Daly, 'Rising to the challenge: fathers' role in the negotiation of couple time', *Leisure Studies*, 25:2 (2006), 201–217.

**They have a bigger gap than we do between what men and women earn.** In the overall 2010 Global Gender Gap Index, created by the World Economic Forum, the UK ranked fifteenth, the United States ranked nineteenth and France ranked forty-sixth.

**men doing household work and looking after children.** According to the French statistics agency Insee.

**and 25 per cent more time on childcare.** According to the US Bureau of Labor Statistics.

**it's hard for me to cool back down.** In a 2008 study, 49 per cent of employed American men said they did as much or more childcare as their partners. But just 31 per cent of women saw it this way. The study is Ellen Galinsky, Kerstin Aumann and James T. Bond, *Times Are Changing: Gender and Generation at Work and at Home*, Families and Work Institute, 2009.

**leaving Simon in Paris with the boys.** Ibid., Alan B. Krueger et al. French women spent about 15 per cent less time doing housework than the American women did.

**A 2006 French study.** Denise Bauer, Études et Résultats, 'Le temps des parents après une naissance', Drees, April 2006.

## 12: You Just Have to Taste It

**Just 3.1 per cent of French five- and six-year-olds are obese.** Nathalie Guignon, Marc Collet and Lucie Gonzalez, 'La santé des enfants en grande section de maternelle en 2005–2006', Études et resultats, September 2010.

**nearly 10 per cent of five-year-olds are obese.** National Child Measurement Programme, June 2010. Figures given are for 2008 and 2009.

**Health is seen as the main reason for eating.** Lemangeur-ocha.com, 'France, Europe, the United States: what eating means to us: Interview with Claude Fischler and Estelle Masson', posted online 16 January 2008.

## 13: It's Me Who Decides

**and it's respectful to the child, Daniel Marcelli says.** In an interview with *Enfant Magazine*, 'Comment réussir à se faire obéir?', October 2009.

**In a national poll.** 'Les Français et la fessée' by TNS Sofres/Logica for *Dimanche Ouest France*, 11 November 2009.

**said they never spank their kids.** 55 per cent also said that they oppose spanking.

**All the French parenting experts I read about oppose it.** Marcel Rufo, a well-known child-psychiatrist based in Marseille, says, 'There are two generations of parents ... Those of yesterday who were spanked and hit and who say, "We weren't traumatized by it." And then there are the parents of today, who I think are much better, because they're more about understanding the child than about prohibiting things. The role of the parent is to give his view to the child, to explain things to him. The child will accept them.' *Le Figaro Magazine*, 20 November 2009.

# 14: Let Him Live His Life

**everything in the house – and in society – that concerns him.**
When French and American mothers were asked to rank the
importance of 'Not let[ting] the baby become too dependent on his
or her mother', American mothers ranked the statement 0.93 out of
a possible 5. French mothers ranked it 3.36. The study, 'French and
American mothers' childrearing beliefs: stimulating, responding, and
long-term goals' by Marie-Anne Suizzo, was published in the *Journal
of Cross-Cultural Psychology* in 2004.

**treating each child's thought as a special contribution.** Raymonde
Carroll writes in *Cultural Misunderstandings* that American parents
'avoid as much as possible criticizing their children, making fun of
their tastes, or telling them constantly "how to do things"'.

**is practically perfect.** Getting 16:20 is a 'rare and outstanding
achievement', according to a report prepared by the University of
Cambridge exam board, for British universities. This was reported in
the *Economist*, 30 September 2010, 'A Chorus of Disapproval'.

**against an ideal, which practically no one meets.** This creates a
problem for social scientists when they try to compare life in
America and France. 'Americans tend to be more emphatic when
reporting their well-being,' say the authors of that study of women in
Ohio and Rennes. Americans were more likely to choose extremes
like 'very satisfied' and 'not at all satisfied', whereas French women
avoided these. The researchers adjusted their findings to account for
this.

**because they're afraid of not succeeding.** Po Bronson and Ashley
Merryman, *NurtureShock: New Thinking About Children*, New York:
Twelve, 2009.

# Epilogue: The Future in French

**that I must always bend to their wills.** 'For Françoise Dolto, a desire is not a need, it shouldn't necessarily be satisfied, but we should listen to it and speak about it, which makes all the difference,' says Muriel Djéribi-Valentin, interviewed by Jacqueline Sellem in '*Françoise Dolto: quand l'enfant est un sujet à part entière*', translated by Kieran O'Meara for *l'Humanité in English*.

# Acknowledgements

I am extremely grateful to Marianne Velmans at Transworld; to my agents, Suzanne Gluck and Eugenie Furniss; and to Ann Godoff and Virginia Smith at The Penguin Press.

My profound thanks go to Sapna Gupta for her astute reading of the manuscript. Adam Kuper gave me advice and encouragement when I needed it most. Pauline Harris provided expert help with research. Ken Druckerman didn't just comment on the early chapters; he also accepted packages on my behalf.

*Merci* to my posse of mother-readers: Christine Tacconet, Brooke Pallot, Dietlind Lerner, Amelia Relles, Sharon Galant, and the heroic Hannah Kuper, who read the chapters on pregnancy while having contractions herself.

For their general support, often in the form of food or shelter, thanks to Scott Wenger, Joanne Feld, Adam Ellick, Jeffrey Sumber, Kari Snick, Patrick Weil, Adelyn Escobar, Shana Druckerman, Marsha Druckerman, Steve Fleischer, and Nancy and Ronald Gelles. Thanks to my colleagues on the rue Bleue for their camaraderie, parenting tips, and lessons on how to enjoy lunch.

# ACKNOWLEDGEMENTS

I am indebted to the many French families who let me hang around with them, and to the people whose introductions made all that hanging around possible: Valérie Picard, Cécile Agon, Hélène Toussaint, William Oiry, Véronique Bouruet-Aubertot, Gail Negbaur, Lucie Porcher, Émilie Walmsley, Andrea Ipaktchi, Jonathan Ross, Robynne Pendariès, Benjamin Benita and Laurence Kalmanson. Thanks to Crèche Cour Debille and Crèche Enfance et Découverte, especially Marie-Christine Barison, Anne-Marie Legendre, Sylvie Metay, Didier Trillot, Alexandra Van-Kersschaver and Fatima Abdullarif. Special gratitude goes to the family of Fanny Gerbet.

It's much easier to write a parenting book when you're blessed with extraordinary parents – Bonnie Green and Henry Druckerman. It's also a gift to be married to someone who's better at what I do than I am. I couldn't have written this book without the encouragement and tolerance of my husband, Simon Kuper. He critiqued every draft and, in so doing, made me a better writer.

Finally, thanks to Leo, Joel and Leila (rhymes with sky-la). This is what Mummy was doing in her office. I hope that one day you'll think it was worth it.

# Index

# INDEX

# INDEX